$\mathcal{A}$dventure Guide™ to
New
Hampshire

Elizabeth L. Dugger

HUNTER

Hunter Publishing, Inc.
130 Campus Drive, Edison, NJ 08818
732 225 1900 / 800 255 0343 / Fax 732 417 1744
e-mail: hunterpub@emi.net

In Canada
1220 Nicholson Road, Newmarket, Ontario
Canada L3Y 7V1
800 399 6858 / Fax 800 363 2665

In the UK
Windsor Books International
The Boundary, Wheatley Road
Garsington
Oxford, OX44 9EJ England
01865-361122 / Fax 01865-361133

ISBN 1-55650-822-0
© 1998 Hunter Publishing, Inc.

Visit our Web site at www.hunterpublishing.com

This guide focuses on recreational activities. As all such activities con-
tain elements of risk, the publisher, author, affiliated individuals and
companies disclaim any responsibility for any injury, harm, or illness
that may occur to anyone through, or by use of, the information in this
book. Every effort has been made to insure that the information in this
book is correct, but the publisher and author do not assume, and
hereby disclaim, any liability for any loss or damage caused by errors,
omissions, misleading information or potential travel problems caused
by this guide, even if such errors or omissions result from negligence,
accident or any other cause.

Cover: *Sculptured Rocks, Groton: Spring Carved by Glacial Meltwater*
© William H. Johnson

Back cover: Echo Lake, Franconia, Bob Grant
Courtesy of the New Hampshire Office of
Travel & Tourism Development (NHOTTD)

All other photos by Elizabeth L. Dugger, except as noted.

Maps by Lissa K. Dailey and Kim André,
© 1998 Hunter Publishing, Inc.

1 2 3 4 5

Contents

Maps

Acknowledgments

Sometimes it takes a village to research a book. Traveling along for this one were Jean, Marion, Heidi, Kathryn, Jesse, Elizabeth O'D., and Kiril and Carly, who helped with the wonderful job of taste-testing in Portsmouth. Readers included Tim and Martha, and a dedicated angler, John. Special thanks go to Ruth and Alex, for extraordinary support. The state of New Hampshire and many towns and chambers of commerce patiently provided endless information; local mail carrier Allen Thresher made sure it arrived. Lissa Dailey's enthusiasm and sharp editing eye were indispensable.

Area Codes

The area code for all New Hampshire telephone numbers is **603**. Most 800 and 888 numbers listed can be dialed only from outside the state.

About the Author

When Elizabeth L. Dugger's mother left New Hampshire to be married in 1950, she brought along copious notes on where all the New Hampshire relatives and ancestors had settled, raised children, and been buried. Returning to explore the state and write this book seemed like the least the author could do in memory of her mother, who was always an ardent explorer. Now Elizabeth L. Dugger lives "next door" in Vermont, "with a lake at my feet and a mountain behind me." Her two sons are nearly grown and also follow their grandmother's and mother's tradition of seeking adventures. Both the *Adventure Guide to New Hampshire* and the *Adventure Guide to Vermont* draw on the excitement of exploration; the beauty of New England and the warmth of its people are also reflected in the author's regionally well-known poetry and fiction. She bought her first pair of hiking boots especially for climbing Mt. Washington, highest peak in New Hampshire, which she describes as an adventure for the soul as well as the feet.

Author's Foreword

A mountain topped with snow, even in June. A river where willows bend so close to the water that the trout practically nip them. A field of wildflowers, and a picnic basket where aged cheddar cheese, fresh bread, and a few bottles of a local microbrew nestle. A wilderness road that leads to a vista of the Presidential Mountain Range, or a village inn where the view includes two mountain ranges at once.

From Boston, the nearest "big city," New Hampshire is less than an hour's drive. How could so many spectacular or charming places still be there? I found the answer at a ranger station in Gorham, the northernmost gateway into the White Mountain National Forest. I had watched a video there of extreme skiers in Tuckerman Ravine, gathered up brochures on campsites and wildlife, and checked out the tracks of deer and moose. Then I stood leaning against the high wooden desk, talking with the national forest ranger, who seemed willing to take all morning answering questions. He'd just come home to New Hampshire after years on the West Coast. What New Hampshire offers, compared to other places, seemed to him remarkable. "The people here chose to set the land aside," he pointed out. "They made the national forest themselves."

Today, when I spread out my New Hampshire road map, the national forest takes up a huge green block in the heart of the state. Private and state preservation groups support even more land being set aside. My guess is that fully a quarter of New Hampshire is maintained as forests and mountains, swift rivers and freshwater lakes, and that even more of the state is charming villages and funky small cities. Even the tiny 18-mile strip of seacoast is almost all saved as rugged beach.

That's how New Hampshire people have chosen to make the place. Take the seacoast, for example. Those stretches of white sand are simply set off with rugged strips of boulders and basic bathhouses for changing into your swimsuit. There's nothing to keep you away from the ocean, and the distant shadow of the Isles of Shoals invites you to jump onto a fishing or touring boat. In the background is the summer resort mood of Hampton

Beach, and you can play in the arcades when you want a dose of flashing lights and sweet treats. At the north end of the seacoast is Odiorne Point, a state refuge with the wild tang of the sea.

From Odiorne Point, the city of Portsmouth is less than 15 minutes away, though you'd never guess it. Just a few minutes of winding sandy roads and you're in a port that dates back to before America was its own country. It's a walker's paradise, compact and colorful, with gutsy coffee shops and savory ethnic restaurants surrounded by colonial-era buildings, a living history park, and boats still plying the port.

There's a pragmatic central industrial strip of the state that includes Manchester, topped by the capital city, Concord. Picture a small town with a statehouse in the middle of it. The Audubon Society pulls together terrific resources here, as do other forest and wildlife groups with statewide energy. It's a good launching point into the open lands and classic villages of the rest of New Hampshire.

For instance, the Lakes District has been a vacation spot for as long as there have been settlers here. A hundred years ago, 200 years ago, even 300 years back, people discovered the open waters you tour or the rocky point where you sun yourself. Yet the husky mountain slopes nearby still have rugged trails where the backs of your legs burn from effort and the hawks soar overhead. Craftspeople quilt with traditional fabrics and landscape painters ache for the afternoon light.

I liked, too, the settled feel of Dartmouth and Lake Sunapee, to the west, where inns and even restaurants are steeped in history, where towns with green-lawned central squares doze in the sunshine. Bakeries abound; so do microbreweries and museums.

Off in the southwest corner of the state, Monadnock raises its rocky head above the landscape. Probably the most climbed peak in New England, it's still a challenge, with its wintery winds, raw rainy days, and rugged rock faces. Somehow development spared the area around it, so there's a wild gorge to descend into, as well as farms with horses to ride, and a lifetime of antique shops to explore.

Part of me came newly alive in the central core of national forest. These are mountains big enough to seize you in their woodlands and endless trails. I met skiers exhilarated from the sweep of snowy slopes, passionate kayak and canoe paddlers shooting the rapids or meandering with the gentler summertime currents, and hundreds of hikers – some in merry groups, some alone, confronting rock and rise. Bed and breakfast inns nestled along sun-warmed rural roadsides, or in winter offered luxurious fireplaces to take the chill off before indulging in superb meals. Bicyclists pedalled determinedly through the mountain passes.

My own best moment came in hiking through the Eagle Pass in Franconia Notch. It's a secluded twist of the trail that leads to Mt. Lafayette. The path winds down among oversize boulders and into a dark grotto of thick green. I paused to find more breath, steady my feet for the ups and downs of rock. Overhead came a fierce cry of "Kek-kek-kek" as a peregrine falcon warned me off its terrain. It flew upward, then dived again toward me. "Kek-kek-kek." A hundred years ago its ancestors probably screeched at the trailblazers here; 200 years ago, at the Native Americans cutting across to the next river.

At last, beyond the mountains, "north of the Notches" as the local residents describe it, the untamed Great North Woods hides hundreds of moose, miles of trout streams, patches of old-growth forest. Snowshoes still make practical sense in the winter months. The shopkeepers talk with local expressions or with French-Canadian accents. Small planes climb the winds, as do ospreys, those huge fish-eating birds of prey. Waterfalls approach two-lane highways or hide deep in gullies where there's ice even in July. Get a fresh map each spring; the back roads (ideal for biking) change from year to year. Really.

It was in a small white clapboard building in Sugar Hill, a tiny town above Franconia Notch, that I realized how deep and old are my own ties to New Hampshire. The historical society's museum there has a neatly organized genealogical collection. I thumbed to the P section: Palmer. I found my mother's distant cousins, and a few not so distant. Photos on the walls reminded me of the ones she saved in albums and cardboard boxes. The white-haired lady at the desk offered me iced tea with a sprig of mint and an oatmeal cookie. I was wearing my hiking boots, carrying my notebooks and camera, obviously not a local resident. It didn't matter. I was welcome – both there and in the field of wildly blooming lupines down the road, where I could look out over the mountains and lie under an immense old maple tree. I looked at the view for a long time, naming the peaks I could recognize.

And picked out a fresh adventure for tomorrow.

In the Shadow of the Mountains

Love in the shadow of the mountains
how it flutters like the pine trees
when the night breezes stroke their spiky hair
quivering into the heartwood.
How it echoes
down the dark lake water
coughs against the low cliffs
in the slap of a sudden southeast gust.
It strains to grow from old rocks
and the roots buckle, thrusting knobby grey ridges
toward the dampness.
Love in the shadow
quick as moonlit deer just vanishing
abrupt as partridge in the cedars
hushed as fox paws padding the trail
where the granite mountains cloak themselves
in shadows.

– *Elizabeth L. Dugger*

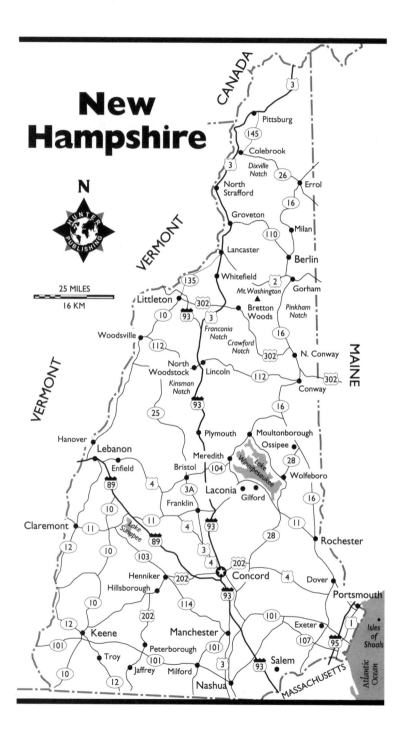

Introduction

New Hampshire is a place for root: roots of massive white pines, and roots of delicate endangered alpine flowers. Roots of mountains, and roots of American independence.

It's also a place to climb peaks: peaks of the White Mountains, and peaks of spiritual delight in vast tracts of woodland, sparkling lakes, and crisp winter air with snow dancing in the wind.

For the adventure traveler, New Hampshire offers a chance to feel alive again. You don't have to hang from your fingers on a cliff face (although Cathedral Ledge is a good place to try it); or pedal a mountain bike up to a phenomenal vista across three states; and you don't have to be splashed with a torrent of spring whitewater on the Androscoggin River to wake you up. Instead, you can climb out of an antique bed with its down comforter in a homey bed-and-breakfast inn, or luxuriate in a grand hotel in the mountains, or wake in a sleeping bag on the ground, listening to the whistle of hawk overhead.

Or you can do what New Hampshire's most famous poet, **Robert Frost**, so often must have done: walk down a country road and think about the stone walls, the generations of farm families, and the open infinity of a night under the bright stars, and find your own words or satisfactions. New Hampshire calls you to the "road less traveled by," and for you as well as for Robert Frost, it may make all the difference.

History

Long before white settlers arrived in New Hampshire, **Native Americans** inhabited the state. Traces of Paleo-Indians from 15,000 years ago remain in a few places, but the more recent tribes were Abenaki, Sokosis, and Pennacook, members of the Algonquin Indians. **Abenaki Indians** were most prominent. The river valleys were vital to their existence: streams and rivers full of fish and shellfish, riverbanks crowded with animals to hunt for food and fur. They also traveled along the rivers, and divers today find artifacts the Native Americans left behind under the cold waters.

They also left behind their names for many places. The name of the Ammonoosuc River means "fish place"; Androscoggin is "fish curing place," a place to smoke and dry food for the winter. Pemigewasset means "swift current," and Saco is "flowing out." These are four of the great rivers of the state; a fifth, the Connecticut, derives from Counitegou for "the long river." Mountain names like Kancamagus and Chocorua evoke the chiefs who lived and died here.

Settlement of New Hampshire began at the seacoast, and there are still homes along the shore that date back to pre-Revolutionary years. The first settlement was at **Odiorne Point**, now part of Rye, in 1623. By 1680 there were four towns in the state – Dover, Hampton, Exeter, and Portsmouth – although the total population was only 3,000. Nearly a century later there were 82,000 people, all of whom eagerly supported the call for independence. More than half of the combat troops at the Battle of Bunker Hill on June 17, 1775, came from New Hampshire. In the war that followed, Portsmouth was a critical seaport and was armed with forts. Today, many villages have changed little in appearance since those early years of settlement: green-lawned common at the center, white-spired church, and trim meetinghouse for gatherings of government and community.

Farther north, the **White Mountains** lured explorers like Darby Field, believed to be the first white man to climb Mt. Washington. After the end of the French and Indian War (1763), settlers headed up the mountain passes and cleared the slopes for crops and pastures. Scientists and artists arrived as guests, and farmers became innkeepers. By the 1850s, thousands were visiting the White Mountains for pleasure, and Ethan Allen Crawford built a pleasure trail to the top of Mt. Washington. As the railroads arrived, grand hotels and inns developed for the guests.

Along with the railroads came the **timber barons**, hungry for profit taken from stripping the mountains. Fires flared in the dry brush left from logging, and thousands of acres burned, scarring the landscape and galvanizing both citizens' groups and government to action. When the **Weeks Law**, named after a New Hampshire congressman, passed in the US Congress in 1911, it meant the **White Mountain National Forest** could be established, buying back land from private hands and starting an immense restoration effort.

The scarred landscape healed. Forests covered the mountains again, and auto touring became popular. Some pockets of virgin timber remained in isolated spots, and the trees around them turned the state green once more.

Travelers interested in **geology** can pick up a publication on the geology of the White Mountains at ranger stations in the White Mountain National Forest. Rock and mineral collectors will find notes in the *Sightseeing* and *On Foot* sections for mountains and trails that may be of special interest to them.

Geography

Rivers, lakes, and mountains make New Hampshire a state of adventure and of contrast. Farthest to the north, along the international border with Canada, mountains isolate the **Great North Woods Region**, where outdoor activities bind local and visitor together in enthusiasm.

The **White Mountain**s occupy the bulk of the state's northern half, just south of the Great North Woods. The highest peak in New England is here, Mt. Washington, its rocky summit 6,288 feet above sea level. It is part of the Presidential Range, a group of imposing mountains that challenge hikers and climbers, and provide dramatic ski slopes and back-country travel on wheels, on foot, on skis and snowshoes, and by air. To the east of the Presidentials is the Mahoosuc Range, and to the west, the Kinsman Range.

South of the White Mountains the land subsides into smaller but still respectable mountains commonly 3,000 feet at the summit, with hundreds of lakes and ponds capturing and releasing the rapidly flowing rivers. The largest of these lakes, like Winnipesaukee, Squam and Ossipee, are the heart of the **Lakes Region**.

The western part of this area of gentler mountains was settled early, with the founding of Dartmouth College in Hanover encouraging cultural assets and the attention of writers and artists. Nearby Lake Sunapee attracted summer residents who returned year after year for generations, creating another source of grace and stability locally. This is the **Dartmouth-Lake Sunapee Region**.

In the southwestern corner of the state is the massive bulk of Mt. Monadnock, its peak a surprising 3,165 feet above sea level, towering over the river valleys and nearby highlands. Villages in these protected valleys escaped the modernization that marched up the interstate highways, and state and privately preserved land became so common that a Greenway of hiking land through the midst of the **Monadnock Region** was easily established recently. Dairy farms, maple sugaring, and horseback riding still abound here.

Rivers determined the early growth of the state. Its largest cities are in the south along the Merrimack River, now also the corridor of Interstate 93, connected with the Boston metropolitan area. Visitors flying into the state generally arrive either in Boston or in the New Hampshire mill city of Manchester, half an hour north of the Massachusetts border. Like Manchester, the state's capital, Concord, arose in the **Merrimack River Valley**; Nashua is the other sizable city, and it too is in this grouping.

The state also has a seacoast, 18 miles long but critical in its Revolutionary history and still remarkably unspoiled. Sandy beaches follow one after another, separated by small strips of rocky tidepool habitat. Whales come close to the shore, seals sun themselves on the rocks, and deep-sea fishermen haul record catches of fighting fish like bluefins. In this book, the **Seacoast Region** is the final chapter.

Climate

New Hampshire's four distinct seasons offer great variety. **Summers** are warm and sunny, with average daytime temperatures in the 70s, and nights are usually cool. **Autumn**, when the mountains and lowlands turn gold and scarlet as the hardwood leaves change color, is a crisp and energetic season loved by most New Englanders. **Winter** begins with the first dusting of snow in late October and approaches ski season by mid-November; the snow lasts until late March at least, with the last few storms considered "sugar snow," prolonging the harvest of maple sap to be boiled into maple syrup and other treats. When **spring** arrives in April it is welcomed eagerly, and blossoms erupt in meadows and on mountainsides.

AVERAGE DAILY TEMPERATURES	
January	21°
February	23°
March	32°
April	44°
May	56°
June	65°
July	70°
August	67°
September	60°
October	49°
November	38°
December	25°
Average monthly precipitation is 3.2"	

The **temperature** range on any day can be quite wide. Not only does a summer day rise to 80° or 90° and drop to 40° at night, but the highest mountains can experience wind, fog, hail, and even snow at any time of year. Alpine hikers do well to prepare thoroughly. Even those touring by car or strolling around the villages and back roads should take an extra layer of warm clothing. Sea breezes along the coast can also be startlingly chilly.

Flora & Fauna

The glorious fall foliage of New Hampshire comes from its maple, beech, birch, and other hardwood trees, whose leaves turn red, yellow, and harvest gold during September. By mid-October the display is over. Trees and farms also give New

Why Socks Are A Good Idea

Poison ivy does grow in some areas of New Hampshire. Walking on established trails will keep you away from it, but if you bushwhack through fields and low shrubs, keep an eye out and remember the old rhyme: leaflets three, let it be.

You'll see plenty of hikers in shorts in the summer, but notice the long socks they are wearing. Even in New Hampshire, ticks are found, and some them, especially in the south and east, may transmit Lyme disease. Wearing socks when you're hiking will save you from a lot of worry afterward; long pants are also a good idea if you're moving through high grass.

Hampshire its characteristic summer green. Fruit trees, like apple and wild cherry, cover the hillsides with spring blossoms.

It wasn't always this way. In the late 1800s New Hampshire's trees were stripped from the White Mountains to feed the growth spurt of the nation. But ardent conservation efforts have restored the forests. In small isolated pockets there are some trees that may never have been cut since white settlers arrived; these are called **virgin forest**, or sometimes simply old-growth trees. In the hiking descriptions, this book points out where you may see some of them.

Above the treeline of the mountains in the Presidential and Franconia mountain ranges are small communities of **alpine plants**. Well adapted for short growing seasons, high winds, and severe winters, these small plants are fascinating to examine. It may take a hundred years for a plant to reach eight inches in height.

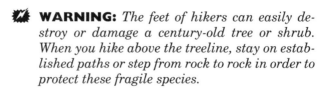

WARNING: *The feet of hikers can easily destroy or damage a century-old tree or shrub. When you hike above the treeline, stay on established paths or step from rock to rock in order to protect these fragile species.*

Especially in danger is *Potentilla robbinsiana*, or **dwarf cinquefoil**, which grows on a barren quarter-acre in the Presidential Range. Larger pockets of this plant have been successfully re-established; recovery plans are also ongoing for some rare **wild orchids** like the small whorled pogonia. Stop at a forest ranger station to get pictures of the plants and information about their survival.

Rare plants are also often found in **bogs**, swampy areas turned acidic through the growth of peat. Many New Hampshire bogs have become plant preserves, with boardwalks so that visitors can see the plants without damaging them.

Wild animals are not confined to the mountains; **deer, raccoons**, **squirrels**, and **skunks** visit the back yards of village residents and even appear in urban areas at times. But it is certainly a thrill to watch them in forests and meadows, and if you walk the back roads at dusk you are bound to meet some close up.

> ✺ **WILDLIFE ALERT:** *Remember that wild animals should remain wild; an animal that approaches you may be ill with rabies, and should be avoided, not petted. It is also critical that hikers and campers not feed bears, even accidentally; a bear that associates food with humans loses its reluctance to approach people and becomes dangerous.*

Two rare animals draw special attention from both visitors and residents: the common loon, which sadly is no longer common, and the moose. The **loon** is beginning to recolonize New Hampshire lakes, and Squam Lake is most famous for these large black and white water birds. The **moose**, like the deer, was rare in the state for a period of time, crowded by changes in the landscape and by hunting. But moose now thrive in any part of New Hampshire that can offer them water plants in summer and mountain browsing on maple and aspen in winter – which means everywhere north of Concord, at least.

Moose are fascinating animals, tall and gangly in appearance but able to move very quickly, and are a symbol of wilderness preservation to many people. They calve in the spring, often with twins, which remain with their mother until the next year's birthing. They can often be seen near roadsides, savoring the salt left over from the previous winter's road treatments.

MOOSE ALERT

Many moose-car collisions take place each spring as the yearlings wander independently without understanding of roads. Remember:

- A moose won't necessarily run away from a car, even if you blow the horn.

- A moose may weigh up to 1,200 pounds; it is big enough to crush the car and should be allowed to move out of the way.

- Moose eyes do reflect light, but because the animal is eight feet tall, your car headlights may not reach the eyes.

- The hood of your vehicle fits under the belly of the long-legged moose, causing the animal's full weight to land on the windshield and hood of a car in a collision. Avoid hitting a moose.

- Moose are more active at dusk and at night. Slow down and look carefully.

New Hampshire is rich in **bird life**, from **great blue herons** to **woodland warblers** to raptors like **hawks** and **eagles**. Ranger stations in the White Mountain National Forest have bird lists, and the Concord headquarters of the Audubon Society of New Hampshire can help you learn bird calls and other forms of identification.

Moose starting to cross a highway in the
Great North Woods region. Would you see him in time?

Travel Information

Winter Travel

New Hampshire roads are well kept in winter, and travel is only seriously restricted during a few snowstorms each year. Ice on the roads is far more dangerous, and state police and local radio stations should be consulted about major highway travel during icy conditions. Here are a few tips for winter driving if you are on back roads or need to travel in heavy snow:

- If you have a choice, get snow tires rather than all-season; it makes a difference if you're doing a lot of snow driving.

- Always add a gas-line "drying" fluid to your tank if the night temperature is going below zero.

- Go slowly. Many difficult road conditions can still be managed if you slow down enough.

- Listen to the weather forecast, the local news and to people at the general stores. If the state police have closed the road or are recommending that people stay home, take it seriously; going off the road on ice makes a trip take much longer and pushes the stress level up to where it's just not fun anymore.

- If you're going to drive in snow for more than a week or so, put a shovel in the trunk and carry a bag of cat litter; these two simple things will get you out of most common problems. (The cat litter goes on the ground to give your tires traction.)

Unpaved Roads

Unpaved roads are common in New Hampshire, and are a wonderful way to see the back country from your car, on a bicycle, or on foot. In early spring, unpaved roads may turn to a gluey mud surface, and this time of year is called **"mud season."** If you are driving through an area, stop and ask at a general store about road conditions before you leave the pavement. Hikers need to stay out of the woods and off the mountain slopes as much as possible during mud season, because boots and shoes compact the wet soil and make it impossible for plants to grow in it – thus encouraging erosion. Mountain bikers also can help protect the forests by staying off muddy trails.

Summer Travel

Summer presents a special problem: **water**. Hikers and other people active outdoors need plenty of water and, sadly, it's just not safe to drink the lovely clear water running at your feet down the mountain slopes. *Giardia*, an intestinal parasite, is present in most outdoor water, spread in part by beavers. So either carry enough drinking water for your activities (hikers need at least two quarts per day, per person), or bring with you filters or purifiers specifically able to deal with *Giardia*.

■ Fall Foliage

Autumn is the season for leaf peeping. Bring plenty of color film. The narrow red leaves you see close to the road on shrubs are **sumac**; the others are **pin cherry** and the familiar five-

lobed **maple** leaf. Golden leaves
can be maple, **basswood**, **beech**,
birch, and **poplar** or **aspen**, as
well as **mountain ash** in narrow-
leaved clusters. **Red oak** leaves
are a hearty brown. Look for the
red berries of the mountain ash,

**NEW HAMPSHIRE
FALL FOLIAGE HOTLINE
☎ 800-258-3608**

too. One evergreen species changes color in the fall: the **tama-
rack**, which turns a clear yellow.

Favorite Foliage Drives

- In the **Great North Woods**, **Route 3** from Pittsburg
  to the Canada border; **Route 145** from Colebrook to
  Pittsburg; and **Route 26** through Dixville Notch.

- In the **White Mountains**, try **Dolly Copp Road**
  (also known as Pinkham B) that cuts from Randolph
  to Route 16 south of Gorham. **Route 302** through
  Crawford Notch and the **Franconia Notch Parkway** (Interstate 93) through Franconia Notch are
  also rich with color. Explore the **Mt. Clinton Road**
  through Jefferson Notch (slowly; the gravel is very
  rough). **Route 142** from Bethlehem to Franconia is a
  winner, as is the road from Franconia through Sugar
  Hill, **Route 117**. And don't miss out on **Route 49**
  from Campton to Waterville Valley.

- In the **Lakes Region**, the roads over and around
  Gunstock Mountain, west of Lake Winnipesaukee,
  are good ones, as is the circuit around the **Squam
  Lakes**.

- For the **Dartmouth/Lake Sunapee Region**, take
  the river roads like **Route 12A** and **Route 10**. Farther south, anywhere around **Mt. Monadnock** will
  offer autumn vistas, and the auto road up **Pack Monadnock** is an easy way to reach a breathtaking
  overview.

Introduction

■ Border Crossings

Border Crossing at Pittsburg, New Hampshire

There's a small border crossing into Canada at the northern tip of New Hampshire, just above the Connecticut Lakes. You must stop there when you return to the United States after visiting Canada. If the crossing is not manned (at night), you must report to the border crossing at **Beecher Falls** in Vermont immediately. The borders are "wired" and your crossing will be noted; reporting in is mandatory.

For the most part, though, border crossings are simply a matter of stating your name and destination and showing a driver's license on occasion; no passport is needed for US citizens entering Canada, but an extra insurance rider is necessary, and you should notify your car insurance agent if you will be going there.

> **WARNING:** *Please don't try to joke with Border Patrol officers; between illegal immigrants, drugs, and ordinary Customs problems, they have little sense of humor and have been known to make extended searches of cars and belongings.*

■ Transportation

The New Hampshire border is half an hour from Boston by car. **Amtrak** trains serve part of the state; call for schedules (☎ 228-8580 or 800-872-7245). There are some long-distance bus routes through **Greyhound/Vermont Transit** (☎ 436-0163) and **Concord Trailways** (☎ 228-3300); Concord and Hanover have public bus transportation, and the Lakes Region in summer has a trolley.

White Mountain hikers can arrange for trailhead-to-trailhead transport with the Appalachian Mountain Club through its Pinkham Notch shuttle service; contact the AMC (see White Mountains Region, Pinkham Notch).

Manchester's airport handles most flights coming into New Hampshire. Continental Express, Delta Connection, United, and USAir fly into Manchester.

▪ Costs

Traveling in New Hampshire can be as economical or as luxurious as you choose. Dollar-sign keys are included with accommodations as a guide to the average room price, and correspond with the accommodations key on the right.

> ### ACCOMMODATIONS KEY
>
> For hotels and resorts, prices are per person, per night, double occupancy. For bed & breakfasts, prices are usually per room, per night. Be sure to ask when you make your reservations.
>
> | | |
> |---|---|
> | \$. . . . . | Up to \$50 |
> | \$\$. . . . . | \$50 to \$100 |
> | \$\$\$. . . . . | \$101 to \$175 |
> | \$\$\$\$. . . . . | \$176 and up |

Foliage season (September through mid-October) is a very busy time, and rates are usually higher then. Be sure to reserve well in advance – arrangements for leaf season accommodations are often made a year ahead.

Special Concerns

Two brief reminders for hikers in particular: Rocky hikes require **hiking boots**. And take plenty of **drinking water** with you.

Campers should pick up applicable rules for **wilderness camping** from a ranger station in the White Mountain National Forest. **Camping** is not allowed above the treeline in the National Forest, and **fires** are prohibited in most areas. Other rules apply. Most of all, in order to preserve wilderness and back-country freshness for yourself and others, practice "leave no trace" camping and hiking.

How To Use This Book

This book divides New Hampshire into seven regions. The first five are best known for their mountains, rivers, and lakes. They are the **Great North Woods**, at the farthest tip of the state, the **White Mountains Region**, the **Lakes Region**, the **Dartmouth/Lake Sunapee Region**, and the **Monadnock Region**. New Hampshire's major cites are found in the **Merrimack Valley Region**, the area you reach first from Boston if you enter the state by car. New Hampshire also has a short but superb **Seacoast Region**, where nearly all of the 18 miles of coast is reserved for public use as sandy beaches and rocky wind-swept ocean promontories. This book is designed to help you explore any or all of these regions, and to plan tours and connect with local resources. Note: All New Hampshire telephone numbers are area code 603.

Each chapter starts with a general introduction to the region. This covers the layout of the major roadways and connections among villages. The sections that follow give specific adventures for each location. There are opportunities for independent explorers, as well as for linking up with knowledgable guides, whether of wildlife, of canoe routes, or of mountain slopes, summer or winter. Your adventures can be as vigorous and challenging or as simple and harmonious as you like. For example, a visit to Lake Winnipesaukee in the Lakes Region could include fishing, sailing on a cruising sloop, mountain biking or skiing on Gunstock Mountain, or exploring the well-worn trails of Mt. Major. On the other hand, photographing the islands of the lake and then visiting the nearby Castle in the Clouds, or exploring colonial history in Wolfeboro may require only a relaxing drive along the back roads.

Suggestions for accommodations and dining are offered in each section, along with useful local phone numbers and sometimes e-mail and Web site addresses. Then, village by village, there's a tour of the sightseeing opportunities – from Federal-era mansions to museums to amusement parks.

Here are brief descriptions of the types of activities explored under each of the categories.

■ On Foot

Hiking, Backpacking, Rock Climbing

You could be looking for an easy scenic stroll to calm your pulse, or a strenuous challenge. New Hampshire's northern mountains offer you more of the up-and-down version, and its villages and farmlands provide restful rambles. You'll be amazed at how much of New Hampshire's greenery has been preserved, either by the state or towns or privately, to ensure generations of access to trees, streams and wildlife. This category will let you know where to go and how to prepare for it: by packing a sunscreen and a comfy pair of sneakers, or toting field glasses and a bird book to tell the hawks apart, or gearing up for fierce weather above the treeline on a mountain peak. There are hundreds of miles of trails in New Hampshire, and countless back roads that are nearly as unpopulated. Those cities, towns, and villages richest in historical architecture and events also offer self-guided walking tours.

Most of the landscape is open to your feet at no charge, although the White Mountain National Forest system is experimenting with modest seasonal use fees with a "passport" that you leave visible in your car. You don't need to check in with a ranger first, although one way to get a passport is to visit one of the national forest ranger stations or campgrounds. Just head out to the start of the trail. If a ranger passes your car while you're up on the mountain, he or she will leave you a mail-in envelope. Your contribution helps make up for drops in federal funding. Count on private recreation areas starting to charge access fees, too; $5 per day is about the highest you'll pay for basic walk-around privileges, but $20 per season is more likely.

A number of the **hikes** in this book are short and simple: half-hour approaches to waterfalls or stunning vistas. Most are mid-range efforts, taking half a day and drawing you up worthwhile climbs that reward with wildlife sightings and stunning views. Lightweight hiking shoes with some ankle support are nice for these, but sturdy walking shoes will also carry you on most daytrips. For mountain hikes, rugged hiking boots with relatively stiff soles are preferable, since they'll keep your feet from being bruised by the rocks underfoot. No matter where you hike, plan to run into patches of mud or wet ground here and there; all those streams and rivers leak now and then, and rain isn't quick to evaporate either!

Rock climbers can get a challenge in nearly any region of the state, but the best-known ledges are in the White Mountains and the Great North Woods, with a few closer to Dartmouth College. The best preparation for rock climbing is to go to North Conway and visit the mountain-climbing shops in town, where there are maps, guides, and up-to-date information on rock slides and avalanche danger (a real threat in winter). This guide mentions some of the traditional climbs, like Cathedral Ledge and Cannon Mountain, as well as a few surprises (see Rumney, page 190, for instance).

> ✹ **CAUTION:** *Fires are generally not welcome in open woods these days unless you're in a campground, but check for details in each region and for each trail. Also, always bring along drinking water; the nuisance parasite* Giardia *infests many streams and lakes, especially if beavers are in the area, and water color and clarity are not real indicators of safety.*

Trailblazing clubs like the Appalachian Mountain Club and the Randolph Mountain Club have opened northern New Hampshire's wonders to hikers and travelers. Also, nearly 50 miles of trails in the southwestern part of the state now make up the Sunapee-Monadnock Greenway. With these advantages, a sense of courtesy to the land and its residents has become critical. In addition, regions above the treeline include precious stands of rare alpine plants that may not look so special at first glance. They also grow tiny wind-dwarfed trees, where a foot of growth could result from a hundred years of stubborn roots mining nutrients out of the rock and dust. Please stay on the trails when you are above treeline, always. Save off-trail exploring for the lower, more richly endowed areas.

A Note About Hunting

Hunting is a specialized outdoor activity, demanding specific skills and a respect for the land and its inhabitants. New Hampshire regulates hunting closely in terms of seasons and methods of taking game. Hunting bears, deer, and wild birds takes up much of the autumn and some of the winter. There are other trapping and hunting seasons also. Please obtain state materials if you're interested in hunting. Many outfitters and guides provide hunting services; this information is so readily available that this book does not list them.

> ✸ **CAUTION:** *If you are walking in the woods in the firearm deer season – generally in November – wear light, bright clothing, preferably the "blaze orange" caps and vests offered in most general stores and sports stores. Deer season attracts many newcomers and inexperienced hunters who may mistake your presence for that of the animal they've waited so long to see. Better yet, stay out of the woods entirely during deer season. You will be doing a kindness to yourself, to the hunters, and to the animals, who need no extra disturbance at this time.*

■ On Wheels

You don't need a four-wheel-drive vehicle to travel in New Hampshire, unless you're headed for the Great North Woods in winter and planning to leave Route 3! In general, even the back roads of the state are well taken care of, summer and snow. Mountain notch roads are often closed in winter, though, like the road through Jefferson Notch, the route called Dolly Copp near Gorham, and the northern end of Route 49 beyond Waterville Valley. If you plan to tour by car or truck in the winter, do look over the suggestions for *Winter*

Driving (page 9) to refresh your memory of (or get acquainted with) some of the standard precautions.

> ❄ **MOOSE ALERT:** *More dangerous than snow-storms in terms of number of car accidents is the state's wildlife, especially moose. These spectacular hoofed browsers aren't tuned in to either headlights or horns as signals to leave the road. New Hampshire advises that you "Brake for Moose" – in other words, stop and let the moose move out of the way. Colliding with a moose at high speed on the highway usually destroys a car as the heavy animal crushes its roof and windshield; you can imagine that the driver suffers, too. Slow down, especially at dusk, and leave extra stopping room at night, too. If you stop to watch a moose or other wildlife, like deer or bears, be sure to pull well off the roadway.*

Biking

Mountain biking benefits from the many hiking trails in the state, although the national forest posts a few restricted-use areas where wheels aren't welcome due to threatened plantlife.

> ➡ **TIP:** *Where trails cross private land, please do stop and ask permission to use them; this courtesy goes a long way toward landowners keeping their land open, not posted.*

The high-tech multispeed bikes with their rugged tires are a perfect fit for even the less active rider, easing the way your legs pump along the rising terrain. And for those who appreciate the unusual, mountain biking on snow is becoming increasingly popular, with local bike shops stocking studded tires and those equipped with chains for traction.

Back road biking offers a different set of challenges. Visitors devoted to just relaxing can enjoy pedaling along tree-lined byways, gazing at old country homes, surprising a grazing deer in a nearby pasture or even meeting one around the corner of a dirt road. The river valleys, especially along the Connecticut, are best for these trips. Many villages offer bike loops, and state parks like Pawtuckaway provide networks.

This book highlights most of the designated bike trails and some especially scenic routes to take among the villages. Also mentioned are supportive bike shops for repairs, rentals, and route planning.

Naturally, you'll want a helmet for bicycling. This is especially important because even a small hill can get your wheels spinning fast enough to carry you into a tree trunk if a stone in the road happens to send you off course. It's also common sense. Other basic reminders apply: Dress for the changes in weather, especially temperature; wear bright colors; carry water with you; and hug the right side of the road.

■ On Water

Loosely speaking, New Hampshire waters are divided into flat water (lakes) and rivers. Canoes and kayaks will take you into real wilderness, and the awkward stance of a blue heron can surprise you at the bend of the river. You can come so close to a loon on Umbagog Lake that you'll see the blank glitter of its beady black eyes (although if it's nesting season, please stay farther back). On Winnipesaukee or Winnisquam, Newfound or Sunapee, there are wide spaces for sailing, motoring and, of course, board sailing, that intensely personal interaction with wind and water.

The Appalachian Mountain Club puts out a *River Guide* to both New Hampshire and Vermont in a single volume, a good notion since the Connecticut River is shared by the two states. State parks on lakes usually have boats available. Rental shops for kayaks and canoes abound in the Lakes Region, and both the Saco River and Umbagog Lake have guide and lesson options for whitewater enthusiasts, new or experienced. The whitewater classification chart on the next page gives information on the skill levels of rapids.

WHITEWATER CLASSIFICATION CHART		
CLASS	SKILL LEVEL	WATER CONDITION
I	Easy	Calm, moving water with occasional riffles.
II	Intermediate	Little bursts of bouncing rapids in clear, wide channels between long stretches of calm.
III	Difficult	Irregular waves through narrower channels where maneuvering around rocks is required.
IV	Very Difficult	Rapids are intense, loud, and long, with complex, rocky obstacles in the way.
V	Exceptionally Difficult	Rapids are long, loud, narrow, and violent, following one after the other without interruption.

Cruising

If you'd rather enjoy the water at a slower pace, check out the larger cruise ships on Winnipesaukee, the Squam Lakes, and Lake Sunapee. Or enjoy a float trip down the Connecticut River.

Fishing

Fishing is a big part of lakeshore and backwoods life, as evident in the general stores closest to boat accesses: Often a special refrigerator is set aside for neat stacks of capped containers, each labeled "worms!" In winter, live bait means minnows, and some shops have their own tanks where you can scoop out a netful. Fly-fishing is a separate art; watch for the occasional roadside sign of a fly-tying pro.

➔ **FISHING LICENSES:** *For freshwater fishing, if you're older than 12, you need a license, junior version, which you upgrade to an adult license after age 15. It's not expensive, and the money goes to the excellent cause of taking care of the lakes, rivers, and streams. Licenses are available at many general stores, as well as through the New Hampshire Fish and Game Department (☎ 271-3421). No license is necessary for saltwater fishing.*

Swimming

New Hampshire waters are safe for summer swimming. Lifeguards are found only at designated patrolled beaches, such as those in the Lakes Region. If you've never skinny-dipped, a secluded backwoods pond can bring you this experience, which is less and less likely in other locations!

🔥 **CAUTION:** *Dipping in a small brook or under a cascade is a special reward for heading up a mountain trail, but beware of slippery rock surfaces.*

Diving

Scuba diving is extra popular on Lake Winnipesaukee, where there are a number of wrecks as well as interesting underwater terrain; river scuba diving is a new attraction, sometimes a way to find Native American artifacts. Ocean dives take place year-round. Classes as well as equipment locations are listed in this book.

▪ With Llamas & On Horseback

You know how to throw yourself into a hike with enthusiasm, how to look over the hillside or the trail across the fields and feel the challenge and freshness of it. Your feet itch to move forward, and your legs already anticipate the steady swing of a good stride. But have you ever considered taking a gentler, less demanding approach? Slowing down enough to savor the sunlight on the trees, the scent of the forest floor, the gentle movement of falling leaves?

Here's where trekking with llamas becomes a gift of serenity that you can give to yourself and your companions. These gentle, mild hiking companions can easily carry a load of about 75 pounds, provided it's expertly arranged, and still keep pace with you along a hillside. They're not for carrying humans; they're for carrying the incidentals that make a trip pleasant. Often a llama trek includes a gourmet meal, complete with tablecloth and dishes, and sometimes even the table. And the steady stamina of the llama inspires its fellow walkers.

Horses were once the pack animal of the White Mountains, and both Crawford and Franconia Notches have former bridle trails that hikers now enjoy. Chances to ride New Hampshire horses are infrequent but exhilarating; check out the stables at the luxurious Mount Washington Hotel and Resort, page 124.

■ On Snow & Ice

Skiing

 New Hampshire offers some of the best skiing in the east, in terms of Nordic trails (which are everywhere!), wilderness skiing in the White Mountains (especially Tuckerman Ravine in the spring), as well as downhill skiing. As early as mid-October there is snow on the highest peaks, and by mid-November there's reliable snowcover in the north. Christmas, New Year's, and the holidays of January and February and even April are downhill skiing delights.

Cross-country skiers, who can enjoy even a few inches of white stuff, make the most of the long frozen season. The White Mountain National Forest has trails open year-round; the state parks also invite Nordic skiers to explore.

Many of the country inns and bed-and-breakfast homes and farms realize how entrancing the countryside is to Nordic skiers, and have their own trail networks and connections to the national and state parks. Try going all the way north to Dixville Notch for the flavor of a grand resort with skiing; the Mount

Washington Hotel and Resort, now owner of nearby Bretton Woods Ski Area, also offers great snow sports and luxurious après-ski environments.

Other Winter Sports

Other snow sports include **snowboarding**, usually done at the downhill ski slopes, **snowmobile riding** (guided tours are available, as well as rentals, especially in the Great North Woods), and the ice specialties of **skating** and **ice fishing** (done through a hole in lake ice, which may be a foot or more thick). And in the mountains, rock climbers spend their winters in the strenuous challenges of ice climbing, which is taught to groups by some of the year-round adventure specialists in the North Conway and Lincoln areas, as well as the Appalachian Mountain Club.

The listings for each region give the established downhill ski slopes and the classic cross-country trail networks. Back roads, especially logging roads where no wheeled traffic enters in winter, can be as glorious to ski as a resort. Maps of snowmobile trails and of the numerous national forest trails are readily available at chambers of commerce and national forest ranger stations.

■ **WEATHER WARNING:** *Remember that weather shifts are extreme; in particular, do not go into unmarked mountain wilderness regions without proper guidance and equipment. Bear in mind that frostbite can occur even at relatively mild temperatures, as long as the wind is blowing. Your best advice may come from the morning's weather forecasts, which can be extensive and will warn of frostbite, wind changes, and severe temperature drops. Even for the snowbunny who loves best the fireplace and the good book, a sense of what's happening outside will enhance each day's pleasure.*

■ In The Air

Scenic Flights, Ballooning, Gliding

 The tiny airports of northern New Hampshire provide a surprising number of small year-round state and private airfields. Small planes offer a fresh view of the mountain scenery, often for a very modest cost (about $25 for a 15-minute scenic flight for two people). There's a flight park in North Charlestown where you can learn to paraglide or hang glide, and parasailing is big at Lake Winnipesaukee.

■ Eco-Travel

 Both the state parks and the White Mountain National Forest provide abundant information on wildlife and geology. Every visit you make to a ranger station or park headquarters will enhance your knowledge of what's in the woods with you. A few special treats are flagged under this heading; don't miss watching the migrating hawks in the Monadnock Region, for example.

■ Where To Stay & Eat

 Country inns and bed-and-breakfast homes line every major route through New Hampshire, and many offer extraordinary cuisine with recognized chefs. Regional listings offer some of the highlights, and give you resources for tracking down more.

 In each region there are tips for sampling some of the less obvious eateries, like tearooms, bakeries, and unusual restaurants. (Your author has a special fondness for the combination of a good hike and a good bakery!) Searching for a special meal can be an enticing adventure; however, if you've been engaging in some vigorous sport or even just traveling on the road for several hours, it's nice to have a good place marked out for dinner and for the night. Microbreweries and the sweeter specialties of chocolate and ice cream shops are also noted.

The finest New Hampshire resorts and hotels are true delights, sometimes dating back to the 1800s; these are listed in each region, as well as a handful of comfortable, country lodgings. Almost all establishments at least offer breakfast, and most are located near restaurants. Listings of bed-and-breakfast homes and of farms open to guests change frequently, so be sure to call ahead. Campgrounds are also noted for those who prefer the fragrance of balsam and crisp night air.

Information Sources

Tourism, Lodging, Etc.

The **New Hampshire Office of Travel and Tourism Development** (PO Box 1856, Concord, NH 03302-1856; ☎ 271-2343) offers a vacation planning kit. US and Canadian residents can get the kit free by calling ☎ 800-386-4664. Lodging information may also be obtained from this office. View their Web site at www.visitnh.com.

The **New Hampshire Campground Owners Association** number is ☎ 800-822-6764.

Many antique shops are mentioned in this guide. For a directory of still more, write to the **New Hampshire Antiques Dealers Association** (PO Box 2033, Hampton, NH 03843), which holds a three-day annual show in August.

The Society for the Preservation of New Hampshire Forests, better known as the **SPNHF**, or just the Forest Society, was formed to encourage creation of preserves. For a lands map and guide to SPNHF properties (now over 100 of them), contact the SPNHF, 54 Portsmouth Street, Concord, NH 03301-5486 (☎ 224-9945); there is a fee. Better yet, visit their headquarters in person and catch up on recent efforts.

Recommended Reading

The books below are mentioned often in this guide, and can be found at or ordered from local bookshops. Some regional guidebooks are also mentioned in the text, along with the addresses of the groups that publish them.

50 Hikes in the White Mountains by Daniel Doan and Ruth Doan MacDougall, Backcountry Publications, Woodstock, VT, 1997.

50 More Hikes in New Hampshire, 4th Edition, by Daniel Doan, Countryman Press, Woodstock, VT, 1998.

AMC White Mountain Guide, 25th edition, Appalachian Mountain Club, Boston, MA.

AMC River Guide to New Hampshire and Vermont, 2nd edition, Appalachian Mountain Club, Boston, MA.

30 Bicycle Tours in New Hampshire by Adolphe Bernotas and Tom and Susan Heavey, Backcountry Publications, The Countryman Press, Woodstock, VT, 1991.

New Hampshire Atlas & Gazetteer, DeLorme, Freeport, ME.

A Guide to Crawford Notch by Mike Dickerman, Boncliff Books, PO Box 385, Littleton, NH 03561.

Autumn Rambles: New England by Michael and Mark Tougias, Hunter Publishing, Edison, NJ 08818, 1998.

The Great North Woods

The region of New Hampshire north of Route 2 is the Great North Woods, a picturesque name for these wide, wild expanses of land available to adventurous explorers. Thick forests, river valley villages, and abundant wildlife characterize the area. Don't be swayed by the fact that paper companies own much of this land; although the loggers and their trucks can be found nibbling at patches of trees, the forest is more than equal to their grazing. An advantage to the hiker or skier is that the massive landholdings are crisscrossed by woods roads, allowing access into the heart of the woods. Moose, bear, deer, brook and lake trout, and birds of prey abound. New Hampshire residents share their passion for the outdoors with visitors, forging a firm bond between old-timers and newcomers.

Getting Around

Enter the Great North Woods from either side of the state: from Lancaster on the Vermont border, or from Gorham at the north edge of the White Mountain National Forest just a few minutes from the state of Maine. The *New Hampshire Highway Map* distributed by the state's Office of Travel and Tourism Development draws a spare outline of roads. **Route 3** traces the Vermont border until it diverges into the center of the state along with the Connecticut River, headed toward the four Connecticut Lakes that are the river's source. From the east in Gorham, **Route 16** also follows a river, the Androscoggin, and brings you north to the frontier-like town of Errol and nearby Lake Umbagog, straddling the Maine border and surrounded by the Mahoosuc Range of the White Mountains. The two north-south highways are connected by rustic **Route 110** as it leads to Stark and West Milan (pronounced MY-l'n), and also by **Route 26** through the rugged mountain pass of Dixville Notch.

Great North Woods

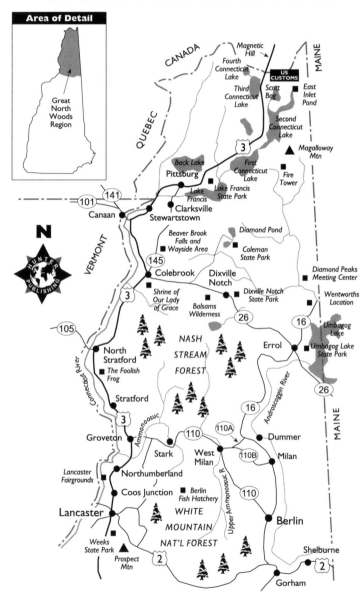

Area of Detail

Great
North
Woods
Region

To fill in the gaps left by the state highway map, start with De-lorme's *New Hampshire Road Atlas and Gazetteer*, which shows a network of secondary roads, many of them graveled rather than paved. The map's weakness is that its printed names of small roads frequently don't match the signs you find while traveling.

Where roads travel over mountains, watch for the occasional road sign that warns, "Not maintained in winter," indicating a road that's more trail than otherwise, a caution for the car driver and a delight for the mountain biker or backwoods ex-plorer.

> ■ **CAUTION:** *It helps to realize the practical rule of the road when the road itself may pass through privately owned timberlands: Logging trucks, with their massive loads of logs and their limited maneuverability, ALWAYS have the right of way. You probably won't meet many of them, but when you do, your courtesy doubles as good common sense (a New Hampshire must!).*

More detailed maps for specific regions can be obtained at gen-eral stores, mentioned in each town description to follow.

The majority of the **White Mountain National Forest** lies south of Route 2, and attracts the most visitors. So the hun-dreds of thousands of national forest acres north of Route 2, in-cluding Mt. Starr King, Mt. Weeks, Mt. Waumbeck, Mt. Cabot, Mt. Pilot, and Deer and Mill Mountains, are less visited, and you have a good chance of finding solitude and a sense of wilder-ness within its bounds. Farther north, beyond Route 110, is the 40,000-acre **Nash Stream Forest**, and next to it a "first" in state history, 24,000 acres of accessible woods owned by the In-ternational Paper Company and now managed for recreation (there's a fee). To the east of both these large forest areas is the **Thirteen Mile Woods**, running along Route 16 and the An-droscoggin River, teeming with moose and birdlife. And north of them all is the **Connecticut Lakes Region**, where the Con-necticut River has its beginning, and where another 300,000 acres of wilderness surrounds the noted lakes.

Great North Woods

It's no accident that Inland Divers is located at the edge of the Great North Woods. The rivers hosted Native American hunters for centuries, even millennia, and diving to the river bottoms can be an archaeological treasure hunt. Paddlers who prefer to stay on the surface also find pleasure in long stretches of wide, easily negotiated water, separated by challenging rapids that in spring swell from snowmelt. The northernmost waters, especially the Connecticut Lakes, are sure spots for sighting moose and hearing the haunting calls of loons. Ospreys, large water-oriented birds of prey, nest near the lakes and rivers, and eagles sometimes soar above, as do hunting hawks and falcons.

There are no recreational ski slopes in this region, but every back yard is a gateway to cross-country ski adventures. Many inns offer their own trails. Even more winter trails are available thanks to the snowmobile riders, who both travel and provide for grooming of thousands of miles of woods trails. Locally rented snowmobiles can carry you with speed and relatively little effort into the deep snow-covered woods for a North Country taste of high adventure.

Many of the small towns of the Great North Woods found airfields a necessity for moving materials in and out, especially in winter, and the legacy of small fields is now a plus for those who like to adventure in the air. Skyrides abound, at surprisingly reasonable prices.

Also found in the small towns are comfortable inns and bed and breakfasts, as well as the dramatic four-season resort of The Balsams in Dixville Notch. In the section farthest north, along the Connecticut Lakes and the Androscoggin River, are traditional lodges for anglers and hunters, also frequented by nature observers and cross-country skiers. Local restaurants specialize in hearty meals and good value, and both Whitefield (near the Vermont border) and Dixville Notch offer dining opportunities with superb cuisine for the traveler who has come so far to find it.

Nearly every road in the Great North Woods offers a summer feast of outdoor riches. Special times to visit are the spring, for moose sightings, and the fall, for brilliant foliage. Winter travel calls for good snow tires and a relaxed attitude about when to arrive at one's destination; weather changes may restrict or slow travel. But a glimpse of the mountain peaks just after a storm makes up for the inconvenience.

A Quick Tour

To spend a day getting to know the region, start in **Lancaster** at the junction of Routes 2 and 3. Weeks State Park is 2.4 miles south of town on Route 3; the stone fire tower on Prospect Mountain at the park gives a stunning overlook of the Connecticut River Valley as well as the mountain ranges to the south and east. Drive north along Route 3 to enjoy the Connecticut River scenery, passing through the busy paper mill town of **Groveton**, where the air is often fragrant with forest products. Groveton's race track draws aficionados of car competitions, especially on weekends.

To reach the wildest part of the Great North Woods, stay on Route 3 through Stratford and North Stratford (watch for the frog museum; see page 54) to **Colebrook**, the shopping town for the northernmost region. Restaurants here offer hearty meals and friendly service, and you can pick up fishing and boating gear in town.

At the north end of Colebrook's Main Street, take the turn for Route 145 and go slowly: The scenery is outstanding, and **Beaver Brook Falls** are only two miles ahead on the right. Sit at the picnic tables and savor the cascade, or climb alongside it for a slippery challenge. There's a small grove to wander through, a self-guided nature trail, and a good fishing stream too.

Thirteen miles north of Colebrook is **Pittsburg**, where the Trading Post sells a trail map that's updated each year by the paper companies, indicating where the logging roads are open to cars, mountain bikes and snowmobiles. If you're headed off the main highway, do buy the map. You can also buy hunting, fishing, and boating (not needed for canoes or kayaks) licenses at this store.

Route 3 rejoins Route 145 here and heads northeast, first arriving at **Lake Francis** on the right, where the migrating waterfowl come close to shore, and then offering a left turn a mile later to **Back Lake**, a favorite local fishing and boating spot. (You can find hand-tied trout flies at small shops here.) Shortly past the turn for Back Lake is the entrance to **Lake Francis State Park**, which has a good campground. Immediately after the state park the river again opens into a lake on the right, this time the First Connecticut Lake, another boaters' haven.

Small woods roads head off to either side of the highway; one of the most interesting is **Magalloway Road**, likely to be unmarked but found by taking the right turn just past the end of First Connecticut Lake 1.3 miles, then taking the right fork followed by two more left forks. In about 1½ miles there's a partly paved road on the left that rises to the **Magalloway Fire Tower**, elevation 3,260 feet, for a great view. Bring field glasses and make the most of it. (This road is also a good moose-spotting area.)

> ✦ **MOOSE ALERT:** *You are in prime moose country now; drive carefully and remember that these big animals are unpredictable. They'll allow you to photograph them, but don't go too close; just because they browse slowly doesn't mean they can't charge rapidly. Especially when driving at night, remember that moose are very hard to see with car headlights. Also, when driving and coming to a stop for moose, recall that other drivers may be endangered if you stop abruptly in the middle of the road.*

Second Connecticut Lake, also to the right as you head northeast, is about 15 miles from Pittsburg and has less-developed access. If you stay in a lodge nearby, your hosts may send you here with their own boat. Logging roads that branch out from the lake may allow mountain bikes (check your trail map for the year), allowing the determined pedaller to reach the Canadian border in 14 miles or so. Remember that if you actually cross the border you're required to report to Customs; the border is well observed, because of smugglers, and your crossing will be noticed.

Stay with Route 3 to reach **Third Connecticut Lake** on the left, and then the Canadian border a mile later. If you have time, check in with the border guard and get the hiking map to tiny boglike **Fourth Connecticut Lake**, the initial source of the Connecticut River. It's now a Nature Conservancy property, and a good spot for birding and discovering bog botany. If you opt to skip the moderately strenuous hike, drive across into Canada anyway to find a great vista less than half a mile down the road, as well as **Magnetic Hill** (see page 55).

Backtrack along Route 3 to Pittsburg and down Route 145 to Colebrook to connect with the **Dixville Notch** drive, Route 145. The left turn for tiny **Coleman State Park**, with its 30-site campground and good trout fishing, is six miles east of Colebrook and well marked. Another four miles east brings you to Dixville Notch, where The Balsams sets high standards in resort lodging and dining. There are good hikes throughout this area, and when you're close to The Balsams you're likely to see hikers on most days.

As you descend the 11 miles from the Notch to the tiny frontier town of **Errol**, watch for the surprising sight of buffalo grazing on the right-hand side; it's a domestic farm, but the massive creatures are worth stopping to look at anyway.

Errol is the outdoors center for the wild lands along the Maine border. North of town Route 16 leads to even smaller **Wentworths Location**, with moose along the roadside and loons in the nearby river and ponds. Southeast of Errol Route 26 covers the few miles to **Umbagog Lake** with its campgrounds and cabins. And the most traveled route out of Errol is Route 16 south, for a serene 18-mile stretch of road caught between forest and river. Route 110 then leads west again through **West Milan** (where there's a nice swimming site) and picturesque **Stark** (home of a noted late-June fiddlers' contest), and connects you back to Route 3 if you want to get back to Lancaster and head south for, say, a theatrical performance in **Whitefield**.

If you stay with Route 16 south, you'll have 13 miles to go to **Berlin** (pronounced BER-lin, to differentiate it from the German city, a choice made during the World War II). You drive through **Thirteen Mile Woods**, a collaborative effort of paper companies, local communities, and the state to provide recreation access to the lands along the Androscoggin River. Watch for the many boat entrances to this great paddling river. And keep an eye out for moose still, especially from supper time to darkness.

Berlin is "the town that trees made," and is still home to Crown Vantage, a large paper company with busy mills along the river. The river itself has been vastly cleaned up in recent years, as had the air, but you'll still catch the sulfurous fragrance of wood chips being digested for future paper. A walking tour of Berlin (pick up the good brochure at the **Berlin Chamber of Commerce**, 164 Main Street, ☎ 752-6060 or 800-992-7480; see *Sightseeing*) will give you a taste of the many ethnic groups lured here during earlier logging booms, including a Russian group with a small and elegant Russian Orthodox church perched on the ridge above town.

Finally, end the day by leaving the Great North Woods and driving another four miles down Route 16 to **Gorham**. If you've timed yourself carefully (and called ahead for reservations, ☎ 466-3103), your 6:30 arrival will connect you with a **Moose Tour** that starts at the small Information Center at the park on Main Street. This 2½-hour air-conditioned van trip makes sure you see a moose or two if you've missed them so far, and includes plenty of history of the logging years, the paper companies, and Berlin itself. Gorham offers a wide range of lodging and dining, and specializes in moose-themed shops. It is also a principal entry town to the White Mountain National Forest, reached either by heading south on Route 16 into Pinkham Notch, or west on Route 2 into Randolph.

Adventures

■ On Foot

Lancaster

A visit to **Weeks State Park**, 2.4 miles south of Lancaster on Route 3, puts the White Mountain National Forest into historical perspective. Congressman John Wingate Weeks, born in Lancaster in 1860, had his summer retreat here. He saw the nearby mountains tragically stripped by greedy timber barons who had no inkling of current woodlot management ideas. In 1911 Weeks' efforts to interest the federal government in preservation bore fruit in the Weeks Act, authorizing Congress to purchase private lands. Fully 11% of New Hampshire eventually became national forest, and many more acres have been preserved through private efforts as well. Without this federal authorization, there could be no national forests or national parks in the eastern part of the nation, which was by then all privately held. At the park headquarters on his 420-acre estate are photographs of the mountains in their desolation, a contrast to the hardwood and spruce-fir forests now covering the estate. A three-mile trail around the base of **Prospect Mountain** makes good hiking, and the stone fire tower is a must for spectacular views of the river valley as well as the Presidentials, Kilkennys, and Percy Peak. The design of the tower makes the climb much easier on those who hate the shivery sensation of openwork fire towers.

For another view of local history, enter the town of Lancaster itself. Lancaster lies on the **New Hampshire Heritage Trail**, a 230-mile route still in progress, designed for walking through some of the state's most historic regions. The 15-mile stretch of the trail though Lancaster starts south of Weeks State Park and includes several village roads. At the **Lancaster Chamber of Commerce** information booth on the village green is a **walking tour** brochure that includes classic 1800s homes and the first two-storied house in Coos County, built in 1780 by Col. Jonas Wilder and now the headquarters of the Lancaster Historical Society at the intersection of Routes 2 and 3 (see *Sightseeing*).

Colebrook

Colebrook is an ideal way station for exploring the **Connecticut Lakes Region**. But don't drive too quickly as you head north. Be sure to stop and admire **Beaver Brook Falls** on Route 145, less than two miles north of town. This is a classic cascade, fresh and exhilarating, and it's easy (although often slippery) to climb along the side and get some great photos. A short walking trail in the glen at the base of the falls leads to the pretty stream, where there's a self-guided nature trail. There's a good picnic area, too. Four-and-a-half miles farther north is a right turn that leads to an old cemetery where one of the area's famous Native Americans, Metallak, was buried. Last survivor of a band of Abenaki on the Upper Androscoggin, the hunter and fishing guide was blinded in 1847 at the reputed age of 120. The cemetery offers an interesting stroll.

Beaver Brook Falls, north of Colebrook.

Connecticut Lakes Region

The town of **Pittsburg**, modest though the village center appears, actually includes 190,000 acres of heavy forest. Paper company ownership of this acreage (about 75% Champion International) has become a boon to hikers because the woods roads are open to day use from late May to mid-October. There's no overnight camping, and no fires. Purchase a trail map (updated yearly by the paper companies) for a few dollars at the Trading Post General Store in Pittsburg. It's your most reliable guide to the miles between here and the international border, although DeLorme's *New Hampshire Atlas & Gazetteer* shows many more small winding roads that you might investigate.

Classic hikes are to the top of **Magalloway Mountain**, where there used to be a fire tower (old signs may still point to the tower), and to Garfield Falls, farther out the same road. Take the right turn just north of **Lake Francis** (4.7 miles north of the First Connecticut dam), and bear right at the fork 1.3 miles in. Two left turns at 2.3 and 2.7 miles in follow quickly and put you on **Magalloway Road**, often not marked. Another 1½ miles brings you to a right turn up to the peak, which is more obvious. It's better not to hike until you reach this turn because the small roads along the way are used by logging trucks. You can probably drive to the 8.3 miles point before you'll have to park and hoof it another mile. Look around for the second viewpoint from the ledges, too. After you've tried the climb, backtrack to the foot of the mountain road and continue away from the highway to the end of the road, passing Paradise Camp on the left. Continue another two miles, and go downhill to a fork in the road, marked by a paper company gate. Leave the car and follow the hiking trail on the other side of the gate to **Garfield Falls**, a 15-minute to half-hour hike depending on where the gate has been placed in any given season. (See why it's so important to get this year's trail map?)

For the hike to **Fourth Connecticut Lake**, the official source of the Connecticut River, a good pair of hiking shoes is advised; it's not a "soft sneakers" trail. Drive to the **US Customs** station at the Canadian Border and sign in as a hiker, receiving the one-page trail map from the Border Patrol Officer.

> ⚠ **WARNING:** *Never make jokes about smuggling, terrorism, drugs, or other border-sensitive topics with the officers who patrol the US border. It's not funny to them, and they may delay your trip considerably as they search for hard evidence.*

You'll be hiking first along the cleared swatch of land that the Border Patrol maintains for visibility, and by signing in, you avoid inadvertently triggering an enforcement chase. Let the officer show you the start of the trail, which is not well marked. The trail is a little more than a half-mile total, and first climbs steeply up brush-covered ledges. Watch for the official border markers: brass tablets three inches across, set in the center of the cleared area at every turn. About three-fourths of a mile along the trail is marker 484-15, which is where you want to take the side trail to Fourth Connecticut Lake. There should also be a sign tacked on a tree saying "4th Conn Lake 300 Yards." Your left turn will take you into the bog that surrounds the small pond. Hike around the east side of the pond to find the outlet, where you can actually step right across the slender start of the Connecticut River. The pond elevation is 2,600 feet; in the short distance that the river flows to Lake Francis near Pittsburg, it will drop 1,220 feet. Over the remaining 380 miles to the sea, the Connecticut River descends the other 1,380 feet much more slowly. This 75-acre site was donated to the Nature Conservancy by the Champion Paper Company.

The Nature Conservancy also manages a parcel at **East Inlet Pond**, with an access road immediately north of Second Connecticut Lake. It's on the east side of the highway; head down it two miles to the pond, then another three miles to the trail to **Norton Pool**, where there's a 143-acre tract of virgin red spruce and balsam fir well worth seeing. Boardwalks help you navigate the bog. Although the public is welcome, the road is a private one (paper company again) and you'll need to give the right-of-way to logging trucks.

Coleman State Park

This modest park (1,685 acres, 33 of them developed) is on **Little Diamond Pond** and is crossed by the **Androscoggin Trail**. Don't expect organized trails or maps, but with a compass and topo map (and, of course, drinking water toted along) you can have a good time within the spruce-fir forest. To reach the park, head east from Colebrook on Route 26 for six miles and take the well-marked left turn at Kidderville for another six miles.

Dixville Notch

Like the other New Hampshire notches, Dixville Notch is a sharp cut in the surrounding mountains. Unlike them, it is formed from vertical strata of rocks, providing great climbing and challenging hiking. Stop at the resort hotel, The Balsams, for a trail map. You get the benefit of the resort's wilderness area, which is a cross-country ski location in winter, as well as the state park.

The most climbed hiking trail in the state park is to **Table Rock**, from which there's a vertical drop of 700 feet. Hiking boots are needed for safety. Take Route 26 from Colebrook about 10 miles to a gravel area on the right, about 150 feet before road reaches the top of the notch. There's a big sign that says "Entering Dixville Notch State Park," and the 0.3-mile trail starts right behind the sign.

> ✹ **CAUTION:** *If the rocks are wet at Dixville Notch, don't try the climb – it gets very slippery and is unsafe.*

There's also a more gradual ascent that you can find by driving back toward the **Balsams Wilderness Ski Area** access road and then measuring 0.2 miles east. Park off the shoulder of the road; the well-marked trail starts some 70 feet before the yellow diamond caution road sign.

Another hike, to **Mount Sanguinary**, begins a mile east of the main Table Rock trail. Look for the **Flume Brook Picnic Area** and park there. The trail is well marked through spruce-balsam forest, about a mile long, and leads to a view from a rocky pinnacle overlooking the resort and its accompanying lake, Gloriette. If you choose, you can continue another 1½ miles to the resort. From the same picnic area is a short trail to a pretty flume, and from the next picnic area east is a trail to Huntington Cascades.

Errol & Umbagog Lake

This area is a canoeist's dream (see *On Water*), but there's also a very private and quiet place to walk: **Big Island**, which divides the 8,000-acre lake's partially developed lower third from its undeveloped upper two-thirds, is preserved by the Society for the Preservation of New Hampshire Forests and is open to hikers. Bring your field glasses and camera; moose and loons abound.

For a more challenging mountain hike, drive nine miles north of Errol on Route 16 to **Wentworths Location** and turn left just past the cemetery onto a dirt logging road, which reaches a gatehouse in one mile. Leave your car and walk across a bridge, then go 1½ miles (with good views) to the rarely occupied Management Center for the property, owned by Dartmouth College and open to the public for hiking. Across the road from the center at the north edge of the clearing is the trailhead for the **Diamond Peaks**. The west peak is reached after 0.8 miles, and the east peak is 1.1 miles from the trailhead; allow about an hour to reach the summit. You'll find several good views from the ledges.

Stark & Route I I0

Phillips Brook is northern New Hampshire's first privately owned hiker's recreation area, provided by International Paper Company in cooperation with Timberland Trails, Inc. There is a no fee for hiking, riding, or fishing, but llama treks and overnight accommodations in a choice of yurt or cabin, lodge, or firetower range from $26 to $100. Call ☎ 800-872-4578, Monday through Friday from 9 am to 4 pm, for reservations and information (no mailing address given). The terrain is challenging, and hikers should bring a topographical map as well as compass, drinking water, and foul weather gear; weather can change quickly, and is often much cooler at higher elevations than you'd guess while driving the roads. The 24,000 acres includes a river, several lakes, and views of the Presidential Range. Over 100 miles of trails and logging roads thread through it. To either side is preserved state land, with opportunities for even longer treks. To reach Phillips Brook, take Route 110 from Route 16 toward Stark and take the right turn marked Paris Road, to the Paris Field trailhead. The lodge is nine miles from the trailhead parking area.

Savor the 40,000 acres of the **Nash Stream Forest**, which was preserved through enormous public and private efforts after Diamond International let it go in 1988. Although it is still managed for timber, it includes high-elevation nature preserves above 2,700 feet, and trails to the **Percy Peaks**. From Stark take Route 110 west for 3.8 miles and bear left on Nash Stream Road. There's a parking area in another 2.7 miles, and the trail starts 50 yards further in. **South Percy** has a wooded summit with fewer views, so the trail heads for the peak of **North Percy** at 3,418 feet. It's a 2.2-mile trail, first on easy grades, then traversing ledges requiring real climbing; rugged hiking boots are a must, and you should hike with a companion in case of an accident. The *AMC White Mountain Guide* has a detailed trail description. Part of the older upper trail is now officially closed, but is a good route for aspiring rock climbers, as it was well laid out by a rock-climbing team across some challenging slabs. (Even this older, closed trail is not a technical rock climb, though; ropes and hardware aren't needed, just skill, care, and confidence.) Rockhounds take note: the Percy Peaks are mineral-rich.

Route 110 has two other possible spots from which to launch hikes: From the South Pond Recreation Area in Stark you can reach South Pond and the **Kilkenny Ridge Trail**, which leads to **Roger Ledge** in 4.1 miles, with a side spur to **Devil's Hopyard**, a boulder-strewn glacial gorge. This is a challenging trail, meant for only those who are in good condition and are well prepared; do read the trail marks thoroughly in the *AMC White Mountain Guide*, and don't mess with bad weather on this very slippery rocky trail. There's also a little-used trail to **Unknown Pond** and **the Horn**, found by going to the York Pond Road between Stark and Berlin and taking the road west to the **Berlin Fish Hatchery**; the trailhead is another two miles beyond the hatchery gate, and the trail to the pond is 3.3 miles, followed by another two miles to the Horn, a 2,905-foot summit with excellent views. Plan to spend a full day, but be careful of your timing, as the fish hatchery locks the road gate some time after 4 pm.

Farther east along Route 110, almost to Milan, is **Milan Hill State Park**. A fire tower with good vistas makes it worth a visit.

■ On Wheels

Road Biking

Road biking in the Great North Woods region is smooth and silky, with most roads recently paved and well-shouldered. A **105.7-mile loop** with only one strenuous uphill ride is found in *30 Bicycle Tours of New Hampshire*. Basically, the loop starts in **Berlin** at the municipal parking lot near city hall, proceeds north, mostly on Route 16, for 30.4 miles to **Errol**, and leads west through the sheer rock walls of **Dixville Notch** on Route 26. **Colebrook** is reached in 22.3 miles, where you change to the southbound stretch of Route 3 to **Groveton** (another 26.9 miles; this is river-bottom riding, gentle and scenic), and close the loop by taking Route 110 past **Stark** to Berlin (the last 25 miles, which has some long ascents and descents).

If you're looking for a shorter ride, pick any of the individual legs of this trip. It's good to know that 13.8 miles north of Berlin in Dummer is the **Pontook Reservoir Recreation Area**, which has parking, pay phones, and toilets, as well as a nifty wooden dam, great fishing, and a planned ecosystem exploration center. You can use Pontook as a start or midpoint for road trips. Keep in mind, also, that Errol has a handful of reasonable motels and hearty dining for the outdoors folks working, hunting, fishing, and boating nearby.

⊙ **MOOSE-WATCHING:** *The Androscoggin River runs along the stretch from Berlin to Errol, with its own wayside and picnic areas; travel this route at dusk between mid-May and late October, and you're almost sure to see a moose grazing near the roadsides, slurping up some calcium salts left from the winter road treatments.*

Looking for the New Hampshire segment of the **East Coast Bicycle Trail**? You won't find any signs for it, but **Route 3** from Groveton to the Canadian border is the road chosen. South of Groveton, the route goes just a tad east to **Lost Nation Road**, a wonderful wilderness excursion that takes you to Jefferson on Route 2 (by a last-minute left turn onto North Road just before Lancaster; check a detailed map like the one in Delorme's *New Hampshire Atlas & Gazetteer*).

Mountain Biking

For mountain bikers the toughest part of the Great North Woods is deciding where to go first. **Pittsburg** is a good place to start, not for pedaling but for getting this year's version of the paper company map that shows where the logging roads are open to trail riding (changes from year to year). There are usually routes near **Second Connecticut Lake** and the nearby bogs and waterfalls that will take you into some of the least traveled land in New England.

> **BIKING TIP:** *Carry plenty of bike repair tools and parts; there are few shops in this area that specialize in bikes, although in a pinch a local garage might give you a hand.*

Also alluring is the **Phillips Brook back-country recreation area** near Stark. To get here, take Route 110 east to the left turn for Paris Road, about three miles east of Stark, and the lodge will be nine miles ahead of you. Call ahead and make sure they're expecting you (☎ 800-872-4578); maps are available at the office. Explore 24,000 acres of spectacular forest, with over 100 miles of trails and logging roads.

> **CAUTION:** *Remember that logging trucks have the right of way; this acreage is owned by International Paper Company and the trucks are there on business, although you're not likely to meet them often if you stay with the trails advised for cycling.*

A third option, especially if you like to find your own way, is the **Nash Stream Forest**, with some 40,000 acres open to day use, down Route 110 in the other direction from Stark. Count three miles west of Stark or four miles east of Groveton, and look for the turn north onto Emerson Road, which reaches the edge of the forest in about 2.6 miles, where it bends sharply right. At that sharp right turn go left instead, onto the Nash Stream Road, which goes all the way through the forest. Trails and logging roads branch off, most often on the right-hand side, following streams. There's no real loop of trails so you'll end up backtracking. A compass and topo map would be a good idea, as well as the usual back-country supplies. Get lost here, and it'll be a long time until someone starts looking for you.

➔ **BIKING TIP:** *Bear in mind that hikers in the North Country aren't yet sold on the idea that feet and wheels belong on the same paths. Help them to learn otherwise, using courtesy in passing pedestrians and staying off the tops of mountains where the alpine vegetation is fragile.*

■ On Water

Canoeing, Kayaking & Boat Tours

The Great North Woods has four large rivers and more large lakes, and enough wildlife to keep your eyes busy any time your paddle slows down. Canoe and kayak paddlers head for the **Androscoggin River**, which flows from Umbagog Lake (where it is also fed by the Magalloway River) to Berlin before turning east into the state of Maine. Dam-controlled and therefore predictable (as much as flowing water ever is), the Androscoggin offers moderate whitewater and year-round flow that makes it a good teaching river. It also has wide stretches of more peaceful travel, few rock hazards and, of course, the pleasures of the wild undeveloped shores of Umbagog Lake as you go to the head of the river. Expect loons calling around you, moose grazing nearby, and the occasional loud slap of a beaver's tail.

⚡ **CAUTION:** *Despite its relative freedom from hazards, neither the Androscoggin River nor any other waterway should be paddled until you've surveyed it yourself or are traveling with someone else who recently paddled it. Blow-downs and the changes of high water can be treacherous. Consult the* AMC River Guide to Vermont and New Hampshire *for additional details.*

Unless you want to explore the Magalloway first, it makes sense to enter the Androscoggin at either **Umbagog Lake** or the ramp by **Errol Dam**. Below the lake the wide slow river is a pleasant paddle to Errol, reaching Route 16 in three miles where there's a launching ramp; another ramp is at the Errol

Umbagog Lake.

Dam three-fourths of a mile later. Class II and III rapids follow the dam, with a large pool at the mouth of Clear Stream that makes it simple to pull out of the river and head back up to re-run the rapids. The river has a nice mix of challenges, especially eddies and scattered Class II rapids, all the way to **Pontook Dam** in Milan, which is followed by two miles of continuous Class II rapids.

> **DAM RELEASE WARNING:** *In Milan, check for the Pontook Dam release schedule, posted on the bulletin board in the parking lot. Any dam-controlled river can have rapid and dangerous changes in water level; be knowledgeable and prepared. Berlin is probably as far as you'll want to stay on the water, as dams and industry multiply after this point.*

Canoe & Kayak Outfitters

- The major canoe and kayak outfitter, Saco Bound, has a branch headquarters called **Northern Waters** in Errol on the river. Classes, trips, and rentals are available; ask about either the whitewater school or canoe trip packet. Northern Waters, Box 119, Center Conway, NH 03813; ☎ 447-2177; www.neoutdoors. com/sacobound).

- **Umbagog Outfitters**, also in Errol, specializes in one-afternoon sessions for those with little prior experience in kayaks, but also offers longer journeys. Owner Jerry Tremblay has unlimited enthusiasm for whitewater kayaking, sea kayaking, and open canoe paddling on the river and in the lake (PO Box 268, Errol, NH 03579; ☎ 356-3292).

- When you're north of Pittsburg in the Connecticut Lakes area, many of the lodges have boats available (see *Where to Stay*). If you'd like to get familiar with the river and lakes with a pro, contact **Connitic Headwater Tours** on Bridge Street in Colebrook (☎ 237-8484) and on Route 3 at the public boat launch on Lake Francis in Pittsburg (☎ 246-3489). Canoe, kayak, and raft rentals and tours are available, along with primitive campsites by the day or week. There are even tepees at some sites! Owners Tom and Jeremy Pichierri offer rafting for groups, and stream touring when the water is high. You can also talk "fish" here.

- Another outfitter on the Connecticut is John Marshall, who runs **River Excitement** (mailing address PO Box 65, Hartland Four Corners, VT 05049; ☎ 802-457-4021; e-mail rvrxcitmnt@aol.com). Marshall's guided drift trips and fishing excursions include delicious streamside lunches.

The *AMC River Guide for New Hampshire and Vermont* offers details for paddling the **Connecticut River**. Unfortunately for those who like to "begin at the beginning," there's just not enough water to bother putting in above Pittsburg. After this point there are intermittent Class I and II rapids, and plenty of action. Be sure to study the *River Guide* in terms of dams at Beecher Falls and Lyman (defunct and changing with each season here). By the time you reach the large backwaters of Moore and Comerford Dams, near Littleton, the river has changed character and is inhabited by those seeking less dramatic thrills: note the sculling and racing around Hanover and Lebanon, as well as sailboats.

For more unusual and challenging runs, although shorter in length, consider the **Nash Stream** (in Nash Stream Forest) or the **Upper Ammonoosuc** (entered by the Nash Stream, and with longer lasting high water).

Fishing

The **Connecticut River** is one of the premier trout streams of the northeast, and the rivers and streams flowing into it – Indian Stream, Dead Diamond River, Mohawk River, Perry Stream, and Swift Diamond River (an angler's prime territory) – all boast fine brook trout. Stick with the Connecticut and the **Androscoggin** if you're looking for landlocked salmon, rainbow trout, and brown trout. The **Connecticut Lakes** (including Back Lake and Lake Francis) and **Umbagog Lake** are trout heavens, too. Even the ponds have brook trout.

> ⊙ **FLY-FISHING TIP:** *Some of the nicest hand-tied flies can be found in small shops around Back Lake north of Pittsburg, like **Wilderness Sporting Goods** (Buster and Carolyn Hutchins, on Beach Road;* ☎ *538-7166).*

An outfitter plying both the Connecticut and Androscoggin watersheds is Ken Hastings of **Osprey Guiding Service**, who offers float and wade fly-fishing trips (PO Box 121, Colebrook 03576; ☎ 922-3800).

Swimming

Swimming in these rivers is as easy as parking the car and stepping into the water. For a real treat of a swimming beach, though, head up Route 110 from the Milan area and look for the **South Pond Recreation Area** turn on your left, about three miles past West Milan. The area is open from 9 am to 8 pm and has a bathhouse and picnic tables as well as boat access. There are hiking trails here, but they're challenging ones that you'll need to prepare for in advance.

Diving

Divers and would-be underwater explorers can visit **Inland Divers** on Route 3, about three miles north of Lancaster, and get ideas about which area rivers and lakes are yielding archeological interest or challenges. Inland Divers provides equipment for dives throughout northern New England, including the seacoast, and can advise experienced divers on quarry and cave adventures as well as deep lake diving. Call ahead (☎ 768-2124) and talk with Ted Ames or Steve Galipeau.

■ On Snow & Ice

 There is only one downhill ski resort in this region, and it won't knock your socks off in terms of terrain or views. However, the 13 trails of **The Balsams Wilderness** in Dixville Notch thread through a scenic woodlands with a respectable vertical drop of 1,000 feet and the resort (see The Balsams in *Where to Stay*) is absolutely unencumbered by lift lines, crowds, or other hassles. A dedicated half-pipe welcomes snowboarders, who can share the other trails as well. Youngsters enjoy a ski-play area. The annual snow index is 250 inches in Dixville Notch, and the resort adds its own snowmaking for 80% trail coverage as well.

In addition to its alpine trails, The Balsams Wilderness offers 76 km of graded cross-country trails to explore, as well as rentals, support, and good food afterward. Its reputation for ski instruction is outstanding. Instructors also lead back-country tours, including up the Table Rock Trail and in moonlight. For snow conditions, call ☎ 255-3951 at the ski area base lodge. There's a video brochure available: The Balsams Wilderness, Dixville Notch, NH 03576-9710; ☎ 255-3400 or 800-255-0600. Ice skaters will also find a welcome at The Balsams.

The Great North Woods has abundant cross-country skiing and snowshoeing available. Many inns and bed-and-breakfast homes offer Nordic skiing "right out the back door." Each state

park and forest also becomes a winter trail network once the
snow settles. **Weeks State Park**, three miles south of Lancaster on Route 3, offers gentle trails around Mount Prospect and
sometimes runs a volunteer-operated rope tow on the mountain.

Phillips Brook (see *On Foot*) offers winter mountaineering, as
well as ski and showshoe trails. Nearby **Nash Stream Forest**
offers the same, but without the staff support that Phillips
Brook has.

The Great North Woods is famous for its snowmobile trails. If
you're not opposed in principle to powered vehicles in the winter woods, you can share the local enthusiasm for both woodland exploration and long-distance rides. There are "ride-ins"
on many weekends, where snowmobilers from a day's ride away
all gather for hot food and good conversation, and there is
plenty of support for rentals and repairs.

Snowmobile Outfitters

- In the Errol area, call **All Seasons Sports** (Route 26,
  ☎ 482-3287); in Pittsburg, **Granite State Power
  Equipment** (Route 3, ☎ 538-6349); and in Colebrook, **Lemieux Garage** (130 Main Street, ☎ 237-
  4377).

- You might want to connect ahead of time with the
  Colebrook Ski-Bees Snowmobile Club (PO Box
  125, Colebrook, NH 03576; no phone; e-mail
  claude@ccslabs. Com).

- Lodges like **Timberland Lodge & Cabins** and
  Sportsman's Lodge (see *Where to Stay*) also offer
  snowmobile trail access.

- **Pathfinder Sno-Tours** in Pittsburg (☎ 538-7001)
  offers guided tours of the wilderness for half- and
  full-day duration, averaging 25 to 125 miles; bring
  your own snowmobile, or rent one here.

- **Northern Enterprises** in Pittsburg (☎ 800-339-
  6352) also offers snowmobile rentals.

➔ **SKI CONDITIONS:** *For cross-country and downhill ski conditions call The Balsams Wilderness at ☎ 255-3400; for snowmobile trail conditions call ☎ 224-4666 or, from outside New Hampshire, ☎ 800-258-3609.*

■ In The Air

At Errol's modest but very necessary airport, **David Heasley** offers sightseeing rides and charters. Other services may be available in the future; ask him about back-country options. Call him at ☎ 482-3323; keep trying until you reach him, as he's a one-person operation.

■ Eco-Travel

Birdwatchers take note: along Route 3 from Pittsburg to the Third Connecticut Lake is a narrow strip of land on both sides of the road called the **Connecticut Lakes State Forest**. This is a great place to look for the Canadian Zone birds, including hawks and ravens as well as warblers. There are loons on the lakes, and First Connecticut Lake in particular hosts migratory waterfowl in spring and fall.

While you're all the way north, savor the two parcels preserved here by the Nature Conservancy: **Fourth Connecticut Lake** and **East Inlet Natural Area**. Unusual bog plants and wetland communities make a quiet but interesting ramble (see *On Foot*).

Looking for one of the really big birds of prey? **Umbagog Lake** is home to ospreys. In May and June, take care not to disturb nesting loons on the shores of the lake and islands. Note that **Big Island** is now a preserve, available for hiking and (by permit from **Umbagog Lake Camps**, PO Box 181, Errol, NH 03579) primitive camping. Loons especially like this area. There's a recently established **national wildlife refuge** on the lake, mostly at the northwestern corner, and much of the rest of the shoreline is protected by conservation easements. If you miss seeing ospreys at the lake, head down Route 16 to **Pon-**

took **Reservoir Recreation Area** in Milan, where the ospreys have also been nesting.

> 🔥 **MOOSE ALERT:** *One of the most unusual animals to watch in the North Country is the moose, and the entire Great North Woods Region is home to these huge gangly-looking animals. They are most often seen at dusk or at dawn, and are notorious for running or walking across roads without regard for traffic. Moose often graze or "slurp" (they eat water plants) close to the roadsides along Routes 16 and 3, where the water contains extra calcium because of its use in winter road salts. Be careful not to stop in the middle of the road to watch, or you'll be as much of a hazard to other drivers as the moose.*

Guided **natural history tours** of the Umbagog Lake area and sometimes of other parts of the Great North Woods, like the Nash Stream Forest, are available through the **Appalachian Mountain Club**, based in Pinkham Notch about 20 miles south of Berlin. You don't have to be a member of the AMC to go on its tours (although members get a small discount), but you do need to make reservations (request the *AMC Guide to Outdoor Adventures* from AMC, Pinkham Notch Visitor Center, PO Box 298, Gorham, NH 03581, open Monday-Friday from 9 am-5 pm; ☎ 466-2727). This is a great way to experience kayak travel around the lakes and rivers and also learn about the wildlife and plants from an experienced naturalist.

Sightseeing

Lancaster

Lancaster's main street is Route 3, and the **Lancaster Chamber of Commerce** has a summer information booth set in a park there (summer information number, ☎ 788-3212; year-round, ☎ 788-2530). There's an iron bridge linking the town with Vermont, and there's a covered bridge five miles southwest of town off Route 135 crossing the Connecticut River. A smaller covered bridge is at the northeast side of town on Mechanic Street. At the intersection of Routes 3 and 2 (the north end of Main Street) is the **Wilder-Holton House**, built in 1780, the first two-story home in Coos (COH-oss) County. This home now houses the **Lancaster Historical Society** and a collection of 18th-century artifacts and Civil War mementos. Reportedly, the house was a stop on the Underground Railroad that helped slaves escape to freedom in Canada during the 19th century. The museum is open during July and August from 2 to 4 pm and from 7 to 8 pm. Make sure you pick up the small leaflet on the town that tells the story of Lancaster's **haunted house** and legendary ghost (now vanished).

Lancaster Area

N

TO
COLEBROOK

3

110

110B

Milan

Groveton

110

16

Lancaster
Fairgrounds

Lancaster

TO
ST. JOHNSBURY, VT

Lancaster
Historical
Society

Berlin

VERMONT

135

Weeks
State Park

Jefferson

16

3

Randolph

2

Gorham

Whitefield

Forest Lake
State Park

116

White Mountain
Reg'l Airport

PRESIDENTIAL RANGE

16

Littleton

93

Twin
Mountain

302

302

Bethlehem

302

3

116

WHITE

MOUNTAIN

Pinkham Notch

NAT'L FOREST

Androscoggin River

Connecticut River

NOT TO SCALE

At the Chamber of Commerce booth is a brochure with a **walking tour** of Lancaster. The back of the flyer has a sketch of the **New Hampshire Heritage Trail** as it winds through the region. Noted on the trail is **Weeks State Park**, three miles south of town on Route 3. This 420-acre state park has breathtaking views of the area, reached by a winding road to the top of Mount Prospect and an easy climb up a 56-foot stone fire tower. The former summer estate also has a poignant collection of photos of the White Mountains as they looked in 1900, when timber barons had stripped them and fires had ravaged the remaining brush and slash. As a US Congressman, **John Wingate Weeks** (born in Lancaster in 1860) was influential in establishing the eastern national forest system in response to the devastation of the mountains that he witnessed. He is especially credited with making the White Mountain National Forest a reality. Think kindly of him as you explore. If he had not moved as quickly and passionately as he did, there would be no old-growth timber stands left.

North of Lancaster on Route 3 is the **Lancaster Fairgrounds**, one mile north of the junction of Routes 3 and 2. The county fair is held here, usually the last week of August (information, ☎ 788-4531; camping reservations, ☎ 837-9146; show ticket reservations, ☎ 636-2845). Country music stars, a demolition derby where local drivers attempt to destroy each other's cars, and farm-oriented favorites like sheepdog trials, oxen and cattle shows, and horse pulling are hot items, and there are also barns full of agricultural competitions and exhibits. You might want to experience rides on the midway and sample traditional fair food like fried dough, sausage-and-pepper sandwiches, and sit-down suppers that end with homemade pies. Be sure to visit the milking parlor if you haven't seen cows milked recently; the machinery is amazing, and the cows formidable. Lancaster's other big events are an enthusiastic small-town **Fourth of July**, a **street fair** on the first Saturday in August (crafters, food, entertainment), and a **winter carnival** in February (confirm dates with the Chamber of Commerce).

A free sugarhouse tour in summer and fall at **Christie's Maple Farm** on Route 2 in Lancaster will also give you a feel for rural skills and traditions; indulge in the "sugarhouse breakfast" on Sundays from 7 am to noon from Memorial Day to Columbus

Great North Woods

Day. Call ahead to double-check times (☎ 800-788-2118). **Lost Nation Orchard and Cider Mill** (☎ 788-3122 for directions) also offers occasional tours; don't miss the apple butter, a Yankee treat.

Groveton

North of Lancaster is the town of Groveton, noted for both its timber industry (fragrant year-round!) and its racetrack. **Riverside Speedway**, just west of Route 3 on Brown Road (☎ 636-2005), holds races from May through September, usually on Saturdays. Race time is usually 6 pm; the track is a quarter-mile banked oval and there's a busy concession stand, as well as free parking and free overnight camping.

Stratford & North Stratford

North of Groveton are the small towns of Stratford and North Stratford; between them (about five miles north of Groveton), on the right, is a small house turned into an eccentric museum, the **Foolish Frog**. It doesn't keep set hours, but you can get in touch ahead of time (RR1, Box 428, North Stratford, NH 03590; ☎ 636-1887), or even stop in, to see the hundreds of frogs in all sorts of media collected by Carol Hawley and Francis McMilleon.

Ten miles past the Foolish Frog, just before you enter Colebrook, is the **Shrine of Our Lady of Grace**, where there are Sunday programs from May to October, including a blessing of the sick. The main monument at the shrine is an eight-foot-high Madonna on a 21-foot pedestal; there is also a Way of the Cross with nine-foot-tall granite crosses, and a Mysteries of the Rosary segment featuring Vermont granite.

Colebrook

Motorcyclists flock to Colebrook each June for the **Blessing of the Motorcycles**, a picturesque and often touching event; contact Rick White, 29 Second Street, Gorham, NH 04581, for the annual schedule and, if you like, a registration form. The **North Country Chamber of Commerce** (☎ 237-8939) in Colebrook is in the back of a house on North Main Street across from Dickson's Pharmacy (167 Main Street). They will also confirm dates and locations of various festivals events in Colebrook, ranging from pancake breakfasts and a great Fourth of July parade to a strawberry shortcake festival and snowmobile events; it's good to keep in touch here.

Just north of Colebrook on Route 145 is the **Beaver Brook Wayside Area** (see *On Foot*, page 36), which is well worth a stop for photos and maybe a climb along the falls.

Pittsburg

Route 145 is the short route from Colebrook to Pittsburg (if you take the longer route, via Route 3 from Colebrook, there's a state-run information center open from Memorial Day to Columbus Day, with rest rooms and picnic tables), a town that was once a nation unto itself. The **Pittsburg Historical Society**, in the town hall and open only on summer Saturdays, memorializes the 1832 "Indian Stream Republic" here. The Republic minted its own coins as well as forming a government that lasted a few years before merging in 1842 into New Hampshire through the Treaty of Washington. Be sure to stop at the **Trading Post** in Pittsburg to get a trails map and browse though the fishing supplies and moose postcards, as well as getting a hearty sandwich for the road.

> ⊖ **MOOSE-WATCHING:** *Pittsburg and Colebrook both take part in a regional **Moose Festival** around the third weekend of August. The event features moose calling, a mock moose parade, a moose cruise, and moose-watchers' breakfasts, as well as dinners, a dance, and more. Advance tickets and information are available from the **North Country Chamber of Commerce** (PO Box 1, Colebrook, NH 03576; ☎ 237-8939).*

At the northern end of Route 3 is a **border crossing** into Canada. It's simple to drive across, with a mandatory stop at the Canadian customs booth on your way north. Go another mile to **Magnetic Hill**, where the magnetic rock underground will actually make your car shift position if you park in neutral with the brake off. The hill also offers a good view. You'll need to stop at US customs on your way back into New Hampshire.

> ✴ **BORDER CROSSING ADVISORY:** *Schedule your return Canadian border crossing for daytime business hours. If the US customs station here is closed, as they are during the night, you'll be required to drive all the way to Beecher Falls, Vermont, when you return across the border – quite a nuisance!*

Stark

The village of Stark, on Route 110 between Groveton and Milan, draws photographers with its **covered bridge** and **Union Church**. Stark housed German prisoners of war in a camp during World War II; the story of the camp is well told in the book *Stark Decency*, by Allen Koop.

Stark also hosts a noted **fiddlers' contest**, traditionally held the last Saturday in June (☎ 636-1325).

Union Church and covered bridge, Stark.

Dixville Notch

Dixville Notch is sometimes called the "Switzerland of the Northeast," with its steep rocky slopes and thick forests. Nestled on 15,000 acres in the notch is **The Balsams Grand Resort Hotel**, which has been welcoming guests since 1866 (see *Where to Stay*). Visit even if you don't plan to lodge there. The restaurant is open to the public and offers a fixed-price menu with exquisite cuisine. The grounds are a series of parks, by turn elegant and wild, mingling Old World grandeur with New England landscape. **Lake Gloriette** rests between Route 26 and the four-story red-roofed buildings; craggy cliffs rise behind the scene. Day visitors are welcome.

Umbagog Lake & Errol

Umbagog Lake is photogenic in any season, with its moose and loons. A new **National Wildlife Refuge** center on Route 16 north of Errol may soon provide additional interpretive material on the region; stop in and meet the rangers, who may tell you where to look for wildlife or special natural history programs.

Berlin

It's hard to leave the mountains, but when you do, follow the Androscoggin River south along Route 16 to Berlin. Here you enter a new excitement: the life of the timber harvesters. Crown Vantage has pulp mills along the river in Berlin, now well-controlled as far as pollution goes except for the pervasive scent of digesting wood (a little like steamed broccoli or cabbage!). Still remaining in the Androscoggin are stone piers that used to be part of a boom system for sorting logs floating down the river. (They're now moved to the mill by trucks.) You can pick up a brochure with a **walking tour** of Berlin at the Chamber of Commerce; to find the office, you'll have to become familiar with the loop of one-way roads in the center of town and get onto the northbound road, Main Street. The **Northern White Mountains Chamber of Commerce** is at 164 Main Street (☎ 752-6060 or 800-992-7480), with helpful staff and plenty of maps. Have the staff show you how to find the **Holy Resurrection Church** at 20 Petrograd Street, an Eastern Orthodox church complete with triptych window and onion domes, proof of the mill-town's once energetic labor recruitment efforts among many European populations.

The new **Heritage Park** (☎ 752-7202), 961 Main Street in Berlin, is gradually opening sections, starting with one floor of artifacts. It will offer interactive displays about the big timber era of 1860 to 1900 as well as about modern-day lumberjacks and pulp and paper mills. Mill tours will be given on Thursdays during the summer. It will take four or five years to complete the park, which will also have a museum, gift shops, tours of a logging site, and a summer lecture series.

> ❷ **MOOSE-WATCHING:** *Drive another four miles south along Route 16 to Gorham, where you can take the **Moose Tour** (leaves the Information Booth on Route 16 at 7 pm; reserve seats in advance, ☎ 466-3103). You'll be entertained by a guide who gives both natural and human history between moose sightings.*

Where To Stay

Lancaster

Three of the four motels in town are open year-round: **Cabot Motor Inn** (Route 2; ☎ 788-3346; $), **Lancaster Motor Inn** (Main Street; ☎ 788-4921; $), and **Four Dorrs Motel** (Route 2; ☎ 788-2501; $). **The Starr King Motel** (Jefferson Road; ☎ 788-2501; $) is open only from June to October with just 10 rooms.

> ❷ **TRAVEL TIP:** *Foliage season reservations are best made months to a year in advance for all Great North Woods lodgings.*

Stratford

Blueberry Hill Bed and Breakfast (Route 3, Stratford; ☎ 636-1964 and 203-599-4716; $$) is close enough to Colebrook and Groveton for easy sightseeing. Hosts Candy and Pete Livingstone share their early Colonial farmhouse on 55 acres of blueberry fields and woods.

Colebrook

Motel lodging here includes the **Colebrook Country Club** (RR1, Box 2; ☎ 237-5566; $-$$); the **Colebrook House and Motel** (Route 3 next to the Congregational Church, 132 Main Street; ☎ 237-5521 or 800-626-7331; $-$$), parts of which date from 1830; and the **Northern Comfort Motel** (RR1, Box 520; ☎ 237-4440; $-$$). The two local bed-and-breakfast inns are highly recommended: **Monadnock Bed and Breakfast** in town, at 1 Monadnock Street (☎ 237-8216; $), hosted by Barbara and Wendell Willard (special welcome to bicyclists and birdwatchers!), and **Rooms With A View**, on Forbes Road in a hillside meadow just outside town (call for directions, ☎ 237-5106 or 800-499-5106; $$), where Charles and Sonya Sheldon offer a wrap-around porch and outdoor hot tub.

Other options near Colebrook are the **Mohawk Cottages**, a half-mile east of town on Route 26 (☎ 237-4310, hosts Phil and Jeannie DeMaio; $-$$), and **Sportsman's Lodge and Cabins** at Diamond Pond (☎ 237-5211 or 800-327-5211; $-$$), which has a restaurant, as well as boats, motors, and canoes for rent and winter trailside snowmobile storage. Hosts are Lee and Linda Spector.

Pittsburg

Lodging in Pittsburg starts with **The Glen** (☎ 538-6500 or 800-445-GLEN; winter, ☎ 508-475-0559; $$), at First Connecticut Lake. This is the biggest of the Connecticut Lakes lodges, welcoming guests for nearly four decades to sit around the wide stone fireplace or outside overlooking the lake. All meals are included in the lodging charge, and owner Betty Falton gives suggestions for angling, birding, and hiking and mountain biking trails. Boat rentals are available. There's a main lodge as well as private cabins, where pets are permitted. Usual open months are May through October.

There are more lodgings at First Connecticut Lake. **Magalloway Cabins** (☎ 538-6353; $$) are year-round housekeeping units owned by Marina Johnson, offering a view from a slope

Great North Woods

above the lake. There's a boat dock, and a special welcome for birdwatchers, as well as sports enthusiasts in all seasons. **Partridge Lodge and Cabins** (☎ 538-6380; $$) has 600 feet of lake frontage (boats available) and seven housekeeping cabins; owners are Gerry and Cathy Boutin, who welcome guests year-round and especially encourage snowmobilers, cross-country skiers, and ice anglers. Fishing and hunting are part of the way of life, and there's also a private fishing pond. Also on the shore is **Ramblewood Cabins & Campground** (☎ 538-6948; $$) with log housekeeping units for two to 10 guests, a wilderness campground, and 180 acres of wanderable acreage including nature trails (Nordic skiers take note); Paul Bergeron is the host. Boat rentals are available here, too.

Finally, note **Timberland Lodge & Cabins** (☎ 538-6613 or 800-545-6613; $-$$), with another long stretch of lake frontage. This four-season "haven" includes 20 cabins, some with four bedrooms, each with a porch with water view or even a dock. Hosts Doug and Linda Feltmate also cater to larger groups for meetings, weddings, and family reunions. In winter they serve breakfast and operate a snack bar for snowmobilers, who connect their trails directly to the lodge. The Feltmates will also connect you with Pathfinder Sno-Tours (see *On Snow & Ice*).

Mountain View Cabins & Campground (☎ 538-6305) is on Back Lake, on the other side of Route 3 from First Connecticut Lake. (You should be picturing a simple two-lane road for Route 3, not a highway!) Cabins can be either on the Connecticut River or on Mallard Cove at Back Lake, and some have fireplaces or woodstoves. Hosts are Merrill and Judy Dalton. Another choice on Back Lake is **Robbins Cabins**, where the housekeeping cabins (☎ 538-6314; $$) are open year-round and motor boats are available from owners Charles and Carolyn Robbins. The **Powder Horn Lodge & Cabins** (☎ 538-6300; $-$$), has fireplaces in some of the eight cabins and plenty of boat rentals; hosts are Dave and Jean Burrill. A Back Lake "Northwoods tradition" is **Tall Timber Lodge** (☎ 538-6651 or 800-83LODGE; $$ to $$$$), which even puts out a newsletter announcing fly-tying weekends, angling records, and a summer fly-fishing school. Call to be put on the "ice out" list, and they'll let you know when the ice leaves the lake and the fish start getting active. Visit their Web site at www.spav.com/progc/ talltimber.

Dixville Notch

The Balsams Grand Resort Hotel at Dixville Notch is a world unto itself. With its red-roofed white stucco buildings caught in a narrow cleft in the mountains, the glimmer of sunlight on Lake Gloriette or on freshly-fallen snow, and the hundreds of miles of surrounding wilderness trails, The Balsams is a magical destination resort. Lodging is by "Wilderness American Plan" where "one rate covers it all from early morning exercise to the last dance of the evening" (lunch excluded). Expect individualized guest rooms with distinctive ambiance and superb cuisine. It's an atmosphere in which people dress for dinner and evening festivities after a day of endless activity, ranging from outdoor adventures to puzzles to reading in the well-stocked library. Three rooms of live entertainment offer everything from billiards to movies to guest speakers to dance bands. In summer there are 27 holes of golf, as well as boating and swimming in the lake. In winter there is alpine and Nordic skiing (see *On Snow & Ice*) and ice skating. Make reservations well in advance, especially for fall foliage season, a breathtaking time to visit. The Balsams Grand Resort Hotel, Dixville Notch, NH 03576-9710; ☎ 800-255-0600 (US and Canada), 800-255-0800 (New Hampshire), or 255-3400; fax 255-4221; www.thebalsams.com; e-mail TheBalsams@aol.com.

Errol & Umbagog Lake

The **Errol Motel** (☎ 482-3256; $-$$) is open year-round. But if you're here to explore, the campground and cabins are appealing, starting with **Umbagog Lake Campground & Cottages** (The Willards, PO Box 181, Errol, NH 03579; ☎ 482-7795; $). Sites are waterfront, off-waterfront, and wilderness – a visit is the best way to pick among the tent sites, camper sites, and housekeeping cottages. There's a small store, a dock with boat and canoe rental and a shuttle service to wilderness sites. The open season is Memorial Day weekend to mid-September.

At the other end of Umbagog Lake, six miles north on Route 16, is the tiny village of **Wentworths Landing**, where the **Mount**

Dustan Country Store offers housekeeping cabins (Rae Waters; ☎ 482-3467; $).

Berlin

The Traveler Motel (25 Pleasant Street; ☎ 752-2500 or 800-365-9391; $$) puts up guests in modern comfort.

West Milan & Stark

Here's a treasure of a country bed and breakfast: **Stark Inn** (☎ 636-2644; $), owned by Nancy Spaulding. You'll cross the Upper Ammonoosuc River by a sturdy covered bridge to reach the inn, which is a large restored farmhouse full of antiques and comfortable furniture. Open year-round, it's a perfect location for a photographer or hiker. As they say in New England road directions, "You can't miss it"; take Route 110 to the covered bridge in Stark and there you are.

■ Camping

Lancaster

 In the Lancaster area, you'll find **Roger's Family Camping Resort & Motel** (RFD2, Box 474, Lancaster, NH 03584; ☎ 788-4885 or 788-3009), which offers a 400-foot waterslide, two swimming pools, and miniature golf, as well as 300 sites (RV and tent). **Beaver Trails Campground** on Route 2 (☎ 888-788-3815) is by the Connecticut River and has rentals for canoeing and fishing. **Mountain Lake Campground** (PO Box 475, Lancaster, NH 03584; ☎ 788-4509) is south of town on Route 3, and offers rustic cabins and teepees as well as 97 sites with varied amenities. It specializes in hikers, bikers, and anglers, with fishing tackle and boat rentals available.

Colebrook

The **Mohawk Valley Camping Area** is at 3 Bridge Street in Colebrook (☎ 237-5756). **Coleman State Park** also offers campsites and is just a few miles out of town off Route 26 (RFD1, Box 183, Colebrook, NH 03576; ☎ 237-4520).

Lake Francis

On Lake Francis is **Spruce Cones Cabins & Campground** (☎ 538-6361 or 800-538-6361; $), where resident owners Gary and Doris Bedell will encourage you to challenge local records for trout and landlocked salmon. If you'd rather wander the hiking trails they'll send you out on land with notions about where to pick berries, too. There are generous trailer/RV sites here as well as tent sites. Lodging is year-round. From early May to mid-December, **Lake Francis State Park** welcomes campers. Each campsite has a fireplace, picnic table, tent site (some with platforms), and parking space; five of the 41 sites are walk-in near the river. Use the boat launch too. No running water after mid-October. Make reservations through the park during the season (Lake Francis State Park, 37B River Road, Pittsburg, NH 03592; ☎ 538-6965; $) and through the North Region Park Office (RFD2, Box 241, Lancaster, NH 03584; ☎ 788-3155).

There's another state-run campground farther north, between Second and Third Connecticut Lakes: **Deer Mountain Campground** (☎ 538-6965; $) is 5½ miles from the Canadian border, with a spring for water, earth toilets, no electricity, and 22 sites. If you enjoy more primitive camping and a chance to have a moose wander past, this is it.

Pittsburg

Private campgrounds around Pittsburg include the ones at Ramblewood, Mountain View, and Spruce Cones lodges already mentioned, and the **Wander Inn Campground** on the Beach Road at Back Lake (☎ 538-6365). Only the Wander Inn and Spruce Cone offer winter camping. Note that no roadside camping is permitted in the area; if you head out into the woods for primitive camping, **fires are by permit** only, available at **Ducret's Sporting Goods** (☎ 237-4900) in Colebrook.

Errol

About four miles south of Errol, on Route 16, is the **Mollidgewock State Park** (☎ 482-3373; season from June to Columbus Day; $), offering 40 campsites on the Androscoggin River with fireplaces, water, outhouses, and perfect access to fishing and paddling.

Stark

Don't forget that there's camping available at **Phillips Brook**, ☎ 800-872-4578 (see *On Foot*). This is ideal for the camper who wants a wilderness experience but may also want a chance to take shelter in a yurt or cabin from time to time!

West Milan

West Milan, also on Route 110, offers **Nay Pond Campground** (send mail to RR3, Box 3193, Berlin, NH 03570; ☎ 449-2122; $), with trailer, tent, and walk-in sites, a private beach on the pond, boat launch, and playground; no open fires. Open June through September.

Where To Eat

There is only one exquisite dining experience in the Great North Woods: **The Balsams** in Dixville Notch, where visitors can partake of lunch or dinner at a fixed price. At dinner, expect such table d'hôte offerings as roasted rack of veal with mushroom sauce, dauphinoise potatoes, asparagus spears, and new carrots, or smoked Ducktrap River trout with horseradish sauce. Desserts range from New England cobblers to sorbets, Swedish profiteroles, and crème brûlée. The resort is noted for its superb luncheon buffet of hot dishes, salads, cheese and fruits, and luscious tortes and tarts. Service is remarkable, and guests savor the opportunity to explore the table d'hôte with fanfare. There's a 300-label wine cellar. Remember to dress for dinner: jackets for gentlemen, casual evening attire for ladies. Menus change daily. Call for reservations (☎ 255-3400 or 800-255-0600).

Groveton

Other eateries in the region are casual and usually serve hearty, fresh-cooked fare. In Groveton, **McKenzie's Diner** (54 State Street, which is Route 3, just north of the center of town; ☎ 636-1404) serves good breakfasts and lunch with excellent coffee, and stays open for early supper (to 7:30 pm) on Thursdays and Fridays. Just up the road on the other side is a family establishment, **Mill Town Restaurant** (☎ 636-6040).

Colebrook

Head for Colebrook for more choices: **Howard's Restaurant** (☎ 237-4025) at the intersection of Routes 3 and 145 (try the poutines, which are french fries with gravy, a full meal), or the **Wilderness Restaurant** on Main Street. Both are open from early morning (about 5 am) to early evening (8 or 9). The **Colebrook Country Club** (see *Where to Stay*) also has a restaurant.

Pittsburg

Pittsburg is casual about restaurants: Pick up a sandwich at the **Trading Post** (☎ 538-6533), or stop for pizza at the **Buck Rub Pizza Pub** (☎ 538-6935) across from the First Connecticut Lake. Just north of town at Back Lake, take the Beach Road to the **Back Lake Tavern and Restaurant** (at North Country Lodge & Cabins, 51 Beach Road, ☎ 538-6521), where breakfast, lunch, and dinner are served through the winter to the snowmobile crowd, but summer hours are often limited to just evenings; be sure to call ahead in summer to check.

Errol

Two competing country fare restaurants sit across the road from each other, and each vies for the best burger description. Try a mooseburger at the **Errol Restaurant** on Main Street (☎ 482-3852), or **Lucy's North Star Café** (☎ 482-3383) for Lucy Nelson's burger with peppers, onions and mushrooms. Stop next door at L.L. Cote Sporting Goods and check out the serious fishing tackle as well as camping supplies. Head out of town on Route 26 toward Dixville Notch for a mile or so, and near the airport you'll find **Bill's Seafood** (☎ 482-3838), with hearty servings of good fresh seafood at reasonable prices. The deep-fried fish and chips are worth the trip.

Berlin

Berlin offers the fast-food restaurants your kids may have clamored for, but resist the pressure and take them to the town's traditional family spot: the **Northland Dairy Bar and Restaurant** on Route 16 just north of the city, with sandwiches, fresh seafood, baked goods and ice cream. Call to check on how full it is if you're headed in at supper time (☎ 752-6210).

Great North Woods

If you're looking for more variety, continue south on Route 16 to Gorham, gateway into the White Mountains, where Italian, Chinese, and New England cuisine jostle elbows along Route 16.

Information Sources

Connecticut Lakes Region Chamber of Commerce, Pittsburg, NH 03592; ☎ 538-7118.

Connecticut Lakes Tourist Association, Pittsburg, NH 03592; ☎ 538-7405.

Dixville Notch Information Center, Dixville Notch, NH 03576; ☎ 255-4255 (May-October).

Lancaster Chamber of Commerce, Lancaster, NH 03584; ☎ 788-3391.

North Country Chamber of Commerce, Colebrook, NH 03576; ☎ 237-8939 or 800-698-8939.

Northern White Mountain Chamber of Commerce, 164 Main Street, PO Box 298, Berlin, NH 03570; ☎ 800-992-7480; e-mail nwmcc@northernwhitemountains.com.

Umbagog Area Chamber of Commerce, Errol, NH 03579; ☎ 482-3906.

Whitefield Chamber of Commerce, Whitefield, NH 03598; ☎ 837-2609.

The White Mountains

Geography

With its snowy peak towering to 6,288 feet above sea level, **Mt. Washington** is the highest mountain in the Northeast. Craggy, unpredictable underfoot, and beset by dangerously shifting weather that includes the highest land winds measured worldwide, Mt. Washington is the symbol of high adventure for visitors to New Hampshire. Cars bearing the bumper sticker "This Car Climbed Mt. Washington" boast about having climbed the winding and precipitous auto road that has brought excursion travelers for more than a century to the windswept summit. Hikers who have climbed the mountain, foot by foot, don't wear the bumper sticker or any other outward notice, but inwardly they are often marked: The experience of walking above the treeline under fierce skies changes many perspectives.

Around this landmark mountain is the **White Mountain National Forest**, and around and within the forest are adventures that range from waterfall hikes to snowshoe rambles, from whitewater canoeing to wilderness birdwatching, from steep and twisting mountain-bike trails to scenic road tours. New Hampshire residents have welcomed guests since the first farmhouses opened the back bedrooms to travelers arriving on horseback. Accommodations include the grandeur of the Mt. Washington Hotel and Bretton Woods, the hundreds of cozy bed and breakfast inns, and the spartan hiking and hunting lodges tucked into the folds of the mountain range. Whether you're asking directions from your host, or questioning a national forest ranger about the avalanche danger or bears, or discovering treasures in an antique shop owned by a family that's held the same land since it was first settled, you're likely to find a warm welcome.

White Mountains Region

1. Santa's Village
2. Six Gun City
3. Twin Mountain Fish Hatchery
4. Mt. Washington Hotel & Resort
5. Tuckerman Ravine
6. Old Man of the Mountain
7. The Frost Place
8. Sugar Hill Historic Museum
9. Cannon Mountain / Echo Lake
10. New England Ski Museum
11. The Flume
12. Attitash Bear Peak & Fields
    of Attitash
13. Mount Washington Auto Road
14. Cog Railway
15. AMC Pinkham Notch Visitor Ctr
16. Echo Lake State Park,
    Cathedral Ledge
17. Hobo Railroad
18. Conway Scenic Railroad

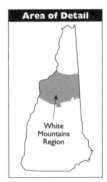

Area of Detail

White
Mountains
Region

Sign describing the Old Man of the Mountain rock formation.

The White Mountains

Considering the White Mountains region in terms of access to adventure travel means looking at it in terms of river valleys and "notches," those places in the mountain range where the land dips down and forms a V-shaped passage between the peaks as if a giant ax blade had notched the land. To the west is the Connecticut River Valley: Flat to rolling farmland enfolds towns whose history goes back well before the American Revolution. Haverhill, Woodsville, and Bath lie peacefully in this river valley, along with Littleton, Bethlehem, Sugar Hill and Franconia, and Whitefield, busy gateway towns from the Connecticut River to the national forest. This area was home to New England's best loved poet, Robert Frost; the stone walls winding along the edges of the fields and the leaf-sheltered trails all recall his phrases, and New Hampshire has even adopted its newest tourist slogan from one of his poems: "The Road Less Traveled."

In **Franconia Notch** is the Old Man of the Mountain, the rock formation that became the state's symbol of independence; the Flume (one of several in the state, but this one is two miles long!) is also in this notch. **Crawford Notch**, farther to the east, was opened to settlement before the Revolutionary War and, thanks to Abel Crawford and his son Ethan Allen Crawford, became a cradle of the modern hiking and environmental movement. **Pinkham Notch** is at the foot of Mt. Washington itself, land of high adventure for hikers, rock climbers, and now mountain bikers, as well as skiers and snowshoe explorers. The **Mt. Washington Valley** and the wild lands along the Kancamagus Highway make up the eastern and southern borders of the region. And little-known **Evans Notch**, shared with the state of Maine, has probably the most challenging hiking in New Hampshire.

The White Mountain National Forest

Exploration of the White Mountains was reported in 1643 when Darby Field became the first non-native person to climb Mt. Washington. Farmers were among the first settlers of the region in the late 1700s, and scientists and artists quickly followed. By the 1850s, thousands were visiting the area each year for scenic travel, and grand hotels were built to serve the passengers that the railroad could bring.

But the railroads also brought a way to transport lumber, and a short 50 years later many of the mountains had been ruthlessly stripped of timber and ravaged by fire, as errant sparks from the locomotives touched off the dry mounds of brush left behind by the loggers. Congressman John Wingate Weeks joined a coalition of citizens' groups, most importantly the newly born Society for the Protection of New Hampshire Forests (SPNHF), to encourage creation of preserves in the region. Passage of the Weeks Act in 1911 allowed the federal government, for the first time, to purchase privately held land. With the SPNHF gathering preservable and vulnerable land areas as quickly as possible, nuclei for the national forest formation arose.

Now the White Mountain National Forest includes nearly 800,000 acres, some in Maine but mostly in New Hampshire. There are over 1,200 miles of trails, along with backcountry shelters, campgrounds, and picnic areas. Some of the most ecologically fragile areas, in wetlands or at the high peaks of mountains, have been further protected as restricted-use areas, where even foot travelers make a difference in species survival by where they place their boots.

Primitive camping is allowed throughout the forest, except in the restricted-use areas, where campers need to stay within designated tenting boundaries. Fires are also banned from restricted areas, and dry weather often raises fire danger enough to advise all hikers and campers to not offer any sparks to the woods around them. But these are really the only restrictions to backcountry use. Hiking, snowshoeing, and cross-country skiing are welcomed. Snowmobilers and mountain bikers are encouraged to stay with established trails – some of them designated for these sports – in order to protect plant life and coordinate use with other trail users. There are six alpine ski areas, as well as the world famous Tuckerman Ravine, where well-equipped and trained skiers can enjoy this "extreme" sport and learn to deal with avalanche danger. Rock and ice climbing are possible in most areas of the forest, with Cathedral Ledge in the North Conway area and Eagle Cliffs in Franconia Notch especially well-known.

There are four designated wilderness areas within the New Hampshire section of the White Mountain National Forest: **Pemigewasset** (45,000 acres), **Presidential Range-Dry River** (27,380 acres), **Sandwich Range** (25,000 acres), and the **Great Gulf** at the north side of **Mt. Washington** (12,000 acres). No vehicles are allowed in these, in order to protect and preserve the sense of wild natural areas.

Bear, moose, beaver, raccoons, squirrels, chipmunks, rabbits, foxes, coyotes, and occasionally a wolf or wildcat may be sighted in the forest. Hawks soar on the thermoclines, warblers call from the trees in lower elevations, and crows and blue jays show off their social skills to campers as well as to each other. Fishing is superb; hunting and fishing are both regulated by state seasons and rules, but may take place throughout the forest.

The White Mountain National Forest is a year-round adventure paradise, full of challenges and scenic rewards. Balancing the hunger for wilderness with the need for trail access and local uses that may include timber harvest is a complex business;

The White Mountains

voice an opinion or seek one in a local general store and you'll be in discussion for hours. Yet the richness of the trails and the overwhelming beauty of the area are beyond debate. All travelers who enter the region have the opportunity to help preserve it for their own use and for the future.

Getting Around

A quick look at the major highways will show the complexity of getting around the mountain peaks. Pull out a map to follow along, as the roads form a series of interconnected loops giving access to the best of the mountain and river scenery.

Visitors arriving from the Boston area or from the trim little airport at Manchester are likely to head north on Interstate 93, which passes by the cities to the south, then the Lakes Region, and crosses into the White Mountains Region just as it reaches **Campton**, a small town best known for being the turnoff to **Waterville Valley** – a busy mountain resort on its own road, Route 49. The White Mountain National Forest boundaries are just beyond Campton. Staying with Interstate 93, the next major town is **Woodstock**, followed by the paired towns of **Lincoln** and **North Woodstock**. Lincoln is a busy summer and winter resort town. Here are the bike and ski shops as well as antique and handicraft galleries, restaurants, and lodging that mark the western center of the region. Roads to the west of Lincoln lead to **Mt. Moosilauke**, a challenging hiker's mountain with peak elevation of 4,810 feet, and to the valley of the **Wild Ammonoosuc River**, a favorite for spring whitewater. To the east is the **Kancamagus Highway**, a 34½-mile wild stretch of Route 112 where every turn of the road seems to shelter a trailhead for hiking or snowshoeing into the Pemigewasset Wilderness. At the end of this beautiful stretch of road is **Conway**: the southern town of the ski center formed by Conway, North Conway, and Jackson, traveling north on Route 16. Beyond Jackson is **Pinkham Notch**, home of the Appalachian Mountain Club's base camp for treks up Mt. Washington and into famous Tuckerman Ravine, where snow may last until July and hikers check for avalanche conditions before setting out in the morning.

The north end of Pinkham Notch is at the town of **Gorham**. Here Route 16 meets Route 2, and restaurants and lodging again cluster. To the east of Route 16 is a stretch of the White Mountain National Forest that includes the difficult hiking and climbing of Evans Notch, on the border with the state of Maine. Route 2 west from Gorham traces the upper boundary of the main block of national forest acreage, meeting in Randolph the major trailhead called **Appalachia**, north of Mt. Washington and its massive neighbors, Mt. Jefferson, Mt. Adams, and Mt. Madison.

Eight miles west of Randolph, Route 2 passes through **Jefferson Highlands**, where Route 115 offers a scenic shortcut back toward Interstate 93. But if you want to explore **Crawford Notch** instead of taking Route 115 all the way to the interstate, there's a left turn onto Route 302, where a scenic railway still rises along the craggy cliffs. You can take 302 all the way to North Conway, closing a tight circle around the ski center; or you can return to where you picked up Route 302 just south of Route 115's intersection with Route 2, and head west instead. Here again are two choices: stay with Route 302 into the old resort town of **Bethlehem** for a good dinner and maybe go on to Whitefield's nightlife afterward, or accept the southwestward twists of Route 2 toward Interstate 93. When you reach the interstate, the northbound side heads up to elegant **Franconia** and its historic and lovely companion town, **Sugar Hill**, and to **Littleton**, another good place for supper and entertainment. On the other hand, the southbound side of Interstate 93 turns into the **Franconia Notch Parkway**. Here is the Old Man of the Mountain, as well as a spectacular gorge called **The Flume**, and trailheads for dozens more of the mountain paths. The southern end of the narrow Parkway expands again into the familiar interstate lanes of Interstate 93 and returns to Lincoln.

The adventures that follow lead from each of the notches into the high mountains, followed by a ramble along the officially dedicated Scenic Byway of the Kancamagus Highway with its ranger station, varied trails, and wild river valley.

The White Mountains

Adventures

■ On Foot

Campton and Waterville Valley

One of the most family-friendly hikes in the White Mountains starts in Waterville Valley and includes two small mountains, Welch and Dickey. Although the peaks are only 2,605 and 2,734 feet high, the views are great and the trails moderate. Even a six-year-old can complete this loop with exhilaration. The loop is 4.4 miles and takes 3½ to 5 hours, depending on kids, birdwatching stops, and how hard you want to push up and down the slopes (surprise, the kids may push faster than you do!). It's an especially good hike for late summer, say August, when the blueberries are ripe. If you're short on time, you can just hike up Welch and back down again in an hour.

> ■ **CAUTION:** *Both Welch and Dickey mountains have bare rocky slopes in places, so don't hike them in wet or icy weather. They get slippery!*

From Interstate 93, take Exit 28 and drive through the tourist-welcoming village of **Campton** (plenty of restaurants and inns) along Route 49. In 4.4 miles turn left onto the Upper Mad River Road, which crosses Six Mile Bridge and goes steeply uphill. Check mileage at the bridge to measure .7 miles to a right turn (onto Orris Road) where a small sign may say Welch Mountain Trail. Parking is another .7 miles down the road. In the woods to the left, opposite where you entered the parking area, the two mountain trails meet. The right-hand one is the **Welch Mountain Trail**. Views along the way include the Mad River and Sandwich Mountain, and when you reach the summit you can see Mt. Tripyramid to the east, Mt. Moosilauke standing tallest to the west. To the north is Dickey Mountain, half a mile farther on the trail, which leads downward and then back up to the second peak. When you get to the summit of Dickey, be sure to go out onto the eastern rocky area for the great view up into Franconia Notch at the **North Outlook**. You can spot Mt. Lafayette, Lincoln, and The Flume to the east of the notch and Cannon

Mountain at its west. Return to the summit of Dickey and take the "highway" direction that leads across an impressive rock slab and then down through the woods and back to the parking area. The stretch down from Dickey has plenty of wildflowers, and you may find blueberries here in late summer. This is a good place to let the kids pick berries, but also an opportunity for them to learn why not to pick the flowers (so many of them are rare, and especially on bare mountain slopes they struggle to survive).

For a generous listing of many more area hikes, long and short, visit **Waterville Valley**, 13 miles up Route 49 from Campton. This self-contained resort specializes in hiking and mountain biking in summer, and offers regular guided treks and rides into the surrounding mountains. At the Waterville Valley Base Camp you can find detailed trail maps. Three more short hikes in this area, designed especially for families with children, are found in Robert Buchsbaum's book *Nature Hikes in the White Mountains*. Trail information and the map "Hiking Trails of the Waterville Valley" are also found in Waterville Valley at the Jugtown store and at the service station on Tripoli Road across from the Waterville Campground.

For a longer hike especially good in early spring before the higher mountains have lost their snow cover, consider **Mt. Tecumseh** (summit 4,003 feet). This is a 4.3-mile hike that will take about four hours. Use the *AMC White Mountain Guide* for this trail and for its neighbor, the **Mt. Osceola Trail** (summit 4,340 feet – the highest in the area, with superb views); both have ends on the Tripoli Road, which cuts to the left from Route 49 about 10 miles from Campton.

Lincoln & The Kancamagus Highway

Return to Interstate 93 from Waterville Valley and head north to Lincoln. Here Route 112 heads east under the name of the **Kancamagus Highway**, named for an Abenaki chief whose name meant *The Fearless One*. You don't have to be fearless to take the many hiking trails that lead from this highway, though. Just cruise through the resort town and head up the flank of Mt. Kancamagus on Route 112 (the road rises to 3,000 feet elevation here). You'll pass **Loon Mountain Recreation**

The Kancamagus Highway

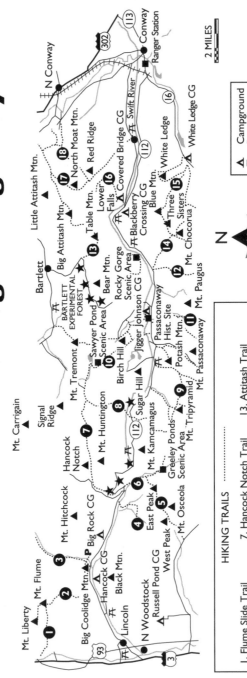

HIKING TRAILS

1. Flume Slide Trail
2. Osseo Trail
3. Wilderness Trail
4. East pond Trail
5. Mt. Osceola Trail
6. Greeley Ponds Trail
7. Hancock Notch Trail
8. Sawyer River Trail
9. Scaur Ridge Trail
10. Sawyer Pond Trail
11. Downes Brook Trail
12. Bolles Trail
13. Attitash Trail
14. Champney Falls Trail
15. Middle Sister Trail
16. Boulder Loop Trail
17. Moat Mtn. Trail
18. Red Ridge Trail

2 MILES

▲ Campground
开 Picnic Area
★ Overlook
P Parking

Area (in winter a ski slope, in summer a superb mountain-biking area; there's also space for plenty of performance events) and enter the White Mountain National Forest. Trailheads are scattered on both sides of the narrow two-lane highway, and there's ample parking. To sort them all out will take some determined study with your *AMC White Mountain Guide*, so here are three of the best, one long and peaceful, one quite short but with a lovely waterfall, and one challenging hike up the slopes of Mt. Chocorua, which is one of the three mountains most often named for favorite climbs in the national forest.

The sign for the **Greeley Ponds Scenic Area** is modest, so start keep an eye out to the right of the highway. When you see the turn for East Pond, Greeley is another mile along, at 9½ miles from Lincoln. Parking is off the road. The entire trail is actually five miles long, reaching the Waterville Valley area, but hiking from the Kancamagus to the Greeley Ponds themselves is just about two miles each way. Walking time is about 2½ hours. (There is swimming at the upper pond from sandy beaches if you like – a nice interlude on a hot summer day.) You'll enter a fragile environment of peaceful ponds, beavers, warblers and white-throated sparrows (listen for the end of the call, three notes at the same pitch) singing from the trees, and reflections of the nearby cliffs and of the spruces and pointed firs. To add a little spice to the hike, continue past the ponds up the steep **Mt. Osceola Trail** for about a half-mile to reach the ledges (rocky, so don't climb them when they're wet or icy), where you can take in a quiet view of the lake below.

From the roadside trailhead for Greeley Ponds, drive another 10.3 miles eastward (toward Conway) on the Kancamagus Highway to reach the turn for **Sabbaday Falls**. Don't miss this one, even though it's rarely a private place; even with a summer-afternoon throng of visitors, these falls are worth seeing. It's a mile from the picnic area to the falls, which include a deep clear pool, a fierce cascade that rushes into a narrow gorge called a "flume," and a cool woodsy walk up well-crafted steps to the top of the falls where you can see how deeply the rushing waters have chiseled the stone.

■ **CAUTION:** *If you're on the walk to Sabbaday Falls with young children, beware of the alluring, climbable railings along the cascade; there's a rocky dropoff.*

From Sabbaday Falls, if you hike southward on the **Sabbaday Brook Trail**, you'll enter the **Sandwich Range Wilderness**. This is a restricted-use area, where no camping or fires are allowed and hikers are expected to help keep the forest looking as untouched by humans as possible. The most interesting landform in this wilderness area is **The Bowl**, a glacial cirque, best hiked to from Wonalancet, a small town south of the national forest border. See the *AMC White Mountain Guide* for details.

The approach to **Mt. Chocorua** is near the eastern end of the Kancamagus Highway. The mountain's pointed rock pinnacle stands out from a distance, and many hikers approach it from Route 16 near Chocorua village. But the approach from the Kancamagus takes you past Champney Falls and the ledges of the Piper Trail before you reach the challenging rocky slopes of Mt. Chocorua. Daniel Doan, in his book *50 More Hikes in New Hampshire*, recommends a loop trail from the Kancamagus that avoids having to retrace your steps, but still puts you back on the highway a hundred feet from where you left it. Consult Doan's book for more detail if you like, or the AMC Chocorua-Waterville Map (Map 7) that comes with the *AMC White Mountain Guide*.

Basically, the route is south along the **Champney Brook Trail** (trailhead 11½ miles from Conway, or roughly 21 miles from Lincoln, on the south side of Route 112), past Champney Falls (reached by a short bypass found 1.25 miles from the start of the trail – beware of slippery rocks and don't try climbing the water chute), and up the steep northeastern side of the mountain. When **Middle Sister Trail** comes in from the left, Champney Brook Trail wings to the right and you go with it over a ledge marked with yellow blazes, entering a spruce and fir woods. Take another turn to the right onto the **Piper Trail**, which crosses the Liberty Trail and (with more yellow blazes) takes you into the alpine zone of rare miniature plants and then up a steep 50-yard craggy climb to the summit.

Views include Mt. Washington and the Presidential Range to the north, and to the west the Sandwich Range. The climb is worth it! Legend says these were the last views seen by Chocorua, who lived in the area around 1760 and may have been a chief of the Ossipee Tribe; he is said to have been killed on the summit as part of a blood retribution for other deaths. When you're done pondering his sad end, and the glorious vista, retrace the trail to the junction of trails at the broken ledge and take the trail on the left, descending. This leads into the **Bee Line Trail** in about 25 minutes, through scrub spruce and over and open ledge (stick with those yellow blazes). Now there's a trail junction again, and you head to the right onto Bee Line until you reach the next trail junction, with a right again onto the **Bolles Trail** so that you're headed north down Paugus Brook and Twin Brook to the highway; a right turn at the road returns you to where you parked.

> ✹ **CAUTION:** *Because this route takes you up and down some steep rocky areas, don't hike it during rain or when the ground is icy. "Discretion is the better part of valor," they say; Chocorua might have learned the lesson if he'd lived longer himself.*

A Note on the Pemigewasset Wilderness: The "Pemi" Wilderness lies north of the Kancamagus Highway, toward the west (Lincoln) side of the area. It is still a wilderness in the national forest sense of the term, meaning that no vehicles are allowed in it (that means mountain bikes, too). But some parts of it are unlikely to provide much taste of the lonely wild mountains these days, as it has been "over-discovered" by hikers, especially along the trails leading toward the Flume and Mt. Lafayette, as well as Thoreau Falls and the Wilderness Trail. If you plan a hike into this area and want a taste of the wild, consider Lincoln Brook, Cedar Brook, and Twin Brook areas, where there's more solitude. And aim for midweek in the spring, late fall, or winter.

The White Mountains

WHAT'S A WILDERNESS?

Sure, you already know: A place where there aren't other people, where there are wild animals, and where you might get lost. New Hampshire's national forest rangers add a few more ideas: A wilderness preserves the primitive environment. And it requires anyone who exists in it to depend exclusively on his or her own efforts for survival. The four New Hampshire designated wilderness areas provide a taste of this way of life, giving hikers privacy and an illusion of being very far away from populated areas. (If you do get lost, you'll find out how far that can feel.)

But wilderness areas today are becoming more frequently visited, and increasingly "touched by human hands" after all. You can help preserve wilderness areas by practicing "leave no trace" hiking and camping.

- Carry out everything you carry in. Bury human waste with a small spade, a minimum of 200 feet from water.

- Speak quietly, move softly, and leave radios at home.

- Travel in small groups, and travel light.

- Wear "earth colors" to be less distracting to other hikers; use this notion for your tent and gear, too.

- Avoid hiking in mud season when spring rains soften the trails. And try not to take shortcuts that will create more paths through the trees.

- Luring wild animals to a campsite is generally a mistake. When bears lose their fear of humans and associate food with people, they become dangerous and may have to be relocated or destroyed. Hang food at least 10 feet off the ground, stored in closed containers.

- Rangers suggest that you leave your dog at home. If you do bring a dog, keep it leashed, and remember that a dog not accustomed to climbing and hiking is going to get tired and sore, just like a human who is not used to such activities. The bigger the dog, the more weight you might have to carry out of the woods if your pet can't handle the trail!

Conway, North Conway, Intervale

It's worth mentioning Conway as the site of the ranger station at the east end of the Kancamagus Highway, and also the start of horrendous traffic jams on summer afternoons. Try really hard to get through this town in the early morning or the evening. There are dozens of outlet stores lining Route 16 from Conway to North Conway, and then a fascinating village of shops, sightseeing, and good food in North Conway; the traffic drawn by all these has never been properly managed.

Behind the ranger station is **Moat Mountain**, where rockhounds are welcome to gather smoky quartz and other minerals for personal use (not for sale). Hand tools only, please, and fill any holes, restoring the area's natural appearance. From the Saco Ranger Station, head over to Route 16 north and at the first traffic light turn left onto West Side Road. After 0.7 mile turn left on Passaconaway Road and go 1.2 miles to High Street (unmarked dirt road) on right. Make the turn and go 1.9 miles (should be mineral collecting site signs) to a parking area at the end of the road. Hike three-fourths of a mile up the marked trail to the mountain site.

There's also a little-known hiking area in Conway called the **Green Hills Preserve** (2,822 acres), managed by the Nature Conservancy. From Conway, head north along Route 302 past the malls and toward North Conway village, watching the roads on the right; you want Artist Falls Road, which turns into Thompson Road. There's parking before the end of the road (the parking at the very end is private); walk to the end and find the kiosk for information and a trail map. The trails range from 1.1 to 2.1 miles in length, and include a unique high-elevation stand of red pine forest, as well as a rare plant community on Peaked Mountain. Obviously, for protection of this vulnerable area, only foot travel is allowed, and no fires or camping are permitted.

North Conway is the home of at least three mountain sports shops, which offer expert assistance and gear for rock climbing. No wonder: Cathedral and White Horse Ledges are just north of town, offering superb climbing, with steep faces drenched in sunlight to counter the deep chill of the rock.

▓ **CAUTION:** *Rock climbers should take these ledges seriously in spite of their popularity as training slopes; there are many difficult routes up the rock walls.*

Climbers on Cathedral Ledge.

Stop at **Eastern Mountain Sports** at the north end of the village (left side of the road in a huge white building that's a resort hotel), just before the left turn to Echo Lake State Park where the ledges are, and check the latest conditions and routes before climbing. At EMS you can also find Ed Webster's book *Rock Climbs in the White Mountains of New Hampshire*, a must-read for technical (hardware-based) climbs. If you're looking for a more relaxed hike, try the pleasant trails in this state park and enjoy watching the climbing teams scale the rock faces.

When you leave North Conway on Route 16, headed north toward the other great notches (Pinkham, Crawford), the first village you enter is **Intervale**. Note the scenic overlook on the left side of the road, with its view of Cathedral Ledge, and pull in for a moment to get oriented. The two roads cross the highway. One is across from the south exit of the scenic rest area, next to the little Intervale post office that's part of a strip of food stores. This road is the Intervale Cross Road; it leads to an old Abenaki Indian encampment (see *Sightseeing*). The other road is farther north, just beyond the north exit of the scenic rest area, and is Hurricane Mountain Road. This leads to two good hiking trails and some fine rockhounding, where even a beginner may find smoky quartz and zircons (Black Cap Mountain), as well as arfvedstonite in quartz with feldspar (Hurricane Mountain). Follow Hurricane Mountain Road east 3.7 miles from Route 16 to the two trailheads, across the road from each other. The **Hurricane Mountain Trail** is the one that leaves the north side of the road and goes half a mile to a wooded summit. The **Black Cap Mountain Trail** goes south instead, 1.1 miles to a summit with views.

> ➋ **TIP:** *For rockhounding, simple tools like a ham-mer and chisel or prybar will likely be enough. Be kind to those who follow you and close up any holes you make as you explore.*

Outfitters

■ **New England Hiking Holidays** has its office in North Conway, and offers a spectacular five-day tour of the White Mountains for hikers who like the re-laxation and relative luxury of fine inns each evening. The tour is repeated a number of times each summer and fall, and reservations are needed (New England Hiking Holidays, PO Box 1648, North Conway, NH 03860; ☎ 800-869-0949 or 356-9696; e-mail NEHH@ aol.com).

Jackson

This gracious village is a base for both **Black Mountain Ski Area** and hikers and skiers headed up to Pinkham Notch. It's also where the trails to Mt. Doublehead start, headed for the north and south summits. David Doan (*50 More Hikes in New Hampshire*) tells of a good loop trail that includes the two wooded summits and the views along the way. There's a sturdy hand-built cabin at the north summit. Doan gives an interest-ing description of how ski trails were once built. The four-mile loop takes a bit more than three hours if you're in good shape. If you'd rather relax for a while, stroll around Jackson and enjoy the covered bridge, park, and gentle New England scenery. In winter this is a picture-postcard village; it's nearly as good in the other seasons too.

The White Mountains

BACK-COUNTRY CABIN RENTALS

By pre-arrangement (at least 14 days in advance) with the Saco Ranger Station, you can pick up keys to either of two back-country cabins. One is on the west side of Black Mountain, reached by hiking 1.4 or 2½ miles (depending on route) from the Black Mountain Ski Trail. The other is on the east side of North Doublehead Mountain, where the access hike is 1.8 miles from either of two established larger trails. These are great winter bivouac spots for snowshoeing and Nordic ski hiking. Get details on the cabins from the ranger station at **Saco Ranger District**, 33 Kancamagus Highway, North Conway, NH 03818 (☎ 447-5448).

Pinkham Notch

Mt. Washington is not the only massive mountain worth climbing in New Hampshire; its neighbors are nearly as tall, and some of the lesser-known peaks like Diamond and Percy have challenges, as does Evans Notch. But let's face it, there's a special appeal to climbing the tallest peak in the state, and the mountain is also known for its capricious and sometimes life-threatening ways. Hikers have died here, victims of drastic weather and slippery rock. But many more hikers have found fresh excitement and delight on these trails. Take precautions, go well prepared, don't hike Mt. Washington alone (really), and enjoy every bit of it.

Mt. Washington reaches 6,288 feet in elevation at the peak, where there is a summit building with food service, public restrooms, telephone, and a post office. No overnight stays are possible at the summit. There is also a weather observatory for what may be the "worst weather in the world" (winter wind chill has been known to match Antarctica's!). Even in summer the temperatures at the summit may be in the 40s in the daytime; at night frost or snow can arrive year-round. There are three basic ways to reach the summit: ride on the coal-powered cog railway that ascends the west slope (this has its own excitement, as the slope is steep and the trestles narrow); drive up in your car on the Auto Road (be ready for tight turns, steep grades, and have good brakes for the trip back down); or hike the trails. Variations include purchasing a ride up in a van at Great Glen Trails, mountain biking up the Auto Road and, believe it or not, running – there's a road race on the mountain every summer!

Pinkham Notch is the spot where many Mt. Washington area hikes begin. Appropriately, the Appalachian Mountain Club (AMC) has a base camp right by the highway, about nine miles north of Jackson on Route 16. Start your hike with a thorough study of the *AMC White Mountain Guide* section on these trails, and a visit to the base camp for maps and gear recommendations. It's called Pinkham Notch Visitor Center and includes a Trading Post with books, maps, and a three-dimensional contour model of the mountain, a lodge with library and meeting rooms, a snack bar, and AMC offices. In the summer there are frequent naturalist-led rambles and lectures. Downstairs are restrooms, showers, and a pack room where backpackers can get reorganized. There's a hiker shuttle van that connects trailheads if you don't want to hike a loop; ask at the upstairs desk for the schedule.

➔ **TIP:** *The ranger station at the north end of Pinkham Notch, just outside Gorham (Androscoggin Ranger Station), has a great display of necessary hiking clothes and tells you why you'll need them.*

If you plan a winter hike, it would also be a good idea to visit the ranger station at the north end of Route 16 (just south of Gorham) and watch the video on Tuckerman Ravine; you'll be better prepared for what to expect. Take the weather seriously, and pack according to the following tips.

The White Mountains

TIPS FOR DAY-CLIMBING
ON MT. WASHINGTON

■ Never climb above the treeline in sneakers or other "ordinary" shoes. The rocks will hurt your feet, and the footing is treacherous without sturdy, built-for-mountains soles. Get a good pair of hiking boots. They'll last for years, and cost less than the deductible on your health insurance. With them you should buy two pairs of socks: polypropylene "liner" socks, which feel great against the skin and help wick moisture away, and wool socks, which cushion and keep your feet warm. The combination of the two pairs means that friction takes place between the socks, rather than between your foot and a sock, so you have much less chance of blisters. Be sure you try your boots with both pairs of socks to get the right size.

■ Once you get above treeline (which is somewhere around 4,400 feet; Mt. Washington's summit is 6,288), the weather can change drastically in as little as 15 minutes. It's not unusual for a summer noon-time hike to include thunderstorms, drenching rain, hail, and thick fog – barely half an hour after a clear-sky start. Temperatures drop swiftly, and wind-chill can be deadly. Aim to stay warm and dry no matter what; then, should the worst happen and you find yourself lost or with a broken ankle, you'll survive until help arrives. More likely, should you simply have the usual challenging weather, you'll still be able to enjoy your hike.

So indulge in today's miracle fabrics: polypropylene long johns (no, cotton is not better, it soaks up moisture and stays wet and cold against you), a synthetic fleece-neck, zippered jacket for warmth, and real rain gear, not just windpants or windbreaker (the wind will blow the rain through these). Other handy layers are a wool sweater, a wool cap (yes, winter version), and mittens or gloves.

■ Water is a must: When you hike vigorously, you sweat and breathe hard and lose moisture. A day's hike means at least two quarts of water carried with you. (Ordinary plastic soft drink bottles with screw tops work well, but the ones with spouts could pop open easily and leak on your clothes.) No, you won't have to go to the bathroom all the time – you're really using this water, and if you don't drink it, you'll get dehydrated, headachy, dizzy, or even sick. Also carry a protein-rich lunch, and several hearty snacks. Chocolate is still a great picker-upper, and granola bars will get you even farther. Dried fruit and nuts are reliable, too.

■ Now add the things you've always heard of as survival gear: a pocket knife, compass, your guidebook and maps, a few first aid supplies (aspirin, Band-Aids), a small flashlight, and toilet paper. If you do use the toilet paper, follow the guidelines for "no-trace" travel: Move off the trail and away from water sources, dig a small hole, and bury the waste thoroughly. Now you see another reason why you want to hike with a buddy: If you have to leave the trail for "the necessary," you have someone standing on it calling you back to the right spot.

■ Biting insects won't be a problem above treeline, but for the part of the trail that's in the woods, especially in moist lowlands, bring some "bug dope." And if you are diabetic or allergic to bee-stings, carry the antidotes you need and let your hiking partner know where to find them in your pack in case you become disabled.

Although this sounds like a lot to tote along, in today's backpacks with padded shoulder straps, waist belt, and chest strap, it's very manageable. Remember, once you've eaten lunch and finished the first quart of water, the weight in the pack will be cut down! Winter hikes, or even those in early spring (May), need much more gear for weather protection and emergencies. Best suggestion: Try your first winter hike with an AMC-sponsored group or other experienced guide, so you can build your knowledge and skills without risking your life or the lives of the many volunteer rescuers on the mountain.

The White Mountains

Two approaches to Mt. Washington are used most frequently: From the east, starting at the base camp at Pinkham Notch, hikers take the **Tuckerman Ravine Trail** 4.2 miles to the summit. From the west, the **Ammonoosuc Ravine Trail** leaves the cog railway station and rises 3.1 miles to Lake of the Clouds Hut, where hikers connect with the **Crawford Path** for the remaining 1.4 miles to the summit. Don't judge the trip by the number of miles, but by the rise in elevation: 4,000 feet. The round-trip will take at least eight hours for the reasonably fit person in good weather. Don't take small children, and don't try to hike this one without building up to it through other hikes.

The **Tuckerman Ravine Trail** is described here, and the western approach is in the Crawford Notch section later in this region. You'll find the trailhead behind the Pinkham Notch Visitor Center (and do check the weather at the peak by stopping at the center). You need to pay close attention to side trails and signs, because many paths split off from the Tuckerman Ravine Trail, especially in the first quarter-mile. After 0.3 mile the trail crosses the Cutler River and begins to climb: the *AMC White Mountain Guide* calls it a "moderate but relentless" climb, but it's steep enough that you'll need hiking boots and you won't want to be carrying on a conversation. There's a good view of the Crystal Cascade before the trail cuts to the right (Boott Spur Trail goes left). You see the Huntington Ravine Trail cut to the right at 1.3 miles, while the Tuckerman goes on to cross first a tributary (at 1½ miles) and then the main branch (1.6 miles) of the Cutler River. Two more trails leave to the right: the Huntington ravine Fire Road (1.7 mile) and the Raymond Path (2.1); stay left. There's a definite crossroads at 2.3 miles, with the Boott Spur Trail heading left, the Lion Head right, and you go straight ahead. You'll reach the buildings at the floor of Tuckerman Ravine in another 0.1 mile, with great cliffs – that you're not going to climb this time. Instead, stay with your trail on the right (north) of the stream to pass through the upper floor of the ravine and reach the headwall. Be careful not to dislodge rocks underfoot; if you do start one rolling by accident, yell loudly to let other hikers know.

Now the trail simplifies a little, with a left turn at the top of the rock slope and a climb up a series of ledges. The Alpine Garden Trail cuts away to the right at 3.4 miles. You'll see many of the flowering alpine plants along your own trail too; remember not to step on them if you can avoid it, as a plant just three or four inches tall may have taken 20 years or more to reach that height). Be careful at 3.4 miles to select the Tuckerman Ravine Trail, not the Tuckerman Crossover; your trail should cut sharply right to start up the steep rocks, where you need to watch closely for paint on the ledges and cairns (rock stacks) that mark the trail. Stick with them to the Auto Road a few yards before the parking area, and climb the wooden steps to the summit area.

> ■ **CAUTION:** *Bad weather on Mt. Washington only gets worse; don't expect it to clear. If fog moves in, and you can see your way back down the trail accurately, go down. Don't cause a rescue team to risk their lives to find you! You can always get to the summit another day; telling the story of having the weather close in on you will still put you into the group of Mt. Washington survivors, and you will have won a round on the mountain, not lost one.*

There are many variations on this approach to the mountain, and many trails heading off to other spots worth visiting, like the Alpine Garden. Use the *AMC White Mountain Guide* to customize your plans.

Shorter hikes around Mt. Washington range from the 15-minute walk from Pinkham Visitor Center up to the Crystal Cascade (well marked, leaves from behind the visitor center), to the slightly longer trail to Glen Ellis Falls (drive 0.7 miles south of the visitor center on Route 16 and park in the marked area on the west side of the highway, where there are restrooms and a picnic area; walk through the tunnel under Route 16 and hike 0.3 miles to the base of the impressive falls). There's also a nice ramble through the Alpine Garden high on the slope of Mt. Washington. The AMC offers guided Alpine Garden tours, well worth the effort and fee (about $60) for the expert botanist who'll introduce you to the plants and their lives above the treeline. If you want to go on your own instead, stop at the visitor center and pick up a book on the plants. If you take the "short cut" by driving to the intersection of the Alpine Garden

Trail with the Auto Road, you'll want good hiking boots to explore the 300 feet of elevation changes on the rocky trail. And you'll need all those pack items listed earlier, especially the rain gear. (Don't let the idea of rain spoil your plan; you can still have a great time exploring the garden, if you're dressed appropriately. Only thunderstorms and heavy fog will make the trip unwise.)

To reach the **Alpine Garden Trail** by car, stop at the visitor center to check on weather at the summit, then drive north on Route 16 for 2½ miles to the Mt. Washington Auto Road on your left. There's a fee for use of the road, which is likely to change from year to year; anticipate spending at least $12 for car and driver, plus more per additional passenger. It's worth it: eight miles of superb views, scary drop-offs but with the road well built and maintained. Look for Milepost 7, and then the Huntington Ravine Trail, which will be on your left; park here and hike the steep Huntington Ravine Trail down the mountain (not up yet!) for 0.3 mile to where it levels out and you turn right onto the Alpine Garden Trail. This is a relatively flat ramble of 1.2 miles across the garden, where you'll struggle to step on stones rather than on the complex and delicate plants. Real botany is best done at plant level: Don't hesitate to crouch, crawl, and lie down in order to see the intricacies of delicate flowers, tiny rootlets, and "pillow" growth patterns that have developed to make life possible on this wind-swept and icy region. If you make it the whole 1.2 miles you get to look down into Tuckerman Ravine, always awesome in its size and splendor, before you retrace the trail to the parking area. (If you don't get that far, you'll still have great views of the Carter Range to the east.) Mid-June is traditionally the best time to see blossoms in the Alpine Garden. Most common are diapensia, which grow in thick dark-green cushions with white five-petaled blossoms. But you can also spot Labrador tea, mountain avens, and dozens more curiously adapted plants; get that guidebook open and have fun!

> ■ **CAUTION:** *Don't pick the plants here. Seriously, you're looking at hundred-year struggles for existence. Hikers are the biggest threat these tiny miracles now face.*

Another good hike for more ambitious walkers is the **Old Jackson Road**, which also leaves from behind the Pinkham Notch Visitor Center and branches away from the Tuckerman Ravine Trail. You'll climb steadily for 1.9 miles to the trail's end at the Auto Road, and can then head up the **Madison Gulf Trail** another 0.2 miles to Lowe's Bald Spot, a superb place for views of the Great Gulf, Mt. Adams, and Mt. Madison. It's a challenging hike that will take about four hours round-trip, mostly through woodlands until the final spectacular view.

Gorham

Between the Pinkham Notch Visitor Center and the town of Gorham to the north are more hiking trails, a ski area (Wildcat), and the region's oldest campground, Dolly Copp. Use Gorham as your "base camp" town for hikes in this region; there are good shops with hiking supplies as well as moose themes (the region's mascot!). This is also a good place to stock up on lunches or plan your supper and lodging (see *Where To Stay* and *Where To Eat*). The fun of the town is the sense of being where the "real hikers" have all visited. Meet Route 2 in Gorham, and turn westward for more adventure in the White Mountain National Forest, or continue north on Route 16 to enter the Great North Woods region.

EVANS NOTCH

From Gorham, most hikers will head either south to the trails of Pinkham Notch and Mt. Washington, or west toward Randolph's busy trailheads and the other hiker havens of Crawford Notch and Franconia Notch. But Evans Notch deserves mention. Least known of all the New Hampshire notches, it lies on the border of Maine, south of Gorham, and is reached by taking Route 2 east and crossing the Maine border, going two miles into the state of Maine, and turning right (south) onto Route 113, which sways back into New Hampshire in a few more miles and eventually connects with Route 302 east of Center Conway. The mountains here are in the Mahoosuc Range (mahoosuc is Abenaki for "abode of hungry animals").

The White Mountains

There's an Appalachian Mountain Club access point called Cold River Camp on Route 113, and from here the trails in New Hampshire lead to the Baldface Mountains: 3.6 miles to South Baldface, 4.7 miles to North Baldface. These slopes were swept by fire in 1903, burning all the way to Jackson. Because of the destructive week-long burn, there are incredible views from these peaks. However, harsh weather is common, and there are no tested and reliable water sources, so this territory is for experienced hikers willing to take some additional risks as well as additional baggage. Consult the *AMC Guide to the White Mountains*; the Forest Service also offers a leaflet on the Baldface Circle and Bicknell Ridge Trail, which can be picked up at the ranger station in Gorham.

Appalachia (Randolph)

From Gorham, Route 2 takes you west along the edge of the main block of the White Mountain National Forest. Route 2 enters the town of Randolph almost immediately, and reaches the Appalachia trailhead for the forest at about six miles from Route 16. The trailhead is on your left, with one of the largest parking areas in the North Country! (That goes to show how important hiking is here.) Although Appalachia is also the name of a small town, most hikers think of this area as part of Randolph – in part because the Randolph Mountain Club does such yeoman work in maintaining and mapping the trails here. (The name has nothing to do with the Appalachian Mountain title; it comes from 19th-century trail builder William Peek, who found some small boys there who'd eaten too many green apples from the orchard and were in pain – hence, "apple-achia.") Pick up the group's trail guide, *Randolph Paths*, at a local shop or at the Pinkham Notch Visitor Center (south on Route 16; see page 85).

Although Mt. Washington beckons as the high peak for the region, Appalachia and Randolph are the true center of hiking trails for the northern White Mountains. South of Route 2 are the so-called Northern Peaks of the Presidential Range: Mt. Madison, Mt. Adams, and Mt. Jefferson. North of Route 2 is the Crescent Range. The earliest hikers' trail was blazed in the 1850s by Gorham mountain guide James Gordon at the urging of Thomas Starr King, the mountain-loving writer who inspired thousands to travel to these peaks. More than 100 miles of trails were laid by a small group of dedicated climbers during the 1880s and 1890s, but the logging of the forests accelerated in 1903-1904, destroying many of the trails. With the establishment of the White Mountain National Forest, countless volunteers and dozens of professional trail crews blazed and built hundreds more miles of trails. Mt. Adams, second highest of the White Mountains (5,799 feet), is a striking sight from a distance and a peak well worth climbing. Mt. Jefferson (5,716 feet) is reached by some of the more challenging hiking trails: the Caps Ridge Trail from Jefferson Notch, the Castle Trail, and the Gulfside Trail and Mt. Jefferson Loop. Although Mt. Madison is the shortest of this group, its 5,366-foot summit offers grand views and more good trails.

These are the peaks now reached from Appalachia, which is only one of six major trailheads listed by the Randolph Mountain Club. To get oriented, check your map and find the secondary road that cuts from Route 16 to Route 2, slicing off a triangle with Gorham at the tip. This secondary road is called both the Dolly Copp Road and the Pinkham B Road (signs may say either or both names). On the Route 16 side, it is the approach road to Dolly Copp Campground, but continues past the campground into deep woods (beware of logging trucks, a sign of the mixed community uses of the forest). It is a more or less level road, and there are designated parking areas along it. The major trailheads start here. From east to west they are:

- The **"height of land"** (highest point) on the Pinkham B (Dolly Copp) Road.

- **Randolph East**, at the Route 2 end of Pinkham B (Dolly Copp) Road, less than a quarter-mile from the highway.

- **Appalachia**, already mentioned, on the south side of Route 2 about a half-mile west of where the Pinkham B (Dolly Copp) Road meets Route 2.

- **Lowe's Store** on Route 2 (north side, about two miles west of the Appalachia parking area). This store is the heart of hiker country, and Randolph Mountain Club activities are listed here. Pick up trail guides and maps as well as supplies. The store, founded by Vernon B. Lowe in 1960, has always welcomed hikers. There are cabins behind it, and plenty of parking (fee charged for overnight).

- **Bowman**, about one mile west of Lowe's Store, also on Route 2 (south side).

- **Jefferson Notch**, reached by taking the Jefferson Notch Road south from the Valley Road in Jefferson (see Crawford Notch).

Randolph Mountain Club trails also start from two former sites of mountain lodges: the Mt. Crescent House site on Randolph Hill Road (which is well marked on Route 2), and the Ravine House Site on old Route 2, now called Durand Road. You can find hundreds of trails and routes listed in *Randolph Paths*, and with these you'll be able to hike not only into the Presidentials, but also north into the less-visited Crescent Range.

To narrow the options for a first-time visit, here are a few favorite hikes of varied length and challenge.

- **Coldbrook Fall**: This hike starts from Appalachia on the Air Line Trail, which you leave 0.1 mile later and turn right onto the Amphibrach (a trail name derived from its original triple blazing in 1883). The trail runs along the edge of a power-line clearing until 0.6 mile, when it bears left onto a logging road. Two other trails cut off to the left, but stick with the Amphibrach to Memorial Bridge at 0.7 miles; this bridge is a memorial to the original path-builders of these woods. You can see the waterfall from the bridge, and walk up the spur trail to get close to it. Round-trip distance for the hike is 1½ miles (you can vary the return by taking Sylvan Way to Air Line, for the same mileage); expect to hike for about 1½ hours.

- **Snyder Brook:** Would you like to see ancient hemlocks, part of the old-growth forest that escaped the logging ax? This is another short hike, just 1½ miles (about an hour) for the round trip, but there are cascades, rapids, and pools on Snyder Brook and the trees are quietly impressive. From the east end of the parking lot at Appalachia take the trail called Falls-way, which runs east a short distance, then turns to cross the railroad bed and enters the woods to run along Snyder Brook. It passes the Gordon Falls (and a related trail loop), then the Lower and Upper Sal-roc Falls, and finally reaches the head of Tama Falls; for more views on the way back, switch trails to Brookbank, which is a somewhat rough trail that returns you to Fallsway.

■ **Dome Rock:** Here's a romantic hike to schedule for a supper picnic. The *Randolph Paths* authors recommend it for a sunset view, followed by a quick descent. The round-trip is 3.2 miles (two hours and 15 minutes) by this set of trails. From Appalachia follow the Valley Way and Brookside to the first crossing of Snyder Brook. Then turn left and climb on Inlook Trail, traversing open ledges with low trees and good views, to Dome Rock. It's worth going another 0.1 mile past Dome Rock on Inlook Trail to see another view, this time from the Upper Inlook. If you're wondering about the name "Inlook," consider that the views here are "in" towards the Northern Peaks, and "out" to the west and north.

■ **Mt. Adams:** The Randolph Mountain Club maintains four places to spend the night on the northwest slopes of this mountain. Two are enclosed lodges: Gray Knob, open year-round, and Crag Camp, where there's a summer caretaker. In addition, there's the Perch (lean-to and some tent platforms) and the Log Cabin (Adirondack-style shelter with one open side). Modest fees are charged for these shelters (even with inflation, figure on $10 or less per night at the enclosed ones and $4-5 at the more primitive versions); you must bring your own sleeping and cooking gear, including camp stove.

But you don't have to stay overnight. Mt. Adams can also be hiked as a challenging day hike of nine miles, or about 7½ hours, provided that the weather is kind, as the trail has some very steep and exposed sections. Start from Appalachia and follow the Air Line Trail into the woods. Trails heading out or across your path include the Link, Amphibrach, Sylvan Way,

Beechwood Way, Short Line, and Randolph Path –
all in the first mile! Stay with Air Line, which begins
to rise steeply to Durand Ridge. This ridge in turn becomes the Knife-edge, where you climb past an overlook of the King Ravine. The ravine is full of huge
boulders and ice caves, and its history includes perhaps being the hiding place for Rogers' Rangers as
they retreated from Canada during the French and
Indian War. At 3.2 miles the Chemin des Dames
("Ladies' Road," once considered the gentlest path
here) rises out of the ravine to meet you. At 3½ miles
the Air Line Cutoff heads over to the Madison Spring
AMC hut (also just called Madison Hut). But stay
with the regular trail another half-mile to a striking
view of Mt. Madison, before turning right to coincide
with the Gulfside Trail. Go 70 yards and turn left to
take a rough rocky route to the summit. You'll pass a
minor summit on the way, named John Quincy Adams for the sixth U.S. president, before you reach the
main peak. Here you lookout over the Great Gulf and
realize why this area was set aside as one of the forest's designated wilderness areas. It is vast and magnificent – but find your own words for it, if you can.

■ For variety on the return trip, take the cutoff to Madison Hut and pick up Valley Way Trail there, descending quickly along the Snyder Brook and offering some
shelter from inclement weather/ Valley Way will take
you all the way back to a right turn Air Line as you get
close to Appalachia.

When you've had enough of running into the many hikers who
head to the White Mountains in summer and during the fall foliage season, try the Randolph Mountain Club paths north of
Route 2 instead. One of the favorite trails in this area is the one
to Ice Gulch, a wild and beautiful place with giant boulders and
very challenging climbing over and among them. Don't miss
Lookout Ledge, either, although it's a short hike.

📖 **SUGGESTED READING:** *For all the hikes north of Route 2, do get the book* Randolph Paths *and the* Randolph Mountain Club's map, *both available at Lowe's Store on Route 2, at the AMC Pinkham Notch Visitor Center, and at Ragged Mountain Equipment on Route 16 in Intervale.*

Jefferson

West of Randolph, Route 2 enters Jefferson Highlands and then Jefferson. Taking the left turn onto Route 115 will lead you toward Crawford Notch, one of the most compact but interesting hiking regions of the forest. Along Route 115 are also two hiking trailheads, for the Owl's Head and Cherry Mountain Trails; see the *AMC White Mountain Guide*.

Crawford Notch

From Route 2, the most direct way to reach Crawford Notch is the left turn onto Route 115 just before arriving at the tourist attractions of Jefferson (east of the town). Route 115 ends at Route 3, where a left turn again brings you to Route 302. At the junction with 302, in the town of Twin Mountain, Route 3 goes south toward Franconia Notch; save that for another day and go left one more time, onto Route 302 as it heads nominally west (actually south) toward Bretton Woods and the Mt. Washington Hotel. Before you reach these landmarks though, you'll see the parking area for Zealand on the right.

Zealand

Zealand isn't actually quite part of the geology of Crawford Notch, as it sits on the higher land above the sharp cut between the mountains. But it is close by, and is one of the most pleasant hiking areas of the White Mountain National Forest. It's especially well liked as a family hiking region, because the elevation changes are gradual and there's plenty to see. The region suffered both logging and two disastrous forest fires, and traces of the earlier settlers can still be found. The **Zealand Trail** includes wooden bridges and an elevated boardwalk, a beaver area, and waterfalls. It takes you to an AMC hut, better described as a mountain lodge, where you can find basic refreshments like lemonade and even (by pre-arrangement) spend the

Crawford Notch State Park

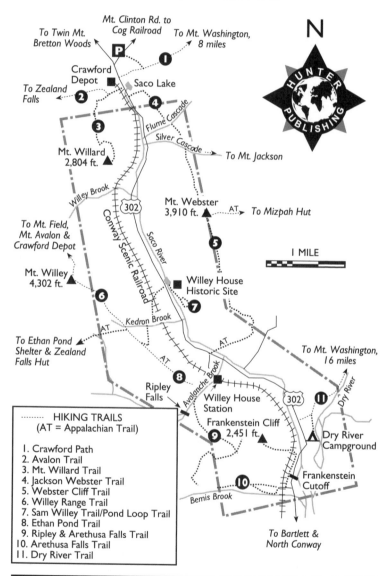

N

To Twin Mt.
Bretton Woods

Mt. Clinton Rd. to
Cog Railroad

To Mt. Washington,
8 miles

P

Crawford
Depot

Saco Lake

To Zealand
Falls

1

2

4

3

Flume Cascade

Silver Cascade

To Mt. Jackson

Mt. Willard
2,804 ft. ▲

Willey Brook

302

Mt. Webster
3,910 ft. ▲

AT → To Mizpah Hut

To Mt. Field,
Mt. Avalon &
Crawford Depot

Conway Scenic Railroad

Saco River

5

1 MILE

Mt. Willey
4,302 ft. ▲

6

Willey House
Historic Site

7

Kedron Brook

AT

To Ethan Pond
Shelter & Zealand
Falls Hut

AT

AT

To Mt. Washington,
16 miles

8

Avalanche Brook

Ripley
Falls

Willey House
Station

302

11

Dry River

Frankenstein Cliff
2,451 ft. ▲

Dry River
Campground

9

Frankenstein
Cutoff

10

Bemis Brook

To Bartlett &
North Conway

------- HIKING TRAILS
(AT = Appalachian Trail)

1. Crawford Path
2. Avalon Trail
3. Mt. Willard Trail
4. Jackson Webster Trail
5. Webster Cliff Trail
6. Willey Range Trail
7. Sam Willey Trail/Pond Loop Trail
8. Ethan Pond Trail
9. Ripley & Arethusa Falls Trail
10. Arethusa Falls Trail
11. Dry River Trail

night in the large bunkrooms. The front porch of the lodge offers an exquisite view, and the nearby falls make for good exploring.

The Zealand trailhead is reached from Zealand Road, which begins two miles from where Route 3 cuts across Route 302 (or if you come from the North Conway area, it's six miles past the AMC's Crawford Hostel at the top of Crawford Notch). Follow the Zealand Road past the campground and on for about 3½ miles to a parking area at the end of the road; the trail is straight past the gate. (Note that the Zealand Road closes for the winter, mid-November to mid-May.) The trail is blazed with blue paint and is well traveled, easy to follow. The round-trip mileage will be 5.6 miles, and you'll spend three hours hiking it (that reflects the ascent involved); if you travel with kids, add another hour. The first part of the hike is a gentle uphill ramble, often along the bed of the old logging railroad. At 0.8 miles the trail arrives at the Zealand River, which it crosses at 1½ miles, then heads across a beaver swamp before re-entering the forest. A major trail, the A-Z Trail, comes in on the left at 2.3 miles, and the trail then wraps along the edge of Zealand Pond until it meets the Ethan Pond and Twinway Trails. A right turn on Twinway takes you to the Zealand Falls Hut in just 0.3 miles, although the last 0.1 mile is very steep (there are steps to help out). When you're ready to visit Zealand Falls, go back to the base of this steep part and take the side trail. This hike can also be extended to include the Ethan Pond Trail through Zealand Notch to Thoreau Falls, another 2.6 miles farther with a 400-foot drop in elevation. If you do opt for the extension, keep in mind that you'll have to climb back up that distance before reaching the "easy" part of your return.

Crawford Depot & AMC Hostel

The history of Crawford Notch includes landslides, railroads, timber barons, grand hotels, and love stories. Today these have mostly vanished, although the railroad is used for scenic train trips several times a week, and romances certainly take place, although not as famous as the ones that the Crawford Notch geographic features are named for. Signs of the busy earlier era can be found, and photos in places like the Crawford Depot building give views of the past hundred years.

But today Crawford Notch is dedicated to hikers, year-round, and the Crawford Depot and adjoining AMC Hostel make up the northern trailhead. The old railroad building, on the right as you enter the notch on Route 302 from the north, is now owned by the Appalachian Mountain Club and has a small museum of photos and artifacts, as well as restrooms and basic hiking supplies. Maps and the route and lodging suggestions of experienced hikers can also be found at the counter here. Trails begin behind the depot, just across the railroad tracks (beware of excursion trains, especially during fall foliage season!). You can also see the modest buildings of the AMC Hostel, where hikers can get a bed for the night (plus free showers and use of a self-service kitchen) for less than $20; reservations are encouraged (see *Where To Stay*).

For a good view of the notch itself, a short hike up Mt. Willard will stretch your legs and get you started in the White Mountains. The **Mt. Willard Trail** is 1.6 miles long but climbs 900 feet, so very small children won't be too happy with it; age five or six is a good time to start. Allow about four hours for the trip, which would take only about 2½ hours for the adult who doesn't stop long at the summit. Kids or not, the view is worth the trouble, as the rocky overlook at 2,815 feet gives a grand vista directly down the notch so that the road and mountain railway unroll before you as narrow lines through the trees and surrounding mountain peaks. Hiking boots are a good idea because the steep parts are alternately rocky and muddy. Have the kids watch for Centennial Pool on the way up, and then start looking for the old culverts still running under the path, possibly dating back to when this was a carriage road for elegant guests more than a century ago. There are no views before the top, just thick woods and plenty of birdsong; June is the best time to see wildflowers like lily of the valley and trillium along the trail. On clear vacation days the trail does collect a lot of hikers, so if solitude is your preference, go early in the morning on a weekday. Rock climbers sometimes head down the sheer cliffs at the top to investigate the small cave a hundred feet down from the summit; there's no other way to reach it, but local tradition has named it Devil's Den and says there were once bones found there! (A later state expedition found nothing of the sort.)

Ripley Falls & Arethusa Falls

Another pleasant hike near Crawford Depot is the one to Ripley Falls, a 100-foot-high waterfall on Avalanche Brook. Continue on Route 302 past the Crawford Depot and the road drops down sharply, passing two waterfalls on the left (there's a parking pulloff on the right if you want to stop a few minutes and admire them). At the "base" of the notch, when the road flattens out again, is the Willey House on your right, which includes a snack bar and small museum as part of the state park. Another half-mile on the right brings you to the turn for Ripley Falls, well marked, and you drive up a short paved road to the trailhead. At first the trail is called the **Ethan Pond Trail** and is marked with white blazes because the Appalachian Trail is also following this section. At 0.2 miles the Ethan Pond Trail goes steeply on ahead, but you make the left onto the **Ripley Falls Trail** and climb far more gradually, with a short drop to the waterfall and the end of the climb; you're going up only 350 feet in all over the half-mile trail, so it's not going to wear you out.

A similar but steeper version is the trail to Arethusa Falls, twice as high (200-foot falls) and about twice the effort to reach. The usual trail to Arethusa Falls is at the south end of the state park here; on Route 302, again go past the Crawford Depot and take the road down through the notch. Pass the Willey House and Ripley Falls turnoffs, driving on the highway until you see the Dry River Campground on the left, and measure 0.5 miles farther down Route 302 to a parking lot on the right. There's a short paved road going up the hill to where the trail begins, 1.3 miles one-way, climbing some 900 feet in elevation.

You can combine the two waterfalls into an all-day hike that will give you a thorough workout and take you down a cliff trail – you won't need ropes and such, but you will want good hiking shoes, and a hiking stick or staff might be helpful. To put this hike together, climb to Ripley Falls from Crawford Depot as just described, then follow the 2½-mile **Ripley-Arethusa Trail** across the height of the land, doing a fair amount of up and down travel on a good trail. (You might see the mounds of golden-brown marble-sized pellets that are droppings from moose, but the large animals are not likely to be close enough for you to see any in the thick woods.) Savor the spectacle of

The White Mountains

Arethusa and give yourself a bit more of a challenge by taking the 0.1-mile footpath to the top of the falls.

> ⚠ **CAUTION:** *Lives have been lost here by falling on the wet rocks and ledges at the top of the falls. It's amazing how much less traction a perfectly good hiking boot has once it gets wet, and a wet surface underneath makes the problem worse. Don't trust these surfaces; stay safe!*

Climb down the spur and go back along the Arethusa-Ripley Falls Trail, climbing 1.3 miles toward Ripley but stopping at the junction with the Frankenstein Cliffs Trail. Head down (to your right) on this trail for a short ways to its first overlook (probably of a snow-capped mountain peak!) and break for lunch, lightening your load for the very steep descent. At 1.3 miles there's an even better overlook of the southern part of Crawford Notch. The Frankenstein Cliffs Trail (named after the local railroad builder, not the monster) takes 2.1 miles to reach the base of the Arethusa Falls Trail, but you can cut this short by about 0.3 miles as you spot the highway through the trees below the railroad trestle. Walk up Route 302 (to your left) the remaining 2.3 miles to the base of the Ripley Falls Trail, stopping to enjoy the Saco River along the way. The total for this double-waterfall-plus-cliffs hike and return to the car is over eight miles, some of it fairly strenuous; make sure you take plenty of water with you.

Crawford Path

Here's a glorious trail for long-distance hikers, one that will take you up to or close to the summits of four peaks in the Presidential Range and let you retrace the pathway first built by Abel and Ethan Allen Crawford in 1819. It was a very rough trail then, and wasn't improved much until 1840, when it was converted to a bridle path that Abel, then 74, traveled for the first horseback ride to Mt. Washington, the highest of the White Mountain peaks. The Appalachian Mountain Club began maintenance of the trail in the late 1800s, and the first part of the trail is now a National Recreation Trail. To reach Mt. Washington is an 8.2-mile hike along this trail, taking a good 6½ hours if you're in shape for it. Obviously, most hikers will use this as part of a backpacking trip that takes more than just a day.

➔ **TIP:** *For this kind of trip, plan carefully using the* AMC White Mountain Guide, *and study weather patterns to try for a safe and relatively dry trip. Best tip: Travel it the first time with someone who has already made this kind of hike and knows how to prepare for it and carry it out.*

But you can hike a great section of the Crawford Path to the summit of Mt. Pierce, also known as Mt. Clinton, and enjoy a six-mile round trip that climbs 2,400 feet of elevation, if you're in pretty good shape and used to the effort needed for steep and rocky trails. The approach to the Crawford Path has traditionally been across the road from Crawford Depot, but there is a new parking lot that makes it simpler. You'll need to locate the Mt. Clinton Road, by heading a short distance back up Route 302 toward the top of the notch and looking for the modest sign on your right, just after Saco Lake.

Turn onto the Mt. Clinton Road; the parking lot for the Crawford Path is on your right. From the trailhead the new "Crawford Connector" joins the Crawford Path in 0.2 miles, where a side trail also leads off to Crawford Cliff; save that one for another day, as you have "miles to go before you sleep" (loosely adapted from New Hampshire's noted poet, Robert Frost). Stay with the main trail along Gibbs Brook, passing another side trail (to Gibbs Falls) at 0.4 miles. There's an information sign for the Gibbs Brook Scenic Area, which includes a 900-acre stand of virgin timber, mostly red spruce and balsam fir. This was a priceless save from the timber companies in the early 20th century! Savor it.

The trail from the AMC's hut at Mizpah Springs enters at 1.75 miles, and you climb back and forth across the face of the Mt. Clinton until you emerge above treeline at 2.75 miles, close to the summit (4,310 feet peak). At 2.9 miles leave the Crawford Path to step aside onto the Webster Cliff Trail to reach the very top of Clinton/Pierce (4,310 feet). You can now loop back via the Webster Cliff Trail and Mizpah Cut-Off.

If you want to extend the hike (to 8.6 miles round trip, and another peak), keep going on the Crawford Path through scrub and low woods with plenty of views from rocky slabs along the

The White Mountains

way, along the crest of the broad ridge that joins Clinton and Eisenhower (political wisecracks certainly allowed, although Mt. Clinton was named long before Bill Clinton led the United States). At 3.6 miles the trail crosses a small brook and begins to climb again, reaching the Mt. Eisenhower Loop at 4.1 miles. Take the left turn to the summit, another 0.2 miles (and 300 feet of climbing) ahead of you. The peak is 4,761 feet in elevation and has fine views. Now you've been to the top of two 4,000-footers in a single day, and may be in danger of catching the syndrome known as "peak bagging," where you make long lists of high peaks and try to climb them all!

There are two small lakes in Crawford Notch: Saco, across from the Crawford Depot, and Ammonoosuc, behind the AMC Hostel. Each has short, interesting trails that can be covered in an hour or two of pleasant walking.

> 📖 **SUGGESTED READING:** *Robert Buchsbaum's book* Nature Hikes in the White Mountains *offers tips for family hikes on these trails, complete with guidance about what to get the kids looking for. But you can just head out onto the trails and discover them for yourself, too.*

Bartlett

This small town south of Crawford Notch is strongly linked with the Mt. Washington valley towns of Jackson, Glen, North Conway, and Intervale. There's a traditional hike here that New Hampshire kids have taken for decades or longer: the hike up **Cave Mountain**, better known for its cave than its climb (the mountain is only 1,335 feet at peak). When you reach the center of Bartlett on Route 302, turn left onto River Street and at the next intersection go straight ahead onto the rough dirt road. The climb to the mountain is a well-worn trail at the end of the road.

Franconia Notch

You can approach Franconia Notch from the north, connecting from Route 2 via Route 3 to the Franconia Notch Parkway, or from the south, arriving from Lincoln. Most travelers are likely to come from the south on their first visit, so landmarks and trails are listed from the southern end of the notch here. Like Crawford Notch, Franconia Notch includes a large state park established through the same local urge for preservation that created the White Mountain National Forest. The state park lines both sides of Route 93 here, and the highway itself narrows to become the scenic two-lane Franconia Notch Parkway for eight miles before again expanding north of Cannon Mountain; don't let the change of road name confuse you. The road passes between the high peaks of the Kinsman and Franconia ranges (the Franconia Range is the second highest in the state, after the Presidentials), and travels within easy sight of the Old Man of the Mountain, the famous rock formation that Daniel Webster and Nathaniel Hawthorne immortalized as a symbol of New Hampshire and the independence of the state's residents. The Appalachian Trail cuts through the notch, and the cliffs here include many traditional rock-climbing routes. The ski area at Cannon Mountain does not offer its ski trails for summer use, but does provide tram rides to the summit (small fee), linking hikers to the trails that head south along the ridgeline.

Trails west of the notch tend to be less steep and rocky than those on the east side, where the bare-rock top of Mt. Lafayette (5,259 feet) and the ridge connecting it with Mt. Lincoln, Little Haystack Mountain, and Mt. Liberty are exposed and dangerous in wet weather. There are trails for every experience and exertion level here, starting with the beautifully laid out handicap-accessible trail to the Basin and extending to the strenuous hike up the Falling Waters Trail to the Franconia Ridge, over the ridge of Mt. Lafayette, and down the Greenleaf Trail and Old Bridle Path. As you can tell from the place and trail names, this notch is full of stories about heroes and explorers; one of the tenderest stories features the actress Bette Davis (see page 111) and the Coppermine Trail, which leads toward Bridal Veil Falls.

Although Route 3 and Interstate 93 both head north from the Lincoln area into the notch, they merge into the Franconia Notch Parkway under the benign gaze of the Indian Head rock formation on Mt. Pemigewasset to the left. The first parkway exit, Exit 1, is for **The Flume**. Visitors to New Hampshire have stopped here for generations, and it's still worth a visit, al-

The "notch" at Franconia Notch.

though on hot summer days it's pretty crowded. The promise of a cool two-mile stroll draws extra company! The parkway exit takes you to a series of parking lots and a visitor center with travel information, restrooms, and snack bar. Pick up a map of the Flume so you'll be prepared for the Boulder Cabin, Table Rock, and Avalanche Falls, as well as the Ridge Path that takes you downhill to Liberty Gorge and Cascades. The Flume itself is an 800-foot natural gorge at the base of Mt. Liberty, with a boardwalk along it that brings you close to flowers, ferns, and mosses. Older hikers take courage: Although there's some rocky and uphill walking here, the Flume was actually discovered by 93-year-old "Aunt" Jess Guernsey in 1808 – follow her example!

Some of the trails from the Pemigewasset Wilderness (described with the Kancamagus Highway earlier) end at the old Whitehouse Bridge, and this trailhead is next along the parkway. A sign for the Basin points you to the next exit; the Basin is part of the **Pemigewasset River**, where there's a small waterfall and at its foot a granite pothole 20 feet in diameter, looking like a bathing spot for wood nymphs and dryads. This elegant little White Mountain sight is easily reached by a rolling path, and even the "modern outhouse" restrooms are wheelchair accessible.

Beyond the Basin a significant hiking trail heads up the slope: the **Cascade-Basin Trail**, which eventually connects with the **Cascade Brook Trail** to approach the spectacular mountain lake a thousand feet higher up, Lonesome Lake. There's an Ap-

Franconia Notch State Park

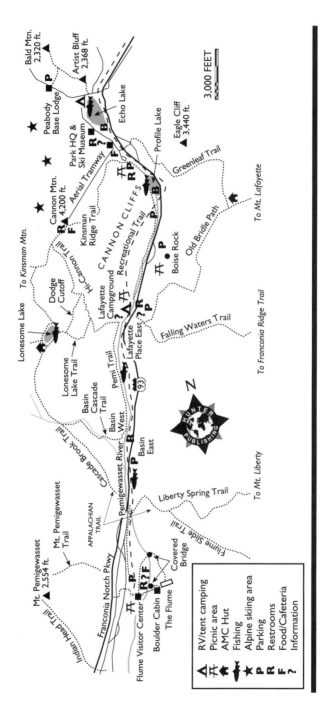

palachian Mountain Club "hut" (snack bar and associated bunkhouses) here, where naturalists offer programs nearly every summer afternoon and evening, and the bunkrooms are small enough (four bunks each) to be used for families to have some privacy. You bring your own sheets, but blankets, plus supper and breakfast, are included. The most recent fee to stay there in the summer was about $60 per adult and about half that for children; off-peak in late May there are no meals served and the price is lower.

The hike to Lonesome Lake is amply described by the *AMC White Mountain Guide* and most other hiking guide books to the region; you can even do this one without a map by just following the signs, but the books are reassuring when the stretches of rocky climbing seem endless. The distance to Lonesome Lake from the Basin is about six miles round trip, but the rise in elevation means it will take about two hours. Wear hiking boots as the rocks are plentiful. Along the way there are cascades and thick woods, and at the summit there are incredible vistas. This trip is worth the effort.

You might also notice the **Pemi Trail** beyond the Basin; it runs along the Pemigewasset River through the notch, a mostly level and comfortable way to hike from one end to the other. Don't hike on the bike trail, though!

Lafayette Place is the next Parkway exit north. There's a campground here, as well as a lodge and visitor center, with displays on the natural and human history of the notch. A shorter, somewhat steeper path, the **Lonesome Lake Trail**, leads from the campground to the AMC hut. It also connects with the Hi-Cannon Trail that climbs Cannon Mountain, a rugged hike of several hours with options on which parts of the peaks to clamber over (including the Cannon Balls at the ridgeline).

On the northbound side of the parkway, two major trails start up toward Mt. Lafayette and the Franconia Ridge: the **Falling Waters Trail** and the **Old Bridle Path**. These are trails for serious hikers, and should be studied in the *AMC White Mountain Guide* in advance (and you'll need dry weather for both safe footing and good views). The Old Bridle Path was literally a pony trail from one of the old resort inns here, and today leads past the AMC Greenleaf Hut (similar arrangements to those of Lonesome Lake Hut) before reaching the crags of Mt. Lafayette's summit.

BOISE ROCK

Few people stop to see Boise Rock, next on the right up the parkway, but the story of the rock is provocative: Thomas Boise was driving his horse past here when he and the animal were caught in a blizzard in the early 1800s. To save his own life, Boise eventually killed his horse and wrapped himself in the hide and sheltered under the rock. Rescuers had to cut away the frozen hide the next day to release the surviving Boise! Nearby there's a spring and picnic tables.

There's a view spot on the northbound parkway to look at the rock formation called the Old Man of the Mountain, but take the next exit instead and park by the snack bar in the "Old Man parking" area. Walk past the snack bar and down the short (one-third mile) trail to Profile Lake, which offers the best view; you'll also be able to see the Eagle Cliffs on the way, a good spot for beginning rock climbers to tackle. The Old Man of the Mountain (also called the Great Stone Face or the Profile) is made of five separate granite ledges slabbed on top of each other, and was formed geologically in a process that started about 200 million years ago. You can't climb it –

Eagle Cliffs in Franconia Notch. The rock spire is called "The Eaglet" and is often climbed.

it's downright dangerous – and the ledges have been reinforced to keep the noted profile in place. North of the Profile (up the notch) is the peak rock formation that resembles the barrel of a cannon and gives the mountain its name.

The **Kinsman Ridge Trail**, which takes a summit trek 16.9 miles to the Lincoln area and Kinsman Notch, has its northern trailhead at the Old Man parking area. You can also take the Pemi Trail from here south through the notch, reaching the Flume five miles later after an invigorating riverside tramp.

Also at this exit is the paved road to the Cannon Mountain aerial tramway. Hikers sometimes use the five-minute ride up the tramway as a launch to the hiking trails at the top of the mountain (4,060 feet), and this is one way to get small children up to the trails with a little less effort. At the foot of the tramway is a snack bar and a ski museum (see *Sightseeing*).

There's a marked road here that leads to **Echo Lake**, the more northern of the two lakes at the foot of Cannon, although you can also reach Echo from the next (and final) parkway exit. The beach here draws a good summer crowd; rock climbers start for Artist's Bluff and Bald Mountain here, as do hikers. The trail is just 1½ miles long and after a steep start is a mostly steady climb that gives some great views of the cliffs and the notch. One of the easier ways to take the trail is by starting at the Peabody Slope (ski area) parking lot and going first to the spur to the summit of Bald Mountain, then down to the trail junction again and heading left to Artist's Bluff. The steep descent is improved with rock steps and takes you to Echo Lake, from which you stroll along Route 18 to where you parked at Peabody.

Coppermine Trail climbs the west side of Cannon Mountain. There's no established trail connection to the notch, so drive around to Franconia (Exit 38 from Interstate 93, just above the north end of the notch) and take Route 116 south from the traffic light at the center of the village for 3.4 miles to park at the foot of Coppermine Road. Walk about 0.4 mile to the trailhead on the left. In another 2.2 miles you'll be at Bridal Veil Falls, a lovely series of cascades. But only a quarter-mile up the trail is the rock with a plaque memorializing a tender interlude in the life of actress Bette Davis. Robert N. Buchsbaum tells the story in *Nature Hikes in the White Mountains*.

BETTE DAVIS

Legend has it that in 1939, the actress, while relaxing in nearby Sugar Hill, fell in love with both the White Mountains and a young Vermonter, Arthur Farnsworth, who was employed at Pecketts, the resort where she was staying. She strayed from a hiking group on the Coppermine Trail, sure that Farnsworth would be the one sent to find her later on. Apparently her ploy succeeded, and she was happily married to the local man until his tragic death three years later when he fell down the stairs in their home. Watch for the plaque to see what the actress said about her beloved. And if you'd like another bit of her history, stop in later at the Sugar Hill Historical Society Museum (see *Sightseeing*).

Mt. Moosilauke

For many New Englanders, a hike up Mt. Moosilauke is an autumn ritual. The mountain peak reaches 4,810 feet, but the challenge is making your way through miles of thick woods before reaching the summit.

> **◆ HOW TO SAY IT:** *Mt. Moosilauke? You can choose whether to pronounce the name with an "ee" at the end or not; you'll hear both versions. The Indian name means "a bald place," referring to the summit, but another local spelling was once Moose-hillock, a very understandable corruption!*

The summit is at 4,802 feet, the most western of the great peaks in New Hampshire, and the view to the east over the White Mountains is superb. The land south and east of the summit belongs to Dartmouth College, which allows no camping or fires there. There was once a stone hotel, Prospect House, at the summit, and remains of a carriage road are still used for trails.

There are several approaches to climbing Mt. Moosilauke, but the most common is to take Raven Lodge Road from Route 118 between Warren and Woodstock (5.8 miles from Route 25 in Warren, or 7.2 miles from Route 112). This access road goes 1.6 miles to the trailhead. Both the **Gorge Brook Trail** and the **Snapper Trail**, which will lead into the old Carriage Road, meet at Raven Brook Lodge (the lodge is not open to the public). You can use these to create a six-mile hiking loop that includes both Mt. Moosilauke's summit and the nearby South Peak. Pick a warm, clear day to go, and be prepared for colder weather and wind; this isn't as challenging in terms of weather as Mt. Washington, but the mountain ridge can be cold and icy year-round. Hiking boots and extra layers are a must. Plan on about 4½ hours for the loop – not counting the time you spend gazing at vistas!

Make the Gorge Brook Trail your uphill choice, as there are a lot of paths diverging from it, but they're not as confusing going up as coming down. The trail first follows a logging road to the Baker River and crosses it on a footbridge, then turns left (0.2 miles; a trail leaves right) for 0.1 mile to a right turn (a trail leaves straight), and another trail, this time the Snapper where you'll later descend, goes left 0.1 mile later. Now you follow Gorge Brook with fewer distractions, crossing the brook twice and at 1.6 miles reaching a plaque for the Ross McKenney Forest. Here the trail has been recently revamped and swings to the right of a former route. When it turns left onto an old logging road at 2.1 miles, you'll have a chance to catch your breath as the grade gets a bit easier, winding up the slope with plenty of outlooks. At 3.3 miles you'll see the summit, and at 3.7 miles the trail joins the **Beaver Brook Trail** for the last 50 yards. The last segment, over the rocks, is marked by cairns.

After you feast on the view (and whatever you toted in your backpack), find the Carriage Road heading south along the ridge. (If weather turns foggy or threatening, though, go back the way you came up.) After 0.9 mile the **Glencliff Trail** enters from the right; look for the spur just after the Glencliff to take a short side trip to the south peak for a fresh view. Return to the Carriage Road for another mile, to two miles from the summit, where you pick up the Snapper Trail back to the lower part of the Gorge Brook Trail.

▲ **CAUTION:** *The first part of the Carriage Road often suffers erosion. Here's where your hiking boots are especially helpful, but do watch your footing on the rocks.*

Lost River

There's some modest hiking to be done at Lost River, off Route 112 east of Lincoln. But since it's really a geological discovery park (complete with waterfalls and caves), see *Sightseeing* for details.

Outfitters
▪ It's hard to pin down **Profile Mountaineering** to one location. Its office is on Main Street in North Woodstock, the mailing address is PO Box 607, Lincoln, NH 03251, and phone is ☎ 745-3106, but the rock climbing, snow and ice climbing, and wilderness treks offered range from Franconia Notch to the Pemigewasset Wilderness to a winter ascent of Mt. Washington. Here's a good way to get support and training for some really challenging adventures. Prices start at about $100 per person for a day, and drop as the groups get larger.

▪ On Wheels

Road Biking

Road touring on bicycles through the White Mountains is surprisingly accessible. Roads were built through valleys and along rivers and streams, and they are still the easiest ways through the mountains, with less severe ups and downs than hikers face. The New Hampshire section of the **East Coast Bicycle Trail** enters the White Mountains at Conway, travels up West Side Road parallel to Route 16 toward Glen, and heads up through Crawford Notch on the wide smooth shoulders of Route 302. The rocky heights of the mountains are well forested, and you pedal through a green wildness, refreshed by the Saco River alongside the roadway. There's a

The White Mountains

steep grade through the notch, but you can take your time, and it's worth the effort. When Route 302 reaches the highly traveled Route 3, the bike trail goes north a short ways on Route 3, then takes the attractive right turn onto Route 115 for terrific views of the Northern Peaks of the White Mountains. The uphill section on Route 115 is mercifully brief, and the downhill swoop is exhilarating; do pause at the scenic overlook on the left. Just past the overlook you need to take the left turn onto Route 115A, crossing the Israel River, and enjoying a low-traffic segment before making a left onto Route 2 itself for a frantic half-mile of dodging high-speed vehicles. Relief arrives quickly with the right turn onto North Road. After about two miles North Road bends to the left and you stay with it another three miles to the right turn onto the Lost Nation Road, sometimes marked at Grange Road at this southern end. The Lost Nation Road lives up to its name: You enter a peaceful rural world set apart from all else, and have 12 miles of the best backroad biking until you reach the paper-mill town of Groveton, entering the Great North Woods region. The best snacking along this trail is in Twin Mountain on the short stretch of Route 3, where general stores cater to hikers and bikers with delights like ice cream, barbecued ribs, and homemade fudge.

Looking for a shorter route, more of a day tour? There's a 37-mile loop described in *30 Bicycle Tours in New Hampshire* that starts in **North Conway** at the Eastern Slopes Inn, heads west across the Saco River to West Side Road (take a right, heading north), then uses Route 302 west for 4.1 miles to reach Bartlett (food break here!), where the Bear Notch Road begins. This summer-only route heads south (left) through 9.1 miles of barely tamed wilderness and takes you all the way to the Kancamagus Highway (alias Route 112; caution: narrow shoulders and fast traffic), which you follow for six miles, probably stopping at some of the river scenic areas. There's a left turn at Blueberry Crossing that takes you through a covered bridge onto the Dugway Road, a narrow and rough road with limited visibility but less traffic and lots of forest appeal; in 6.1 miles it reaches Allen Siding, where a left and 0.2 miles takes you to a railroad crossing and another left. Just 0.4 miles later you're back on West Side Road, which in 4.6 miles connects with your right turn onto River Road and brings you back to the start at the inn.

Another day loop uses Route 142, which connects Route 302 in **Bethlehem** with Franconia through a relatively undiscovered forested region. Use Route 116/18 to connect with Route 302 to the west of Bethlehem and cycle back through the town, which includes some pleasant eateries as well as the sights of an early resort town, complete with old inns whose wide porches often shelter visiting Hassidic Jews from more urban regions. Bethlehem is visitor-friendly and includes antique shops and a terrific little theater.

It's also worth noting that the **Kancamagus Highway** (Route 112) offers 34 miles of uninterrupted scenic wilderness to bike; drawbacks are the narrowness of the shoulders in many areas, and the heavy summer and fall foliage traffic. You'll need a mind that's both relaxed and very alert to make this ride enjoyable, but the numerous side trips along the route are a lot of fun. Don't miss Sabbaday Falls! And catch a swim at Rocky Gorge.

A short and smooth tour can be found in **Franconia Notch** on the paved bike path that runs south from Skookumchuck Brook all the way to the Flume; it's 8.8 miles long and has plenty of attractions, although there are also plenty of people around them, especially in midsummer. The northern terminus is at Route 3 and Skookumchuck Brook, and the southern one is at the Flume exit from the Franconia Notch Parkway. There are only two brief "bike walk" areas in the high-pedestrian sections. Bike rentals are available at nearby **Cannon Mountain** (☎ 823-5563) and in Franconia at the **Franconia Sports Shop** (open seven days a week, ☎ 823-5241; in-line skate rentals, too).

Mountain Biking

Mountain bikers have some great challenges in the White Mountains. The nine-mile-long bike trail through **Jefferson Notch** is rough and steep at times, but offers quality views, thick forest, and has been blessed by the White Mountain National Forest authorities specifically for wheels. It is now part of a 25-mile loop recommended for mountain biking and offers three waterfalls and great views. Start at the trailhead three miles east of Twin Mountain on Route 302 in the parking area 200 yards beyond the entrance to Zealand Campground (elevation 1,506 feet). Leave from the east side of the trailhead using Lower Falls Hiking Trail. After one mile go left onto the Cherry Mountain Road (unpaved); if you want to add a 3½-mile side trip to the summit of Mt. Martha, take the Cherry Mountain Hiking Trail when it splits to the left at the "height of the land." Otherwise, keep going past several private cabins and turn right onto the gravel road, Mill Brook Road, marked FR93. After one mile more, find the gated Mt. Mitten Road on the left, where foot and bike travel are welcome. This road goes through remote country for several miles and reaches Jefferson Notch Road, where you turn right (uphill) and may meet cars. Don't try the Caps Ridge Hiking Trail, it doesn't work for bikes; stay with the Jefferson Notch Road past Bretton Woods Cascades and finally meet the paved base Station Road, where you go right (west) for five miles to find Route 302. A right on Route 302 brings you back to the trailhead.

Two lesser-known trails, the **Tunnel Brook Trail** and the aptly named **Mountain Bike Trail**, run north-south between Warren and Route 116, offering a pleasant stop at Long Pond and plenty of stream crossings as you slip between the mountain peaks to either side. A White Mountain National Forest map helps to find and pursue these trails; you can get one at any of the ranger stations (Laconia, Gorham, Conway, and the National Forest Information Station at Campton, which is Exit 28 from Interstate 93), or by writing to the Forest Supervisor at 719 Main Street, Laconia, NH 03246; call ahead (☎ 528-8721) and check this year's fee for the very comprehensive trail map, which should be $5 or less.

Meet fellow bikers at the annual **Mt. Washington Valley Fat Tire Festival** at Bear Notch Ski Touring Center in Bartlett, usually the third weekend of September (confirm at ☎ 374-2277).

Resources

There's a map specialized for wheels: the ***Mountain Bike Map of the Mount Washington Valley,*** put out by Mountain Cycle Guide Services and available for about $6 at the AMC Pinkham Notch Visitor Center as well as many bike shops in the region. The map includes a number of expert and remote trails, like the

Livermore Trail from the Kancamagus Highway at Lily Pond along Flume Mountain, and the trail over Cranmore Mountain to Black Cap Mountain from North Conway (see *On Foot*). The map also details trails like the Lower Nanamocomuck Ski Trail, which starts from the Bear Notch Road, and the Hales Location Trails off West Side Road outside North Conway.

And the village of Jackson offers its own recreation map and guide, describing five mountain bike rides on town roads and approved trails, plus road biking loops that range from 5½ to 45 miles. Call the **Jackson Resort Association** to purchase a copy (☎ 383-9456 or 800-866-3334).

For a breathtaking downhill adventure, the ski areas in the region will hoist you and your wheels to the top of the peak and send you flying down: Attitash Bear Peak (☎ 800-223-7669), Bretton Woods, Cranmore, Loon Mountain, and Waterville Valley. Waterville Valley (base camp, ☎ 236-4666), in fact, offers a tremendous range of mountain-biking trails and guided rides, as well as a top-notch bike shop, and has unusually low family prices that include bike, in-line skate, and canoe use with the lodging; see *Where to Stay*.

You can blend bike touring with elegant evening lodging and dining through **Bike the Whites** (Box 37, Intervale, NH 03845; ☎ 800-448-3534), which sets up self-guided tours that travel inn to inn, about 20 miles a day. Your luggage is transported for you each day, your bicycle gets stored under cover at night, there's emergency assistance, and bike rentals are available too. Participating inns are The Forest (Intervale), Snowvillage Inn (Snowville), and the Tamworth Inn (Tamworth). Now that's a vacation! Visit their Web site at www.bikethewhites.com.

> 🔥 **WARNING:** *Designated wilderness areas are off-limits to bikes, for the sake of often fragile plants. This includes the Great Gulf, Pemigewasset, Presidential Range / Dry River, and Sandwich Range Wildernesses. The good news is that each of these regions is surrounded by miles of open cycling terrain. And the White Mountain National Forest ranger stations will help with route planning, too.*

The White Mountains

Bike Shops & Outfitters

Almost all the region's bike shops are open seven days a week, year-round, and provide rentals and repairs.

- **Boarder Town Bikes**, in North Conway (Route 16) and in Glen (Route 302), ☎ 888-860-3561.

- **Joe Jones Ski and Sports**, in North Conway (Main Street in the village center), ☎ 356-9411.

- **The Bike Shop**, in North Conway at Mt. Valley Mall Blvd., ☎ 356-6089.

- **Ragged Mountain**, three miles north of North Conway on Route 16/302, ☎ 356-3042.

- **Sports Outlet**, on Main Street in North Conway, ☎ 356-3133.

- **Red Jersey Cyclery**, in Glen at the junction of Routes 16 and 302, ☎ 383-4660.

- **Ragged Mountain Equipment** (Route 16/302, Intervale, ☎ 356-3042) offers a free leaflet with three local mountain bike rides.

- **Moriah Sports** at 101 Main Street in Gorham (☎ 466-2317) is an experienced bike shop. Mike Micucci, who wrote *Mountain Biking in the Northern White Mountains*, operates a guide service here. The shop, open year-round, has expertise in both mountain and road bikes, and provides route planning especially for mountain bikers on the hundreds of miles of nearby logging roads and mountain trails.

Outfitters:

- Loon offers the **Loon Mountain Bike Center** in Lincoln from Memorial Day to late October (☎ 745-8111), with cross-country trails along the Pemigewasset River.

- At **Bretton Woods** (☎ 800-232-2972; www. Brettonwoods.com) there's a "summer park" with a lift-serviced and cross-country trail network and rentals of front and full suspension bikes.

- **Cranmore** in North Conway (☎ 356-5543; sports center, 356-6301) also has a full-service rental shop.

- Another specialized biking resort is **Great Glen Trails** on Route 16 in Pinkham Notch, north of Gorham, ☎ 466-2333. This is also the center to contact about road races on Mt. Washington. Shuttles are available; trail fees and bike passes run under $10 per day per adult, and season passes are a great deal.

- If you prefer a guided adventure on wheels, hitch up with **Northern Extremes Bike Tours & Water Sports** (☎ 383-8117 in Glen, next to Patch's Market on Route 302).

▪ On & In The Water

Boating

 Canoe touring or whitewater? Take your pick. Or kayaks! **Saco Bound Downeast** has been providing rentals, route planning, and guided trips and tours for years. Its headquarters is on Route 302 in Center Conway, ☎ 447-2177 (www.neoutdoors. com/sacobound). At Great Glen Trails on Route 16 in Pinkham Notch, north of Gorham, **Mad River Canoe** (☎ 466-2333) is establishing a demonstration site, so count on Great Glen for more support and rentals.

> **CAUTION:** *If you're going out on the rivers alone, study the* Appalachian Mountain Club River Guide *first, then walk or (second best) drive the route to check on recent blowdowns and especially on changes in old dams and other water-related structures. Whitewater in the North Country takes expertise; if you're new to the sport, join a guided group first or paddle with someone who has already run the river this season.*

The rivers most interesting to run in this region are the Pemigewasset (starts in Franconia Notch as a stream and builds quickly south, until it gets interesting around Waterville Valley); the Mad River (runs through Waterville Valley and Campton, with miles of continuous rapids); the Ammonoosuc (famous for whitewater; runs from Bretton Woods/Twin Mountain area all the way to Woodsville to the southwest); the Gale (Franconia to the Ammonoosuc); the Swift (incredible whitewater along the Kancamagus Highway); the Saco (exciting whitewater for expert paddlers; rafters love this one too); and the Ossipee, which meets the Saco. For all of these, the most dramatic thrills are during spring runoff, but it's not a time for beginners to test the water. There are sections of the Gale, the Mad, the Pemigewasset, the Swift, and the Saco that rate Class IV difficulty on the whitewater runs, and for several, covered boats are necessary. Go for it – but go prepared.

For a whitewater run of more moderate difficulty, try the **Saco** from Bartlett to North Conway. The put-in is at the iron bridge in Bartlett, where there's parking and access. The first stretch of eight miles has a swift current with frequent rapids, and suffers from fallen trees in the stream at the outside of many turns. The river changes to quickwater rather than rapids at Humphrey's Ledge, just beyond the eight mile point. There's a possible takeout 3½ miles later at the North Conway bridge, but if you have time, keep going for another eight miles to the covered bridge at Conway, with some excitement just before the end as the Swift River comes in and the rapids start. Another finish is 2.75 miles farther at yet another covered bridge, in Center Conway.

For a relaxed summer paddle, head for the **Waterville Valley Resort** (☎ 236-4666), where you can paddle comfortably on Corcoran's Pond (rentals available). If that's too gentle, check out **Ski Fanatics** in Campton just down the road on Route 49 (☎ 726-4327) for a "funyak" rental (a sort of modified kayak) and head for the Pemigewasset River. Ski Fanatics also has a rental shop for the Saco River, located next to Eastern Slope Campground on Route 16 in Conway (☎ 447-5571); they rent canoes there and have river shuttles to get you back to where you started.

You can have a family-friendly lake paddle in Franconia Notch at **Echo Lake,** where canoes and paddleboats are rented (☎ 823-5563) and there's a nice swimming beach.

Canoe & Kayak Outfitters

There are plenty of places to rent canoes and kayaks around the Saco River. Here are a few:

- **Northern Extremes Bike Tours and Water Sports,** Route 302, Glen, ☎ 383-8117 (also rents river tubes and inflatable boats).

- **Saco Valley Canoe** at the State Line Store, Route 302, Center Conway, ☎ 447-2444 or 800-447-2460.

- **Saco Bound Canoe & Kayak**, Center Conway, ☎ 447-3801.

- **Saco River Canoe Rental Company**, Conway, ☎ 447-2737.

- **Canoe King of New England**, North Conway, ☎ 356-5280.

- Rubber raft rentals: **Joe Jones North Shop**, Route 16/302, Intervale, ☎ 356-6848.

Fishing

Fishing has always been one of the big draws of the White Mountains; trout still abound and make for challenges of mind against instinct. There's good lake fishing in the Waterville Valley area at Russell Pond on Tripoli Road and at Campton Pond at the lights; the nearby Mad River is stocked with trout. To enhance your success at fly-fishing, take a course at the **Waterville Valley Base Camp** (☎ 236-4666). Waterville Valley's town recreation department on Noon Peak Road rents fishing poles (don't forget your state license). Call ahead to the Rec. Department at ☎ 236-4695 and find out about fishing programs for learners as well.

Another trout-stocked water body is **Profile Lake**, where you can quietly angle under the gaze of the Old Man of the Mountain; no motors allowed. Farther north, around Lincoln and North Woodstock, take to the streams at the **East Branch of the Pemigewasset**. And when you reach the Conway region, there's **Conway Lake**, **Crystal Lake**, and targeting trout and salmon on the **Swift** and **Saco Rivers**.

Boating on Profile Lake at Franconia Notch.

The **Connecticut River** offers trout fishing and more: Check out the lakes at Comerford and Moore Dams outside Littleton for big-fish angling. These are also good for **ice fishing,** and large enough for sailboats to enjoy, too.

Lake Tarleton in Warren was about to become part of the White Mountain National Forest as this book went to press; ask at the ranger stations for information on boating there. It will be the largest lake in the national forest. The lake is a wonderful trout fishing spot.

For a truly luxurious fishing vacation, consider the 65-acre estate at **Nestlenook Farm Resort** in Jackson (☎ 383-0845), where Emerald Lake is privately stocked with trout, and gear can be rented.

Outfitters

■ On Route 16 north of North Conway village, **North Country Angler** (☎ 356-6000) offers equipment as well as fly-tying school and fly-fishing instruction at Nereledge Inn (see *Where to Stay*).

Swimming

Swimming is possible in every stream and river. At **Echo Lake State Park** in North Conway, reached by heading north of the village and turning left on the River Road (look for the state park signs); you can watch the climbers on White Horse and Cathedral Ledges between plunges into the water. **Rocky Gorge** on the Kancamagus Highway doesn't really allow swimming but will give you a midsummer treat with cool river water to wade in and plenty of hot sunny rocks for sitting and sunbathing. At Franconia Notch there's a lovely swimming beach at the smaller **Echo Lake,** accessed by exits 2 and 3 from the Franconia Notch Parkway. And there's nothing to stop you from having a relaxing dip at the **Moore Dam** picnic area at Exit 44 from Interstate 93. Riverside campgrounds offer good places for swimming too; in Gorham, **Moose Brook State Park** even includes a warming pool and a swimming pool as it taps into the Perkins and Moose Brooks (see *Where to Stay*). And the **Jefferson Inn** on Route 2 in Jefferson promises the "world's best swimming pond" across the road, stream fed and clean with a sandy beach and floating dock; call ahead for reservations (☎ 586-7998).

For a really different dip, duck into the cascades and pools at **Jackson Falls** in the village of Jackson next to Route 16B just above the Jackson Community Church. Or slip down to the **Saco River** in Glen: From the junction of Routes 16 and 302, take 302 south for 2.2 miles and turn left onto West Side Road, measuring another 2.4 miles to where the river comes close to the road – if you park on the right you can scramble down the bank and cross the river to the gravel beach on the other side, a spot called Humphrey's Ledge.

■ With Llamas & On Horseback

Horseback Riding

Many of the early trails in the White Mountains were first traveled on horseback. The grand inns offered carriage rides to the summits of the peaks, too.

Today most horseback travel is based at the inns, with a few stables scattered around the North Country. If you love to watch fine horseflesh perform, you'll be deeply satisfied with the **Equine Festival** on the third weekend of August at the Fields of Attitash in Bartlett; a $50,000 prize on the last of the five days of the festival is an additional draw.

The White Mountains

Starting from the south end of the region, there's **Waterville Valley Riding Stables** (☎ 236-4811) with guided trail rides during summer and winter, as well as pony rides for children, and hayrides. **Loon Mountain** (☎ 745-8111) in Lincoln also offers trail rides at varied paces, and self-designed rides for experts. **Attitash Bear Peak** (☎ 800-223-7669) in Bartlett on Route 302 has daily horseback riding. In Franconia both the **Franconia Inn** and the **Mittersill Resort** provide horses to ride; see *Where to Stay*.

An impressive stable at the **Mount Washington Hotel** (☎ 278-1000) on Route 302 in Bretton Woods lets experienced riders head out on the trails for scenic rambles. Or head for the **Franconia Inn** in Franconia, where experienced guides take you trail riding through the Easton Valley (reserve rides by calling ☎ 823-5542; the inn is two miles south on Route 116 from the center of Franconia, reached from Exit 38 of Interstate 93).

Horse-Drawn Excursions

For a twist, consider riding in a carriage or wagon or even buggy. These abound in the Conway area: **Horse n' Around** (☎ 356-6033), **Farm by the River** (☎ 356-2694), **Nestlenook Farm** (☎ 383-0845 in Jackson, Victorian carriage), and **Madison Carriage House** (☎ 367-4605 in Madison, south of Conway).

With Llamas

Finally, walking with a llama is perhaps the ultimate relaxation. The llama – gentle, strong and slow-paced – carries the food and comforts and slows you down enough to really appreciate the mountains around you. **Snowvillage Inn** (☎ 447-2818 or 800-447-4345) in Snowville, south of Conway, puts together occasional llama hikes; call ahead for scheduling.

Open Door Bed and Breakfasts, a consortium of Mt. Washington Valley inns, sometimes offers llama trekking; write to them at PO Box 1178, North Conway, NH 03860 (☎ 800-300-4799).

■ On Snow & Ice

The splendor of autumn in the White Mountains comes from the glorious fall foliage, red and gold across the slopes and along the rivers, and also from the crisp clear air that promises snowflakes a few weeks away. For ski, snowshoe, and winter hike lovers, that autumn air raises the adrenaline and the expectations: Excitement is a mere turn of the season away.

Figure on winter arriving by the end of October in the mountains, and early November in the valleys. It definitely lasts through March and, in the higher elevations, often into May. Tuckerman Ravine on Mt. Washington starts its ski season in March and may continue into July!

Being well prepared for the cold and wind makes winter a lot more enjoyable. The other key to winter fun is to get outside and do things; that way your time snuggling next to the fireplace is a well-earned reward and a perfect contrast to the day's events. You can start by choosing and even cutting your own Christmas tree at a tree farm like The Rocks in Bethlehem, taking a moonlight snow walk on the trails around a country inn, or shopping in the festive evening atmosphere of ski resort towns like North Conway and Waterville Valley. Sleigh rides abound all winter.

Or you can get more active: Every country inn, and nearly every bed and breakfast inn, is close to or even includes trails for cross-country skiing. The entire White Mountain National Forest is open to skiers and snowshoers. There are downhill ski slopes with thousands of feet in elevation to explore. And there's the formidable challenge of extreme skiing, especially in Tuckerman Ravine but also on other mountain slopes. Snowboarders will find a variety of slopes available too, whether sharing with the skiers or on special halfpipes and other boarding specialties.

So, what are you going to try first?

The White Mountains

Waterville Valley Resort Area

The numbers speak for themselves: 255 acres, 2,020 feet vertical drop, 96% snowmaking coverage, 4,004 feet elevation, 49 trails, and 12 lifts, including a high-speed detachable quad. In addition to the ski shop and snowboard shop, Waterville offers a base camp that it calls "nature's own theme park," where cross-country skis and snowshoes take you out onto trails around the White Mountains. Waterville Valley was built exactly for this, the dream child of one of the first and foremost ski developers in New England. The beautifully designed resort enhances the valley. There's also an ice skating arena and athletic club. The resort passport provides access to all of these, plus lodging, a shuttlebus, and entertainment such as fireworks, magic shows, bonfires, and rides on the trail-grooming "cats." For kids, there are age-specialized ski programs, and two lifts are dedicated to little beginners and novices.

A number of prestigious snow races take place at Waterville each year. There's also a course for recreational racing. And the resort offers an adaptive ski program that gets mentally and physically challenged children out onto the slopes, free from wheelchairs or braces. Check out their Web site at www. waterville.com or call ☎ 800-468-2553 for information and reservations.

The **White Mountain National Forest** also provides cross-country skiing near Waterville Valley Resort. If you take Exit 28 from Interstate 93, head east on Route 49 for 5½ miles and look for the parking area. Another access is at the 8.1-mile point, also providing parking. Both lead to the **Smarts Brook ski trails**, which vary from 0.5 to four miles long and are designated for intermediate and advanced (not beginning) skiers. Some are designated for one-way travel. Difficulty ratings are posted at each trail junction. A map of the trails is available from the National Forest Information Station at Exit 28, as well as at most of the other White Mountain National Forest ranger stations. From the first access point at 5½ miles from Interstate 93 there's a choice of four trails; the second access point, farther away from the highway, is to the **Old Waterville Road Trail**, which you'll have to ski for about two miles before you reach the other loops of trails.

There's another national forest ski trail that's even closer to the Waterville Valley resort: **Livermore Road ski trail**. Note that the resort charges a fee for its trails (which are groomed), so if you ski over into that area, be ready to pay up. To reach this trail, from I-93 take Exit 28 to Route 49. When you reach the start of Tripoli Road on your left, follow Tripoli Road 1.3 miles to the access road for Mt. Tecumseh ski area, where you bear right and go 0.5 mile. Turn right and cross the bridge, bearing left to the parking area. When you take the right-hand fork you are on the Livermore Road ski trail, which heads northwest toward the Kancamagus Highway; when you take the left fork instead, you're headed for the **Greeley Ponds Cross-Country Trails** and will reach the lower pond in three miles. Use caution on the last 0.3 mile to the pond, which can be a slippery descent.

Loon Mountain

It's hard to choose between Loon and Waterville Valley on the basis of ski facilities: Loon has a 2,100-foot vertical drop, peak elevation of 3,050 feet, 43 trails on 250 acres, and 97% snow-making coverage. The Children's Center has lots of space. Skiers can glide all the way down into town on two recently built trails. Snowboarders appreciate the 100 x 300-foot half-pipe and the snowboard park.

Choose instead on the surroundings. Where Waterville Valley is a self-sufficient resort enclosed by mountains, Loon is more open, and close to town. Condominiums nestle on the hillsides along Route 112 (a.k.a. the Kancamagus Highway), and there's the Mill at Loon Mountain, an event grandstand and shopping extravaganza par excellence. By the way, Loon offers special three-day clinics for "women at play," as well as weekly "Flying 50s" programs for mature skiers. Other pluses: a wildlife theatre, a children's theatre, and night tubing on a beginner trail with lights. There's also a cross-country center with skis and snowshoes available, as well as a skating arena. Children especially remember the storytelling by the Mountain Man and Friends, a long-time area tradition.

The resort specializes in lift-and-lodging packages; call ahead at ☎ 745-8111, ext. 5400, to reserve tickets and services. For snow conditions, ☎ 745-8100; for cross-country information, ☎ 745-8112.

Kancamagus Highway

Nordic skiers will exult in the great cross-country access along the Kancamagus. The Greeley Ponds Cross-Country Trails can be accessed here, 9.3 miles east of Interstate 93 (Exit 32); look for the marked parking area, and the trailhead is 0.2 mile farther east.

About six miles farther away from the Lincoln end of the Kancamagus, or 18 miles west of Conway, is Lily Pond, where there's a small parking area on the north side of the highway. The **Upper Nanamocomuck** starts to the east of the pond at an elevation of 2,070 feet, and includes a steep downgrade plus a narrow bridge at the end of the "run," making the trail challenging for even advanced skiers. (This difficult stretch is only a mile long, so you can take it slowly if you like.) The entire trail is 9.6 miles long and comes out at Bear Notch Road, the scenic connector between the Kancamagus and Route 302. There's a plowed turn-around and roadside parking on Bear Notch Road, about 0.75 mile north of the Kancamagus. You will have descended to 1,340 feet, a respectable drop! Occasionally there may be some logging in the winter woods; you'll know it's a tree-harvesting year if part of the route is actually plowed for trucks, in which case it's up to you to keep an ear out for the heavily laden vehicles (although they are rare). Otherwise, listen for chickadees, blue jays, and red squirrels, and you may even see a moose near the ponds.

> ⚡ **WARNING:** *Don't try to cross the Swift River at places that aren't marked as crossings; the water doesn't freeze, despite an occasional glaze of ice, and the current is swift and cold.*

A third cross-country section is closer to Conway, just 12½ miles west of the Saco Ranger Station. There's a 10-car parking lot by the skier symbol on the south side of the Kancamagus Highway, and the East Loop (two miles) of the **Oliverian/Downes Brook ski trail** starts here. Novices may prefer the West Loop (1.35 miles), which has its own trailhead and parking area another 1½ miles west on the Kancamagus. There's a connector (0.5 mile) between the two loops.

> ⚡ **CAUTION:** *Note that these back-country ski trails are not patrolled; take someone skiing with you, and be sure to leave your route and planned return time with someone at home in case of trouble. After all, if you want a wilderness adventure, you're going to have some risks that a groomed trail wouldn't have.*

Snowmobile travel doesn't suit everyone, but local residents will assure you there's no quicker way of getting out to the winter woods or going cross-country to the jamborees that local clubs put together. If you want to look into the sport, stop in East Conway on Route 113 to visit the **Town & Country Polaris Snowmobile Rental Center** (☎ 939-2698). To get there, you'll take Route 16 to where it meets 113 and actually leave New Hampshire briefly as Route 113 enters Fryeburg, Maine – then heads to the left (north alongside the Fryeburg Post Office) and goes 1½ miles to the snowmobile center. In addition to rentals, there are guided snowmobile tours take an hour to a week; call ahead for guide availability.

North Conway & Intervale

Cranmore (☎ 356-5543, 800-786-6754; www.cranmore.com) calls itself New England's hottest family resort, set in the heart of New England's oldest and favorite ski town. The resort is located off Route 16, north of the town. It can justly claim to be a birthplace of American skiing under the leadership of Hannes Schneider. Although the vertical drop is a modest 1,200 feet, the 36 trails include sunny southwest exposure, there's 100% snowmaking coverage, the six lifts include a high-speed detachable quad, and there's night skiing on Thursdays, Fridays, and Saturdays, as well as holidays. A snowboard half-pipe and snowboard park add to the fun. Count on great views of the White Mountains and lots of attention for kids and other beginners. Slopeside lodging is available (☎ 800-SUN N SKI).

Cross-country skiers in the North Conway area can take advantage of a 65-km **trail network** put together by Mt. Washington

Valley Ski Touring. This is basically an inn-to-inn set of loops, with two centers: one on Route 16 in Intervale at Joe Jones North, a ski and sports shop with instructors; and the other on Route 16A, parallel to 16 but just to the east, where there's an official ski touring warming hut and waxing room and the New England Inn. Full moon ski tours, a chocolate festival, and a free ski week are set season-to-season, so call for dates (☎ 356-9920). Day passes for the trail network cost about $10 or less; season passes are a great buy.

Bartlett

Attitash Bear Peak has 45 ski trails to swoop down 1,750 feet of vertical drop at Attitash and 1,450 feet at Bear Peak, with 10 lifts to get you back to the two peaks. Snowmaking covers 98% of the trails. There's also a brand-new slopeside hotel, the Grand Summit, picking up on the area tradition of luxurious mountain lodging. Snowboarding hits are scattered among the trails. There are two base lodges, and plenty of ski and snowboard programs, including versions that guarantee you'll swooping the slopes in just one day (age seven and up). Both information and reservations are at ☎ 374-2368 or 800-223-SNOW; www.attitash.com. The resort is on Route 302. Recent additions include a new triple chairlift and 52 more acres of expanded ski areas that should give the resort the most skiable terrain in New Hampshire, according to its managing director.

Jackson

Black Mountain (☎ 383-4490 or 800-475-4669; e-mail ski@ blackmt.com) is a small ski resort on Route 16B north of Jackson village, and its family-friendly atmosphere and low lift prices make it especially attractive for novices and family vacations. The Jackson Academy of Skiing, a base lodge with cafeteria and day care, and children's programs are added to a variety of ski-and-stay programs using local inns, hotels, and condominiums. There's even a special slope reserved for snow tubing, where you must rent your tube, and you get a snow tube lift ticket. The vertical drop is a respectable 1,100 feet, with four lifts serving 30 trails, and nearly complete snowmaking coverage. Look for the gentle learning slopes and the more traditional winding trails with scenic views.

Winter is a romantic time at **Nestlenook Farm Resort** (☎ 383-9443 or 800-659-9443) in Jackson, on Dinsmore Road. Horse-drawn Austrian sleigh rides take you through the Emerald Forest. There's also ice skating on Emerald Lake, and snowshoeing over the 65-acre estate. Rentals are available by the hour or day; the resort recommends the trail to Widdlesworth Overlook, for a view of Mt. Washington.

Jackson Ski Touring Foundation on Route 16A provides more than 150 km of groomed trails that interlace the village and lead to mountain vistas and through river valleys (up to 154 km total). Daily use is about $10 per adult, with children nine and under free; there's a good annual membership rate if you're staying a while. Call for reservations and lodging information (☎ 383-9355; for snow conditions, ☎ 800-927-6697; www.xcski.org/jacksonxc). Stay-and-ski packages connect with local inns. There are new extended trails that take in changes of elevation to challenge more experienced skiers, too. And a special three km of trails near **Nestlenook Farm** have been reserved exclusively for snowshoers, including hills that give views of the Ellis River Valley up to the summit of Mt. Washington (call Nestlenook for information specific to snowshoe trails: ☎ 383-0845). Keep in mind that Jackson has a winter carnival week, usually in mid-January, when things will be even more festive (and maybe a tad crowded; confirm the dates at ☎ 383-9356 or 800-866-3334).

Pinkham Notch

Love the drama of a great drop? **Wildcat's** 2,100 vertical feet and fierce double-diamond trails are a must for adventurous skiers. The resort boasts "glorious glades" and a choice of groomed or untouched powder, with 174" of snowfall each year. Six lifts serve 40 trails, and snowmaking gives complete trail coverage. Best of all, you look across Pinkham Notch at Mt. Washington itself from the peak of Wildcat. Call ahead for snow information and lodging (snow and weather, ☎ 888-SKI-WILD; lodging and reservations, ☎ 888-4-WILDCAT; information ☎ 800-255-6439; www.skiwildcat.com).

If you can give up the ease of lifts and tows in exchange for wilderness skiing, the **AMC Pinkham Notch Visitor Center** is your base camp. Always check in here to find out about avalanche and snow conditions in Tuckerman Ravine and other changeable parts of Mt. Washington before you start out. There's also a logbook to sign if you want to leave a record of when you headed out and where you planned to be, although it's not checked by staff unless there's an emergency reported. Spring skiing at Tuckerman is New England's most intense adventure, and needs careful preparation and the right gear – weather on this mountain is unpredictable and often life-threatening, and if you get lost or need rescue, you'll probably have to pay some part of the bill for rescue services. So start with a buddy who's already experienced with winter ski touring or ravine skiing, take appropriate precautions, and consider signing up for an AMC guided introduction to the winter wilderness before it's just you and the mountain vying for control.

Avalanche warnings at Pinkham Notch Ski Area.

Get in touch with the AMC at Pinkham Notch Visitor Center & Lodge, Box 298, Gorham, NH 03581 (☎ 466-2727) or take a planning visit to both the visitor center (on Route 16) and the Forest Service Androscoggin Ranger Station (☎ 466-2713; will give avalanche bulletins and weather conditions) at the north end of Pinkham Notch, where there's a video to help prepare you. And remember, this isn't the only direction for ascending Mt. Washington: for spring skiing especially, when the Tuckerman Ravine crowd makes the Pinkham Notch center seem overloaded, consider heading up the west side of the mountain to the cog railway base and skiing from there.

MORE ABOUT TUCKERMAN RAVINE

The Forest Service Androscoggin Ranger Station (300 Gen Road, Gorham, NH 03851) has a brochure on Tuckerman Ravine that answers some of the basics: Tuckerman spring skiing begins in late March, there are no lifts, and you're carrying all your gear from Pinkham Notch. There are limited shelters at Hermit Lake, with reservations advised. This is the only camping area in the ravine. The mouth of the ravine is at 3,800 feet elevation at Hermit Lake, 2.4 miles up the Tuckerman Ravine Trail from the base camp. Another half-mile of trail takes you to the floor of the bowl, which rises from 4,300 to 5,100 feet. Expect to hike an average of three hours to get to the beginning of a ski run! And you may still have to wait for others to get out of the way on narrow sections of trails, as this is a crowded time. If all you want to do is watch, head for the jumble of boulders at the north side of the ravine called the Lunch Rocks. Pay attention to avalanche and falling ice warnings posted along the way.

CAUTION: *Tuckerman's avalanches, falling ice, and boulders with great holes in the snow mean it's a hazardous place to ski. Most avalanches occur right after a snowstorm or during it; check warnings and, if in doubt, don't go. Expert skills, proper equipment, and good judgment are needed to ski it safely. Best recommendation: Always hike up the way you're going down, so you can see this day's obstacles and dangers. And ski out before the afternoon gets late enough to cast shadows that create treacherous ice.*

The White Mountains

Randolph & The Northern Presidentials

For a taste of **wilderness skiing** that's a tad more moderate than Mt. Washington's version, Randolph offers superb lower altitude back-country skiing, cross-country, and snowshoeing on many of the trails described in the book *Randolph Paths*. Snowcover is reliable. Refer to *On Foot* for a description of some of the trails that lead from Appalachia and the other Randolph-area trailheads. South of Route 2 there are sparkling vistas of winter woods and frozen waterfalls on trails like the Valley Way, Amphibrach, Link and the Sylvan Way. North of Route 2 there are loop trails in the vicinity of Randolph Hill, as well as a lumber road that runs from east to west about a half-mile north of Randolph Hill Road; connect to it with the Carlton Notch, Mount Crescent, and Ice Gulch Trails and the Cook Path.

Another plus of skiing the Randolph side of the Presidentials is that the Randolph Mountain Club keeps its Gray Knob lodge open year-round, on Nowell Ridge on Mt. Adams. All three of the adjacent mountains, Adams, Madison, and Jefferson, develop excellent snowfields for expert skiers (but you also need to be able to assess avalanche danger).

> ■ **CAUTION:** *If you ski above the treeline, your skis should be made for back-country use, which means sturdy fiberglass; skins (a rougher surface added to the ski bottoms) help with the uphill climb, although red wax or Klister can also be used. Skills required for the downhill slide are sustained snowplowing, quick jump turns, or telemark step turns – you've got to get safely around those trees!*

By the way, **ice climbers** head for Randolph to reach King Ravine and Great Gully; these are gorgeous climbs with deep solitude, and require expert skills and preparation.

For a slower but just as picturesque winter tramp on the mountain trails, get those showshoes on. Remember to bring ski poles, as you're in deep snow. Also recall that winter activity can easily dehydrate hikers. Drink at least two quarts of water per day, which you need to bring warm, in insulated containers, so it won't be ice by the time you need it.

Bretton Woods

Downhill or Nordic? Bretton Woods offers ample facilities for both sports. Alpine skiers take advantage of the **Bretton Woods Mountain Resort** (☎ 278-5000) on Route 302, about four miles east of its Twin Mountain junction with Route 3. Bretton Woods downhill features a vertical drop of 1,500 feet (peak elevation 3,100 feet), 32 trails, 98% snowmaking coverage, and five high-capacity lifts. There are two special treats: the view, and the restaurant at the top of the quad chair lift offers mountaintop dining for lunches and Saturday dinners. On Fridays and Saturdays in December through February the resort has night skiing, too, as well as entertainment in its slopeside lounge. This is skiing, resort style!

Across Route 302, based at the elegant Mt. Washington Hotel less than a mile east of Bretton Woods downhill slopes, is the **Bretton Woods Cross Country Ski Area** (☎ 278-5181 or 800-232-2972). This is a 100-km network that circles the hotel, climbs into the national forest, and even includes (for expert skiers) a mountain cabin where you can stay overnight by prior reservation! For a nifty twist on the usual trails, you can take the quad lift at the downhill resort and work your way down a cross-country trail that requires intermediate-level skills. The cross-country center offers rentals and a cafeteria, and you can lodge practically on the trails (☎ 278-1000 or 800-258-0330).

When you're at Bretton Woods you're at the north end of Crawford Notch, where there's plenty of winter wilderness experience waiting for you. The Appalachian Mountain Club offers **cross-country skiing and snowshoeing workshops** that start at the Crawford Notch Hostel (AMC workshop information: ☎ 466-2727, Monday through Saturday). **Ice climbers** also head for Crawford Notch, with the most popular routes ascending the east face of Mt. Willey, the south face of Mt. Willard, and the Frankenstein Cliffs in the southern part of the notch. Arethusa Falls, a 200-foot waterfall a little farther south, is also an ice climber's challenge.

The White Mountains

Twin Mountain

This might as well be a sister town to Bretton Woods, just four miles northwest on Route 302 where Route 3 intersects. Twin Mountain calls itself the snowmobile capital of the east, and offers 100 miles of groomed trails in the heart of the White Mountains. Write for a trail map: Twin Mountain Snowmobile Club, Dept. M, Box 179, Twin Mountain, NH 03595. Trail and parking area use are free, and many lodging and service establishments offer midweek specials to encourage snowmobilers to come then. Trail conditions can be checked by phone (☎ 846-2273 or 800-258-3609). **Garneau's Garage** (☎ 846-5790 or 800-750-5790) is the local spot for snowmobile sales and service, as well as trailer parts and hitches; it's located on Route 302 just west of the junction with Route 3. Also helpful is **Foster's Crossroads** next door, where there is snowmobile clothing along with some parts and accessories. Both businesses issue snowmobile registrations, which you'll need to run your rig in New Hampshire. **Snowmobile Rental of New England** is based at the Seven Dwarfs Motel on Little River Road, off Route 3 south of the intersection with Route 302 (☎ 846-5535).

Beaver Brook Ski Trails

Between Twin Mountain and Franconia Notch on Route 3 is a state wayside area called Beaver Brook. It's four miles from Twin Mountain (eight miles from Franconia) on the south side of the road. Here is the access point for a challenging set of trail loops through hardwoods and spruce-fir forest. The three trails are flagged with blue diamonds to distinguish them from old logging roads and open spaces in the woods. At the wayside parking area three trails meet. The one furthest to the right is the only one that's headed out (the other two are one-way toward you), so start there for the 2.3-km **Beaver Loop**, easiest of the three; at 0.8 km take the left fork, which will return you to the parking area. The right fork will put you on the **Badger Loop**, more of a challenge at 3.1 km long, returning to the parking area as the central trail. To connect to the Moose Watch Trail you go from Beaver to Badger and then, at 1.5 km from the parking lot, bear right; there are views of Garfield Ridge, Mt. Hale, North Twin Mountain, Haystack Mountain, and the Sugarloaf Mountains, with a high point 615 feet above the parking lot.

🔥 **MOOSE ALERT:** *Watch for evidence of moose browsing on the twigs and bark of woody plants, especially near the clear cuts in the woods. If you see one of the animals, don't get too close, as they are unpredictable and powerful.*

Cannon Mountain & Franconia Notch

Cannon Mountain (☎ 823-5563; snow conditions, 800-552-1234; www.nhparks.state.nh.us/cannon_mt) is the downhill slope for Franconia Notch, accessed from Exit 3 of the Franconia Notch Parkway (the sign says "Peabody Lodge"). For such a little-known resort, the vertical drop is astounding: 2,146 feet. The summit is 4,180 feet. This is no-frills, rapid, flat-out skiing, swooping down direct trails that don't waste time winding around the woods. There are six lifts, including an aerial tramway that has a separate base area (don't miss the nearby ski museum; see *Sightseeing*). The base lodge is friendly and rugged; there's a ski shop and a practical ski and snowboard school, as well as basic day care and cafeteria.

Nordic skiers can find a lot of cross-country trails and centers nearby. There's free access to the **Franconia Notch Recreation Trail** from Cannon Mountain to start with. Then there's the **Franconia Village X-C Ski Center** (☎ 823-5542), based at the Franconia Inn on Route 116S at Exit 38 of Interstate 93. It offers 65 km of groomed trails that loop among the local inns and lodges. Staying at Lovett's Inn or the Mittersill Resort (see *Where to Stay*) will put you on this trail network, as will the Pinestead Lodge, Cannon Mountain House, and the Horse & Hound.

Above the village of Franconia is **Sugar Hill,** where 30 km of cross-country ski trails, horse-drawn sleigh rides, snowshoeing, and tobogganing add up to unforgettable winter adventures at **Sunset Hill House,** an elegant inn and resort with incredible views. Treat yourself by staying there (☎ 823-5522 or 800-SUN HILL; see *Where to Stay*), or just stop by and register at the inn or warming hut before you use the historic trail network. Dinner at the inn could be a glorious finale; you'll want to dress up for the occasion.

The White Mountains

Between Cannon Mountain and Franconia village are the **Lafayette Ski Trails,** a network provided by the White Mountain National Forest, unpatrolled and with a few good challenges. The main trail is the 2.1-mile Notchway, which is on an easy grade but gains 441 feet in elevation. Some shorter side-trails like the Scarface and Bickford trails are more difficult. To find the trails, from Interstate 93 take Exit 36 onto Route 141 and go east about 100 yards. There's a metal sign on the south side of the road, along with parking. The other end of the network is accessed from Echo Lake parking lot at Cannon Mountain.

Mt. Moosilauke

There are no established facilities for winter activities at Mt. Moosilauke, and the steep slopes and icy weather make it a risky place to hike if you're not already experienced in snow survival. But it's worth mentioning as a wilderness goal for hardy adventurers; check each year for possible Appalachian Mountain Club guided winter hikes there as training, or connect with a local guide firm like **Profile Mountaineering** (Lincoln; see *On Foot*) for support and suggestions. The *Dartmouth Outing Guide* also gives suggestions for winter hikes here, with cautions on which trails are toughest.

Along the Connecticut River Valley

An unusual guided tour service for snowmobilers, cross-country skiers, and snowshoers is given by **Northern Land Services of Bethlehem** (☎ 869-2634), where vacations can be customized by connecting with local guides and establishments. Bethlehem is also the site of two Christmas tree farms: the **Rocks** (☎ 444-6228), and **Finnegan's Fine Firs** (☎ 444-6275).

■ In The Air

Glider Rides

 Soar near the summit of Mt. Washington in a three-seat Schweizer **glider** when you take off from **Mt. Washington Sky Adventures in Gorham** (☎ 466-5822 or 800-353-2873; home, 466-3650). This unique air operation also includes a 1942 Stearman biplane and a six-passenger twin-engine Piper Aztec. The airport is on Route 16 as it bends through the town and intersects with Route 2.

Franconia Airport offers warm-weather airtime at **Franconia Soaring Center**, ☎ 823-8881, specializing in glider rides but also offering a scenic and exciting ride in an authentic 1939 Waco UPF-7 biplane. There's a picnic area at the airport where your friends or family can relax as you take to the air.

Both airfields use federally licensed pilots and have incredibly reasonable prices for an adventure that most people will never have the equipment to try out on their own. Call ahead for reservations and options, which may vary according to weather conditions.

Scenic Flights

There's a one-man air operation at Whitefield, working from the Mt. Washington Regional Airport, a small strip southeast of town; take Route 3 south 1½ miles to Colby Road, where you turn left and go another 1½ miles to Airport Road. **George Graber** offers 15-minute scenic flights over Mt. Prospect and the Weeks Estate (☎ 802-892-6109).

Sightseeing

Heading north into the White Mountains on Interstate 93, Exit 28 provides both a state information center and a national forest one. It's a great stop, even if you're not planning to take Route 49 on into Waterville Valley, where a large and lovely valley resort provides access to hiking, mountain biking, skiing, and year-round trails in the White Mountain National Forest.

North Woodstock & Lost River

Exit 33 from the interstate takes you into North Woodstock, home of **Clark's Trading Post** (one mile south on Route 3; ☎ 745-8913). This vacation attraction (open mid-May to mid-October) dates to 1928 and is a summer playground of steam railroad, bumper boats, and a Main Street of early Americana along with a "mystical mansion." There's a family of native black bears, trained to entertain and clearly enjoying themselves. And there's the largest gift shop in the mountains. You get a chance to dip candles or be photographed in frontier-style clothes, all enlivened by music from restored nickelodeons. It's a light-hearted New Hampshire vacation tradition.

Take Route 112 west from Exit 33 for six miles to reach **Lost River**, ☎ 745-8031, where you'll climb through caves and around waterfalls, and have a chance to explore the geology of a stunning natural gorge where the river plays hide-and-seek with the rocks. The self-guided tour takes about an hour. Do wear clothes that can handle a trail of ups and downs (picture boardwalks and stairs) and optional cave crawling, plus there's a nature garden, ecology trail, and historical display. The gift shop is next to the cafeteria. This unusual attraction is actually owned by the Society for the Protection of New Hampshire Forests, which is why the natural history displays are so well developed. Open mid-May to mid-October.

By the way, in North Woodstock village there's an **indoor climbing wall** for extra practice before you head to the slopes; it's at the **Pemi Valley Rock Gym** on Main Street at the Alpine Village (☎ 745-9800, summers). This is a good rainy-day diversion, and outdoor instruction is also available in rock climbing (basic and intermediate) from **Profile Mountaineering** (☎ 745-3106).

There's a great **water park** for the hottest days of summer in North Lincoln, also reached from Exit 33: the **Whale's Tale** (☎ 745-8810) is a half-mile north on Route 3 and is open from mid-June to the first weekend of September. Tubes, slides, wave pools – all kinds of ways to be wet and wild!

Lincoln

It's easy to flow from North Woodstock to Lincoln, as the two are closely connected. If you're arriving directly from Interstate 93, though, take Exit 32 and turn east onto Route 112, the Kancamagus Highway. There's a White Mountains Attractions **visitor center** immediately on the right, and when you head east into town you'll find a series of craft shops and art galleries on the left. Immediately after those shops is the left turn onto Connector Road that takes you to the **Hobo Railroad** (☎ 745-2135, information year-round), a turn-of-the-century-style station where you can catch a scenic ride though the woods along the Pemigewasset River. There are also special dinner trains, fall foliage excursions, a July 4 party train, and trips where gold panning is taught! Although the railroad is mostly a summer and fall excursion, it often has "Santa trains" from the end of November until Christmas.

The next opportunity for sightseeing from Route 112 is on the right: **The Mill at Loon Mountain** (☎ 745-6261), which is both a cluster of lodging options for the nearby ski resort and a mall full of shops. Also at the Mill are the **Papermill Theatre** of North Country Center for the Arts (summers only; ☎ 745-6032 or 745-2141), and **East Branch Outfitters** (☎ 745-4806), where you can rent kayaks and canoes and ride a shuttle to the Pemigewasset River. The Mill at Loon Mountain hosts the Royal Lippizaner Stallions each September. Across the highway from the Mill is the **Upper Pemigewasset Historical Museum**, open Sunday and Wednesdays from 2 to 4 pm from mid-June to mid-September. Here you can bone up on early resort hotels, pulp and paper manufacturing, and founding families of the town.

Route 112 starts to ascend into the mountains, and **Loon Mountain ski resort** (☎ 745-8111; snow phone, 745-8100; www.loonmtn.com) is on your right. Held here each September are the **New Hampshire Highland Games** (for specific dates and tickets, call ☎ 800-358-SCOT). Even if you're not up for skiing or hiking, the **gondola** at Loon Mountain will give you a spectacular view of the region. The resort also showcases music year-round, ranging from jazz to rock to impressive concerts. Call for information and dates.

Kancamagus Highway

This scenic highway, also known as Route 112, stretches 38½ miles from Lincoln to Conway, from the Pemigewasset River, along the Swift River, to the Saco River. It climbs to nearly 3,000 feet near Lincoln as it passes over Mt. Kancamagus. Weather permitting, it's open year-round; there are no gas stations on most of the route, so it's wise to fill up the car's tank before you start up the road.

KANCAMAGUS

Kancamagus (can-kuh-MAG-us; "the Fearless One") was a Native American chief, grandson of Passaconaway and nephew of Wonalancet. He lived around 1684 and was the third and final Sagamon of the Penacook Confederacy. He was unable to keep peace between Native Americans and pioneers, and after much bloodshed the confederacy tribes scattered, with Kancamagus and his followers going north to upper New Hampshire or Canada. Many of the mountains in this region are named for significant Native Americans.

Driving Route 112 from Lincoln takes you past the Loon Mountain Recreation Area (ski resort that in summer is a hiking and biking haven) and past scenic overlooks and trailheads for hikers, mountain bikers, and skiers into the White Mountain National Forest. To the north are Big Coolidge Mountain and Mt. Hitchcock and Mt. Huntington; to the south are the noted peaks of Osceola (named for the great chief of the Seminoles), Kancamagus, and Tripyramid. Sabbaday Falls is a scenic treasure not to be missed, about halfway along the highway on the left side of the road; park and take the short hike (see On Foot) for one of the region's lovely treasures.

After Sabbaday Falls comes the **Passaconaway Historic Site**, where you can explore the **Russell Colbath House,** built in the early 1800s. The poignant story of Ruth Russell Colbath's 39-year nightly vigil of lighting a lamp for her missing husband is best appreciated when you see the very isolated and simple surroundings in which she lived.

For a little-traveled and deeply forested scenic drive, look for the left turn onto Bear Notch Road; it will take you to **Bartlett,** beyond North Conway, and you'll have seen deep woods not usually accessible by car.

If you stay on the Kancamagus Highway, the next point of interest is **Rocky Gorge**, a scenic area on the left. This is especially striking in spring when the high turbulent water makes the river swell and roar; in the summer it's often crowded as people enjoy sitting on the rocks in the cool stream.

As the wild part of the Kancamagus Highway ends, on the right there's a brightly painted totem pole followed by **Baldy's Store** (☎ 447-5287). Owner Treffle Bolduc is a snowshoe maker; he is now in his eighties and has wonderful stories to tell of the Huron Indians in Canada who taught him his art. In the back of the store is a two-room Indian museum, jammed with treasures he has collected, including wonderful snowshoes and a birchbark canoe. The store and museum are open daily through the summer and fall, although hours may change as needed to keep up with the snowshoe trade.

The final stop is on your left, the **Saco Ranger Station**, where there's a huge relief map that puts the scenic road into perspective, and Forest Service rangers will help with route and adventure planning.

LEGEND SAYS...

To the south of the last part of the Kancamagus is **Mt. Chocorua** (shuh-COR-oo-uh), although its rocky, pointed peak isn't visible from this angle. There are many legends about the Sokosis chief for whom this peak was named. The best-known version declares that he left his son to stay with a family of settlers named Campbell. When the chief's son died, possibly from poison used for foxes, the chief took revenge by murdering most of the Campbell household; the settlers then chased him to the top of the mountain that bears his name, and he jumped to his death from the highest ridge. Hiking Mt. Chocorua is a New England summer and early autumn tradition; see *On Foot*.

The White Mountains

North Conway & Intervale

There's nothing as frustrating as a classic North Conway traffic jam, which can extend miles north and south when shopping at the outlets lining the road south of the village is at its peak (many summer days and early fall). After all, who can resist a visit to the outlet for **L.L. Bean** (☎ 800-4-TANGER), long a leader in outdoor clothing and gear? And there are dozens more clothing, household goods, and gift outlets and shops to investigate. Try to miss the midsummer crunch.

Antiquing in the Mt. Washington Valley

NOT TO SCALE

1. Ellis River Antiques
2. Intervale Farm
3. Antiques & Collectibles Barn
4. Sedler's Antiques
5. Main Street Antiques
6. Sleigh Mill Antiques

On the other hand, there's a lot of fun to be had in wandering the village of North Conway at any season. Visit sports shops and restaurants, prowl antique shops, and rub shoulders with other adventure travelers in the cream of New Hampshire's mountain climbing centers: **Eastern Mountain Sports** (☎ 356-5433) at the north end of the village in the Eastern Slopes Inn, and - **International Mountain Equipment & International Mountain Climbing Store** (☎ 356-7013) on the other side of Main Street. Anglers take note: **The North Country Angler** (☎ 356-6000) provides a great fly-fishing shop (farther north on the left side of Main Street just past the hospital turn).

In the middle of the village on Main Street is the **Mt. Washington Valley visi-**

tors center, a good place to examine restaurant menus and also to check the weather conditions at the top of Mt. Washington. Across the road, on the other side of the park, is the **Conway Scenic Railroad** (☎ 356-5251 or 800-232-5251), where you can ride a train to Conway or Bartlett and back. Be sure to check the dining car schedule if you want to have lunch or dinner on board. The valley train runs on weekends as early in the year as April, and becomes daily from mid-June to mid-October. There's also a notch train to Crawford Notch, daily during fall foliage season and five days a week earlier in the summer. Reservations are a good idea. Access to the cars is easy, and there's boarding assistance for passengers needing special help. Special Christmas-season evening trains include memorable storytelling.

If you're not planning to rock climb, it's still fun to watch the climbing teams tackle **Cathedral Ledge** just west of town at Echo Lake State Park. Look for the state park sign and turn left on River Road at the north end of the village, and the park and ledges are less than a mile ahead. Climbing equipment may be purchased at **Wild Things**, back on the highway heading north. And at 1½ miles north of North Conway village is one of the area's most popular antique shops, the **Antiques & Collectibles Barn** (☎ 356-7118).

ANTIQUING IN THE MT. WASHINGTON VALLEY

From Conway to Intervale, antique shops line Routes 16 and 302. Just a few are listed here.

- **Ellis River Antiques**, Route 16, Jackson (☎ 383-4307), has unique furniture and antiques for the home, from rustic to primitive to Victorian.

- **Intervale Farm Antiques,** Route 16A, Intervale (☎ 356-5134), offers ephemera, vintage postcards, sheet music, and shop tools.

- **Antiques & Collectibles Barn,** 1½ miles north of North Conway (☎ 356-7118), and **Main Street Antiques,** North Conway (☎ 356-3342) are multi-dealer establishments.

The White Mountains

- **Sedler's Antiques**, North Conway (☎ 356-6008 or call the main shop in Georgetown, Mass., ☎ 508-352-8282), has dolls, jewelry, tools, and furniture.

- **Sleigh Mill Antiques**, Snowville (☎ 447-6791), specializes in 19th-century lighting.

Birchbark tepee at site of Native American Indian encampment, Intervale.

When you leave North Conway on Route 16/302 north, you come to Intervale, where there's a scenic vista overlooking Cathedral Ledge on the left. Across from the vista parking lot is a small cluster of shops, and at the south end of the cluster by the post office is Intervale Cross Road. Up this small side road is a partially preserved **Native American encampment** where an Abenaki scholar, Stephen Laurent, had a small shop; the shop may no longer be open, but the encampment, with its authentic birchbark tepee, is worth a thoughtful visit.

A handful of summer attractions cluster along Route 16 next: Ragged Mountain outdoor equipment and clothing, a miniature golf park, and on the left, **Hartmann Model Railroad and Toy Museum** (☎ 356-9922 or 356-9933), where there are American and world railroads laid out for fun and collecting.

New Year's Eve is a special time for North Conway, as well as for nearby Conway, Bartlett, and Jackson, with a family-centered **First Night** celebration from noon to midnight. Expect to buy an admission button and then participate in song, dance, games, art, history, and outdoor events. There's bus service between the participating towns.

Glen

When Routes 16 and 302 separate north of Intervale, it's just another quarter-mile to a pair of theme amusement parks: Story Land and Heritage New Hampshire. **Story Land** (☎ 383-4186) is a family park featuring nursery rhyme and classic bedtime stories, ideal for small children – ages four and under enter free (strollers available free), and ages up to 10 will have fun with the rides and shows. **Heritage New Hampshire** (☎ 338-9776) takes you into the state's history, where you can meet settlers and revolutionaries, explore their homes and businesses, have a photo taken with a Civil War balloonist, and play with steam engines and trains. The park is wheelchair accessible. Both parks are summer and foliage season attractions, not winter; call ahead for prices.

Bartlett

In the summer, **Attitash Bear Peak** turns into a wild vacation spot with waterslides, the White Mountain Observation Tower, scenic chairlifts, and guided horseback rides along the Saco River. There are also big events like an early June **soccer tournament**, and in August a **blueberry festival,** a high-excitement **equine festival**, a **rodeo**, and at the end of the summer the **White Mountain Jazz & Blues Festival.** Call to confirm dates, which may change from year to year (☎ 374-2368).

Jackson

One of the nicest parts about Jackson in the summer is that it's not flashy: just a simple, lovely village enjoying the sunshine on the hills, fields, and rivers. **Walking** through the covered bridges and around the park is a peaceful luxury.

Pinkham Notch

Glen Ellis Falls are about 9½ miles from Jackson Village. The falls are so close to the road that it's not fair to call them a hike! They're most impressive in spring or right after a rain storm,

The White Mountains

but lovely any time. Park in the Glen Ellis Falls parking area on the left, then go through the tunnel under Route 16 and down the stone walkway and stairs (you are on work done by the Civilian Conservation Corps in the 1930s) – note that there are more than 150 steps to go down. There are several overlooks before the falls, only a third of a mile from the road; the falls drop 66 feet.

Next on the left is the Appalachian Mountain Club **Pinkham Notch Visitor Center** (☎ 466-2727). This is the base camp for hikers and skiers headed up Mt. Washington from this side of the mountain, and is also a fascinating spot to stop and visit. The Trading Post sells trail guides, maps, and identification guides for plants and animals, especially the hard to find alpine plant guides. Sit on the porch and watch the wide variety of hikers go in and out; across the path is the Joe Dodge Lodge, where mountain visitors can spend the night for a small fee (see *Where to Stay*). If you'd like to go up the mountain but not on your own feet, head a little farther up Route 16.

Wildcat Mountain (☎ 466-3326), on the right as you go north up Route 16, turns pussycat with summer weather: The ski area 11 miles north of Jackson on Route 16 offers a 12-minute gondola ride to the summit, with nature trails at the top, and invites guests to run back down the 2,100-foot climb if they choose! This is also a good foliage stop, with a view of Mt. Washington.

Great Glen is on the left about 1½ miles past the entrance to Wildcat. Great Glen is the location of both a trail network and the privately owned auto road up Mt. Washington. Most recently, fees were $15 for a passenger car and driver (including an audio tour on cassette) plus $6 for each adult passenger and $4 for each child aged five to 12. Or you can ride in a van with a tour guide for $20 (children five to 12, $10). Children under five ride free. Hikers can also register at the stage office for a ride back down the mountain! This is a breathtaking ride, with narrow roadway, grades averaging 12%, and remarkable views, especially above the treeline. The summit house at the top of the mountain has restrooms, a snack bar, and a post office. You won't be able to go into the weather observatory at the peak, but you'll be able to see some of the records. Auto road questions can be answered at ☎ 466-3988; the season is mid-May to late October, opening at 7:30 am each day. Van tours take about 1½ hours round trip, including 30 minutes on the summit.

Great Glen Trails (☎ 466-2333; www.mt-washington.com), next door to the auto road, is an all-season recreational trail park. Designed for hikers, mountain bikers, and cross-country skiers, the trails range from beginner level to challenging. All equipment can be rented at the base lodge. Summer programs include archery, a concert series, moonlight events, and nature tours. Winter ones add guided wildlife tours, races, and a Sno-Cat shuttle for sightseers, Nordic skiers, and snowshoers that takes you halfway up Mt. Washington and lets you stride and slide back down. There's a ski school, trail patrol, child care, and dining.

At the north end of Pinkham Notch, just before reaching Gorham, is a left turn for **Dolly Copp Campground**. The road is called both Dolly Copp Road and Pinkham B. It cuts across through the forest and emerges on Route 2 in Randolph, without ever going through the bustling town of Gorham. It's a pleasant shortcut, and a scenic drive.

Gorham

This little town (population only 3,100) hosts tourists with enthusiasm, offering at last count over 600 motel rooms and 16 restaurants. About the only time it's quiet is during "mud season" (early spring, April to mid-May), and even then there are expert skiers passing through town to get to Tuckerman Ravine.

Gorham offers visitors the **Northern Forest Moose Tours,** which leave the town information booth at the park on Route 16 daily from mid-June to mid-October (reservations advised, ☎ 752-6060 or 800-992-7480). These tours take no more than 24 passengers at a time in an air-conditioned van, traveling through the town's northern neighbor Berlin and up the bank of the Androscoggin River as dusk falls, generally finding from two to 20 moose per trip (97% success rate in the past season). The van stops for passengers to climb out and take pictures of the large wild animals; if the moose are not close enough to see well from the roadside, the tour guide focuses a telephoto-lens

Taking moose lightly in Gorham.

video camera on the amazing creatures so passengers can see them "close up" on a video screen inside the van. This is also a great way for those not comfortable hiking the river banks to see active moose. The guide is knowledgeable about moose, and even more so about local history; when it gets too dark to see animals, the van turns back toward Gorham, stops briefly at Pontook Dam for restrooms and a stretch, then makes the return trip with a video on paper company and logging history shown in the van. The latest fee was $10 per person; the tour starts at 7 pm (check in at the booth by 6:30), and lasts 2½ hours.

Gorham carries the moose theme through two moose gift shops and a miniature golf course with a giant moose statue in front. Just one June or July drive up along the Androscoggin River will convince you that the town really is a moose capital.

> **MOOSE ALERT:** *Remember to slow down at dusk and after dark; moose are hard to spot because the bulk of their bodies is higher than car headlights hit. And a moose-car collision usually totals both.*

Randolph

Vyron D. Lowe was a Randolph guide and founded **Lowe's Service Station and Store,** located on Route 2 about two miles west of the Appalachia trailhead. The general store is still a family business and includes a service station, garage, and overnight cabins. Stop here to check on announcements of events by the Randolph Mountain Club, and to step into White Mountain tradition yourself. If you park at the store to go hiking, there's a fee. Nearby is the start of Lowe's Path to Mt. Adams, as well as the Vyron D. Lowe Trail to Lookout Ledge and Randolph Hill.

Jefferson

If you're headed to the hiking trails of the notches, you might not even go through the center of Jefferson. There are two theme parks here that kids have explored for years: **Six Gun City** is a Wild West and frontier show full of animals and deputies, plus rides on a pony, a burro, a log boat, or a bumper boat. It's open from mid-June to Labor Day and weekends to mid-October. It's a family business; the Brady family will even help plan your visit (☎ 586-4592).

Santa's Village (☎ 586-4445; e-mail hisanta@moose.ncia.net; www.santasvillage.com) starts its season at Father's Day weekend. It's always Christmas here, with Santa to talk to, elves to visit, and rides on the Skyway Sleigh and the Yule Log Flume. Petting the reindeer is a favorite activity. Both parks are best suited to children under 10 and their families. Call ahead for this season's admission prices.

Twin Mountain

When you take Route 115 south from Route 2 in Jefferson Highlands toward Twin Mountain, Route 115 forms a "T" with Route 3. To reach this busy outdoor-adventurer support town you take a left. To stop first at the **Twin Mountain Fish Hatchery**, turn right and go north on Route 3 about a half-mile. The public part of the hatchery is to your right; park and walk along the raceways to the visitor center with its classroom and restrooms. This hatchery uses the springs that form Carroll Stream as a source of oxygen-rich water to nurture brook trout, as well as rainbow and brown trout. You'll see the trays of fertilized eggs, and the brood fish that become part of the state stocking program after they reach three years of age. The fish and wildlife center is open daily from May to October (9 am to

4:30 pm); for guided tours you need an appointment (☎ 846-5108; Hatchery Superintendent, Twin Mountain, RFD1, Whitefield, NH 03598).

When you take the turn south on Route 3 you arrive at Twin Mountain's major intersection, the traffic light crossing of Routes 3 and 302. There are plenty of restaurants and lodging here. The town recreational field recently started hosting a **Native American Cultural Weekend** each July; to check dates, ☎ 800-245-TWIN. This festival features dance, drumming, storytelling, and historic lectures, and costs a token fee for adults, with children admitted free.

Bretton Woods

The showpiece of Bretton Woods is the **Mount Washington Hotel and Resort**, a grand hotel surrounded by New England's highest peaks. The hotel carries on a tradition of luxurious lodging in Crawford Notch, and is the last of the grand hotels to survive the years of fire and loss. Its opening on August 1, 1902, was attended by Abel Crawford himself, trailblazer of the notch. Built to the directions of railway tycoon Joseph Stickney, the hotel's elegance came partly from the efforts of Italian master craftsmen skilled in masonry and woodworking. The hotel was later owned by Stickney's widow, whose second marriage made her the Princess Clarigny de Lucinge; two owners later, in 1944, the hotel was the scene of an international gathering of financiers from 44 countries to reestablish world monetary exchanges following World War II. The Bretton Woods International Monetary Conference set the gold standard at $35 an ounce, gave the postwar world a badly needed currency stability, and put the hotel into history books.

Today the hotel's Victorian elegance is protected as a National Historic Landmark and by a group of New Hampshire businessmen who now own it. It is still a vacation residence of poets, presidents, and princes, and can be visited more casually during special events like the Independence Day fireworks celebration; call for events open to the public. The Mount Washington Hotel & Resort, Route 302, Bretton Woods, NH 03575; ☎ 278-1000 or 800-258-0330.

An unforgettable way to visit the mountain peak that rises behind the grand hotel is to ride the **cog railway** to the summit of Mt. Washington. The railway station is not far from the hotel: Head west on Route 302 toward Twin Mountain and you'll find a well-marked right turn that leads to the Base Station in about five miles. There are trains daily from early May through October, although they run less frequently in cooler weather; call ahead for the day's schedule and to make reservations (strongly recommended; ☎ 846-5404 ext. 6, or 800-922-8825 ext. 6). Check on current fares, too; adult fares were recently about $40 per person, with discounts for seniors and children. The round trip lasts three hours, including a 20-minute stop at the summit. Dress warmly for the chill winds and occasional fog at the peak! Expect the train trip to be dramatic and a little bit scary: The coal-fired engines puff their way over a narrow track, suspended in places on trestles. One trestle, called Jacob's Ladder, climbs a 37% grade, which you may never have experienced in a moving vehicle. Don't forget your camera.

Crawford Notch

One day in 1771, Timothy Nash was tracking a moose on Cherry Mountain. When he climbed a tree to see his location better (and maybe the moose), he noticed a break, or notch, in the mountains ahead of him. He walked through the cleft in the mountains where the Saco River flowed, and made his way to Portsmouth to tell the Royal Governor, Benning Wentworth (for whom many New Hampshire places are named), about his discovery. According to Matt Dickerman's version of the story in *A Guide to Crawford Notch*, the skeptical governor insisted that Nash prove the passage by bringing a horse all the way through from home. This task required the help of Nash's friend Benjamin Sawyer, in order to hoist the horse and lower it on ropes when the rocks were too precipitous in places, but horse and men survived the trip. As a result, the two men received a land grant in Crawford Notch, named Nash and Sawyer's location, and began work on a road and encouraging a settlement.

Look at the later period of the notch, when grand hotels lined it, in the photographs displayed at the old railroad station now owned by the Appalachian Mountain Club on Route 302 at the head (north end) of the notch. Wander on the short and scenic paths by Saco Lake and Elephant's Head Rock across the road from the AMC Crawford Hostel, then drive down the steady descent of Route 302. Two waterfalls come down to the left side of the road; there's parking on the right. Farther down is the Crawford Depot, headquarters of the state park here, with a museum and picnic site as well as seasonal gift shop. There's also a nature trail here. All around you are hikers huffing and puffing up the peaks and along the ridges; if you're not in the mood to climb up there yourself, you can enjoy a lot of Crawford Notch from the road and its adjacent scenic areas.

Franconia & Sugar Hill

These two communities at the north end of Franconia Notch make up a lovely and poetic site for a day trip, weekend, or relaxed week of exploring. The center of Franconia is at the intersection of Routes 18 and 116. If you arrive from Exit 38 of Interstate 93, Route 116 is straight in front of you. Take it for another mile to find the right-hand turn to a farmhouse where poet **Robert Frost** lived and wrote. Soak up the scenery, and if you dare to discover the more discouraging parts of the poet's personal life, pay the modest museum fee and browse among stories of his hard times. Check in advance on schedules for poetry readings at **The Frost Place**, which in late July hosts a conference of some of America's finest practitioners of the writing art. For information, contact Director, The Frost Place, Ridge Road, Franconia, NH 03580, ☎ 823-5510. Open weekends from Memorial Day to the end of June, then all week except Tuesdays, 1 to 5 pm through Columbus Day weekend.

When you return to Route 116 by the loop road that the museum signs point to, you won't be far at all from Franconia's small but active airfield (offering summer glider flights) and the delights of the Franconia Inn; turn right for both, or left to return to Franconia village.

From the same intersection in the village, Route 18 winds southeast along the Gale River, passes a well-stocked information booth, then leaves the village and begins to climb toward **Cannon Mountain.** Stop to explore the **Mittersill Resort** on your right, a recreation of Austrian chalets in a small village with stupendous mountain vistas.

If your village choice is the other direction of Route 18, past the small grocery store on the right and the bicycle shop on the left, you find **Garnet Hill** on your right in half a mile. This is the famous mail-order natural fiber clothing manufacturer whose catalogs you may have seen; the business is not open to the public, but in late July each year it offers a weekend tent sale at Loon Mountain in nearby Lincoln, where seconds, returns, and no longer current items are sold for prices that draw an astounding crowd. Immediately past Garnet Hill on the left is the last standing stone **iron blast furnace** in New Hampshire, dating to the mid-1800s when the desperate need for iron for national expansion and for the Civil War drove the local industries of iron mining and smelting, with sits companion, charcoal manufacture. There's a brief roadside explanation of the furnace and its history; for more details, check the Sugar Hill Historic Museum (see next page).

New England's last remaining stonework furnace, once used to smelt iron from ore.

The White Mountains

To reach Sugar Hill, drive past the iron furnace and take the left onto Route 117, which climbs steadily uphill. If you're here in June and early July you can see the fields of lupines blooming in pink and purple along the roadsides; these adjoining towns hold a two-week **lupine festival** in mid-June with events like tea parties and garden tours. Advance tickets and information, ☎ 823-5661 or 800-237-9007. On your right watch for the Sugar Hill Inn, then make a steep climb up the mountain. On the right you'll find **Polly's Pancake Parlor** (see

Where To Eat), which offers a good view across the road from the parking lot. On the left is the startlingly narrow church of St. Matthew with its bright yellow door. At the crest of the hill there's a noticeable business on the left called **Sugar Hill Sampler** (☎ 823-8478), a historic inn with a large gift shop, well worth a visit. The same left turn will take you to **Sunset Hill House** (see page 169), an elegant inn with walking trails and exceptional golf course; visit even if you don't plan to dine or lodge or use the trails, just to see the magnificent panorama of both the Presidential and Kinsman Ranges.

Route 117 then descends into Sugar Hill proper, where the library and museum are on the left. On the right is **Harman's Cheese & Country Store** (☎ 823-8000), which has possibly the state's best cheddar, aged at least two full years. The **Sugar Hill Historic Museum** is open from July 1 to mid-October, usually afternoons (☎ 823-8142 or 823-5336) and features changing exhibits that recently included weddings from five generations of one of the town's families; the iron industry; and the great hotel era of the 1800s. One room of the museum is a replica of a 19th-century tavern with original furnishings. In the sleigh barn you can find the elegant sleigh owned by actress Bette Davis, who vacationed here for years (find her story under *On Foot*, page 111).

Franconia Notch

The attractions of Franconia Notch have been described in *On Foot*: Cannon Mountain's **tramway** to the summit, the short trail to Profile Lake to view the famous rock formation called the **Old Man of the Mountain,** the dark leafy coolness of the gorge called **The Flume**. There's also the **New England Ski Museum** (☎ 823-7177) at Exit 2 of the Franconia Notch Parkway, open noon to 5 pm daily from December 1 to March 31 and from Memorial Day to Columbus Day (free admission). Don't miss the vintage ski films! The **Lafayette Place**, farther south on the parkway, has exhibits on the natural and cultural history of Franconia Notch, as well as interpretive programs at the adjacent campground throughout the summer.

Along the Connecticut River Valley

When you've had enough of challenging the mountains and want to relax or indulge in some summer theater, head for the small towns along or near the Connecticut River Valley.

Littleton

Littleton is a gateway town to the White Mountains at the west side of the state, and has good bookshops and a small but very interesting **historical museum** that features old stereoscopic slides. It's in the lower level of the town office building at One Union Street, open Wednesdays and summer Saturdays, 1:30 to 4:30 pm, or by appointment, ☎ 444-6586, -2419, -2980, or -2637. Littleton's **Chamber of Commerce** offers a walking tour brochure of the small town, as well as a map of several nature trails around the town. Don't miss the hike up to **Kilburn Crags** (from Main Street go west 1½ miles from the post office, turning left with Route 135 and parking on the left after one mile more), where there are Devonian fossils to be found nearby, as well as mineral discoveries.

Bethlehem

Bethlehem is four miles east of Littleton; its village mood and many antique shops are charming, and for many year the town has been a summer for visiting Hassidic Jews; be sure to visit **Bretzfelder Park**, owned by the Society for the Protection of New Hampshire Forests and home to a magnificent old memorial white pine, as well as nature trails and summer evening lectures. The **Bethlehem Flower Farm**, three miles east of town, offers daylilies all summer (☎ 869-3131).

ANTIQUING IN BETHLEHEM

Antique shops melt sweetly in and out of business in town, but at any given time there may be close to a dozen. Some of the latest shops are:

- **Country Collectibles**, selection of wood stoves, glass, linen furniture, tools; next to post office, ☎ 869-3991.

- **Sanborn's Little Shoppe**, antiques and collectibles, across from People's Bank, ☎ 869-2292.

- **Checkered Past**, 154 Guider Rd. (Exit 40 from I-93), multi-dealer group shop in 1820s barn. Open year-round, ☎ 444-6628; e-mail Kscope@ConnRiver.net.

- **Carousel Antiques**, across from the Colonial Theater. Bedroom, dining room and parlor sets, plus china, crystal, Nippon, decorative pieces, ☎ 869-5755.

- **3 of Cups Antiques**, vintage clothing, furniture, prints, linens, kitchenware, across from Colonial Theater, ☎ 869-2606.

Many shops are open summers only, and on only a few days each week. Call ahead to be sure!

Whitefield

About 10 miles from both Littleton and Bethlehem is Whitefield, where the **Weathervane Theatre** offers professional-level repertory (☎ 892-9322, open July and August, reservations strongly advised).

Haverhill, Orford & Piermont

Farther south are the very photogenic river-valley towns of Haverhill, Orford, and Piermont. Orford is especially striking with its **Ridge Houses**, seven strikingly handsome houses built between 1773 and 1839. Piermont has a **polygonal barn** (a change from the classic round ones!), and Haverhill offers a **village common** (an unusual double common with white board fence), with lovely gardens around it, as well as Federal-era and Greek Revival houses. Just north of Haverhill is a turn worth discovering: a small road headed toward the Connecticut River and little-known **Bedell Bridge Park**. This may be the most peaceful spot in the river valley, with a dirt road winding among wide green fields and wetlands, ending at a picnic spot by the foundations of a long-gone bridge.

Warren

The little town of Warren can be reached via Route 25 from Haverhill or Route 25C from Piermont; there's a state **Fish and Wildlife Center** here, open May through October from

9 am to 4:30 pm (☎ 764-8593), with interactive exhibits looking at wildlife habitat and the life cycle of the Atlantic salmon. Check out the hatchery and see the fish up close. Then take a drive into the white-clapboard village to see its curious monument, a space-rocket booster towering over the common.

The Mount Washington Hotel & Resort, Bretton Woods.
(Photo courtesy of the resort)

Where To Stay

Bretton Woods & Twin Mountain

 The single luxury resort of the White Mountains is a treasure of gracious and elegant vacationing. With a rich history and lush surroundings, the **Mount Washington Hotel & Resort** nurtures a mood of lavish leisure and playful diversion. From the 900-foot white veranda you can gaze across the rolling grounds to the nearby mountain peaks. The hotel offers a Modified American Plan (MAP) for lodging, which includes full dinners and breakfasts; options vary from the grand hotel to the adjacent townhomes, country inn, and motor inn. There are many vacation packages, too, including golf, carriage rides, and romantic touches like fresh flowers and candlelight. Write to or call the hotel for a packet of descriptive literature. Mount Washington Hotel & Resort, Route 302, Bretton Woods, NH 03575; ☎ 278-1000 or 800-258-0330. $$-$$$$. The resort is worth a visit even if you don't stay there.

In addition to grand Mount Washington Hotel are some comfortable and historic lodgings. Probably the most famous is the **Notchland Inn** at the south end of Crawford Notch. The 1860s granite mansion has housed not only hikers but trailblazers, and there's an eclectic library to bone up on the inn's history (it was originally the Bemis Mansion), as well as the region's. The Davis Path, which ascends Mt. Crawford and links to other trails leading to Mt. Washington, starts across the road from the inn. Rates are MAP, breakfast and five-course dinner included (☎ 374-6131 or 800-866-6131; e-mail Notchland@aol.com; $$$$).

Twin Mountain is full of small motor inns and motels; two of them are **Carlson's Lodge** on Route 302 a half-mile west of the junction with Route 3 (☎ 846-5501 or 800-348-5502; $-$$), and **Northern Zermatt Inn and Motel** on Route 3 north of the junction (☎ 846-5533 or 800-535-3214; $-$$).

Waterville Valley & Campton

Recall that the town, ski slopes, and adventure camp of **Waterville Valley** are all part of a single resort designed for year-round activities. There are inns, lodges, and condominiums offering moods that range from country charm to grand resort to practical and modern. A flat rate for a family includes adventures and equipment use. Reservations and information, ☎ 800-468-2553; e-mail wvlodging@waterville.com; $-$$.

Nearby Campton, a bit closer to Interstate 93, offers other options: Start with the warm and friendly **Campton Inn** (a country home dating to 1836), with innkeepers Robbin and Peter Adams; RR2 Box 12, Campton Village, NH 03223; ☎ 726-4449; $$ for two. A second inn, the **Mountain-Fare Inn**, offers nine rooms plus a carriage house annex, all in the village. Innkeepers are Susan and Nick Preston. Mad River Rd., Box 533,

Campton, NH 03223; ☎ 726-4283; $$ for a room and hearty breakfast.

Woodstock & North Woodstock

Looking for a country inn with a lot of entertainment? The **Woodstock Inn Bed & Breakfast** has traditional country inn comforts and adds a microbrewery and live entertainment year-round. Ask about vacation and retreat packages and the November brewer's weekends. 135 Main Street, Route 3, North Woodstock, NH 03262; ☎ 745-3951 or 800-321-3985; e-mail relax@woodstockinnNH.com; www.woodstockinnNH.com. $-$$, depending on season.

Jack O'Lantern Resort and Golf Course offers another approach to keeping guests busy. In addition to the 18-hole, par 70 golf course, there's a Cabana Club with heated pool and Jacuzzi, sauna, and game room. Reserve ahead with the Keating family. Woodstock, NH 03293; ☎ 745-8121 or 800-227-4454; $$.

Options in North Woodstock are the **Wilderness Inn**, a bed and breakfast (☎ 745-3890 or 800-200-WILD-20; $-$$), where there's also afternoon tea served; **Autumn Breeze** motel units (☎ 745-8549 or 800-684-3543; $-$$); and **Three Rivers House**, a country inn (☎ 745-2711 or 800-241-2711; $-$$).

Lincoln

Home of Loon Mountain, an impressive ski resort with year-round activities, including hiking directly into the Pemigewasset Wilderness, Lincoln has plenty of lodging. **The Mill at Loon Mountain** is a four-season resort village that includes the Mill House Inn, Rivergreen Resort Hotel, and Lincoln Condominiums (for all three, ☎ 745-6261 or 800-654-6183; $$, many rooms are suites), and the Lodge at Lincoln Station (☎ 745-3441 or 800-654-6188; $$, many suites). All have access to the vacation packages of the Mill at Loon Mountain, including restaurants, theatre, and events like the month-long Christmas celebration, or the Scottish Highland Games in October.

Nearby is the **Mountain Club at Loon**, a resort hotel that includes a fitness center and an unusual outdoor whirlpool (☎ 745-2244 or 800-229-STAY; $$$-$$$$).

A traditional family favorite in the area is the **Indian Head Resort** on Route 3, 1½ miles north of Exit 33 from Interstate 93. Indoor and outdoor pools and a thorough kids entertainment program add to the spas and lounge (☎ 800-343-8000; e-mail info@indianheadresort.com; www.indianheadresort. com).

You can also choose among the **Drummer Boy Motor Inn** on Route 3 (☎ 745-3661 or 800-762-7275; $$); **Parker's Motel** on Route 3 (☎ 745-8341 or 800-766-6835; $$); the **Franconia Notch Motel** on Route 3 bordering the Pemigewasset River (☎ 745-2229; $$); **Red Doors Motel** on Route 3 (☎ 745-2267; $$); **Kancamagus Motor Lodge** on the Kancamagus Highway (☎ 745-3365 or 800-346-4205; $$); **The Beacon** on Route 3 (☎ 745-8118 or 800-258-8934; $$-$$$); and **Profile Motel & Cottages** on Route 3 (☎ 800-282-0092; $$-$$$).

For a more rustic ambiance, try the **Mt. Liberty Motel and Cabins on the River** (☎ 745-3600; $-$$) or **Cozy Cabins** (☎ 745-8713; open May through October; $-$$).

Conway

Hostelling International offers 43 beds in a New England farmhouse off Route 16 in Conway. Reservations are advised (☎ 447-1001; $; closed in November). A continental breakfast is served. There are also rooms for families. Write to the hostel at Hostelling International-White Mountains, 36 Washington Street, Conway, NH 03818.

Highly recommended is the **Darby Field Country Inn & Restaurant**, a friendly getaway spot. Call for directions, ☎ 447-2181 or 800-426-4147; e-mail marc@darbyfield.com; www. darbyfield.com; $$.

North Conway & Intervale

Skiing at **Cranmore**? Contact the resort to put together a ski-and-stay package that includes condominium lodging (☎ 800-SUN N SKI; North Conway, NH 03860; www. cranmore.com; $$-$$$$). In town, visit the **Eastern Slope Inn Resort**, a National Historic Site on 40 acres with 134 rooms, suites, and townhouses (☎ 356-6321 or 800-258-4708; www. journeysnorth.com/easternslopeinn/esi.html; $$-$$$). The contrast of this elegant inn with the high energy of the Eastern Mountain Sports shop tucked right behind the inn lobby says a lot about the fun of adventure in the White Mountains!

Other large hotels in the North Conway area are the **Four Points Hotel by ITT Sheraton** (Route 16 at Settler's Green, ☎ 356-9300 or 800-648-4397; e-mail 4points@nxi.com; $$-$$$), and the **Green Granite Inn & Conference Center** (Route 16, ☎ 356-6901 or 800-468-3666; e-mail granite@nxi.com; $$-$$$). There's also a Best Western called the **Red Jacket Mountain View** on Route 16 (☎ 356-5411 or 800-752-2538; $$-$$$).

There's lots of enjoyment in savoring the country inns (which range from elegant to country comforts) in the region. For instance, the **1785 Inn** offers a view of Mt. Washington as well as exquisite dining and a Victorian lounge (innkeepers Becky and Charlie Mallar; ☎ 356-9025 or 800-421-1785; e-mail THE1785INN@aol.com; $$-$$$). **The Buttonwood Inn** is a secluded 1820s Cape-style building with its own hiking and Nordic ski trails (hosts Claudia and Peter Needham, ☎ 356-2626 or 800-258-2625; e-mail button_w@moose.ncia.net; $$-$$$). **Cranmore Mt. Lodge** includes "lovable" farm animals, evening fireside piano, and theater presentations by innkeepers Dennis and Judy Helfand; there's a dormitory-style hostel also available (☎ 356-2044 or 800-356-3596; e-mail helfandd@nxi.com; $$-$$$). Or get a taste of Scotland with the clan names on the rooms, plus some Scottish cuisine, at the **Scottish Lion Inn & Restaurant** with chef/owners Michael and Janet Procopio (☎ 356-6381; $$-$$$).

Also in North Conway are the **Victorian Harvest Inn** (hosts Linda and Richard Dahlberg; ☎ 356-3548 or 800-642-0749; $$-$$$), the **Eastman Inn** (hosts Peter and Carol Watson; ☎ 356-6707 or 800-626-5855; $$-$$$), and the **Village Inn** (the Bliss Family; ☎ 356-3345, $$-$$$). To the west of town on the Saco River, on 65 acres of forest and pastures, is **The Farm By the River**, which has been owned by the same family for over

The White Mountains

200 years. It has its own cross-country skiing, fly-fishing, swimming, and horseback rides. Hosts are Charlene and Rick Davis. 255 West Side Road; ☎ 356-2694 or 888-414-8353, $$-$$$.

Nereledge Farm (hosts Valerie and Dave Halpin; ☎ 356-2831; www.nettx.com/nereledge.html; $$-$$$) is also west of town on the River Road but within walking distance of the village. The bed and breakfast home dates to 1787 and offers an English-style pub room with darts, as well as views of Cathedral Ledge, almost close enough to hike over for a rock climb or ice adventure. Walk to the river for swimming, canoeing, and fishing.

Stonehurst Manor, a turn-of-the-century mansion on 33 acres of pine forest, offers two- to five-day hiking tours. Amenities here include a library lounge and four dining rooms with gourmet menus. The inn has a history of "English country manor" style. PO Box 1937, Route 16, North Conway; ☎ 356-3113 or 800-525-9100; www.StonehurstManor.com; $$-$$$.

At the north end of North Conway, where the town actually becomes Intervale (although you'll barely notice the name change), are more inns: **The Forest** offers Victorian charm and has been a haven for travelers since 1890. The rooms are furnished with antiques, and there's a stone cottage with four-poster beds and fireplace (innkeepers Lisa and Bill Guppy; ☎ 356-9772 or 800-448-3534; $$-$$$). The **Wildflowers Inn** is a Victorian summer cottage with wonderful views and flowers everywhere (☎ 356-2224; $$).

You'll have to go out of town in the other direction for two more outstanding inns: one is the **Riverbend Inn**, a 14-acre colonial estate in Chocorua, south of the Conway area but close enough to get back to town for events and activities (hosts Noreen Bullock and Russ Stone, ☎ 323-7440 or 800-628-6944; $$-$$$). The other is located in Snoville, a tiny village south of Conway with a small swimming beach on a pristine lake. The **Snowvillage Inn**, high above the village, has views of Mt. Washington, its own cross-country ski and snowshoe trails and, in summer, award-winning gardens. All this is in addition to their gourmet food, candlelight dining, and hearty breakfasts. Hosts are Barbara and Kevin Flynn. The inn is six miles from Conway, in Snowville; ☎ 447-2818 or 800-447-4345; $$-$$$.

Glen

The Bernerhof is a small hotel with cuisine that gets featured regularly in magazines. They feature Middle European traditional delights like wiener schnitzel. In addition to award-winning chefs, the inn offers a cooking school. Send for details: The Bernerhof, PO Box 240, Route 302, Glen, NH 03838; ☎ 383-4414 or 800-548-8007; $$$-$$$$.

Bartlett

Attitash Bear Peak has condos at the foot of the slope and vacation packages that even include sleigh rides (☎ 800-223-SNOW). The resort offers a new slopeside luxury: The Grand Summit Hotel and Conference Center, with 143 rooms, health club, year-round heated outdoor pool and whirlpool, and more. It's available year-round for White Mountains enjoyment and is especially handy for summer and fall events at the Fields of Attitash (not to mention that water slide, which isn't just for kids!). And when you're there in winter, ski in and out right onto the slopes and trails. Route 302, Bartlett; ☎ 374-0869 or 888-554-1900; www.attitash.com; $$-$$$$).

Jackson

Skiing at **Black Mountain**? Ask about a ski-and-stay package that includes an inn, hotel, condominium, or bed-and-breakfast inn nearby (☎ 800-475-4669; e-mail ski@blackmt.com; www.blackmt.com; $$$). One of the favorites is **Whitneys'** at the foot of the slopes; this restored 1840s farmhouse includes a well recommended restaurant (☎ 383-8916 or 800-677-5737; $$$).

This is such a picture-perfect village that it's no surprise to find exquisite inns with superb dining here. The queen of the Jackson inns is **The Wentworth,** an elegant and award-winning resort hotel dedicated to the comfort of its guests. The architecture is lovely, the decor exquisite, the cuisine outstanding. The inn dates to 1869 as a luxurious vacationing experience and includes an 18-hole golf course as well as swimming pool, ice skating, 150 km of cross-country ski trails, and sleigh rides (Jackson Village; ☎ 383-9700 or 800-637-0013; e-mail wentwort@nxi.com; $$$-$$$$).

Escape to the different elegance of **Nestlenook Farm Resort**, a 65-acre estate offering horse-drawn carriage and sleigh rides as well as flower gardens, mountain views, and seasonal choice of either trout fishing or ice skating on Emerald Lake (☎ 383-0845; $$-$$$).

One of the most romantic inns in North America (according to the *Los Angeles Times*), the **Inn at Thorn Hill** offers Victorian decor and social rooms as well as luxuriously furnished lodgings in the main inn, plus a comfortable carriage house and a three lovely cottages. Don't miss the award-winning dining, with entrées like medallions of venison in a red wine-juniper berry sauce and parsnip pancakes. Innkeepers are Jim and Ibby Cooper. Thorn Hill Road, Jackson; ☎ 383-8062 or 800-289-8990; e-mail thornhll@ncia.net; www.innatthornhill.com; $$$-$$$$.

Other choices include **Paisley & Parsley,** a "retreat for self-renewal," where hosts Bea and Chuck Stone pamper guests (☎ 383-0859; $$-$$$); the **Inn at Jackson** (innkeeper Lori Tradewell; ☎ 383-4321 or 800-289-8600; $$); **Christmas Farm Inn** (hosts Sydna and Bill Zeliff; ☎ 383-4313 or 800-HI-ELVES; $$-$$$), which is a family resort; the **Carter Notch Inn** overlooking the Wildcat River Valley (innkeepers Jim and Linda Dunwell; ☎ 383-9630 or 800-794-9434; $$-$$$); and the **Village House**, with 100 years of traditional hospitality (innkeeper Robin Crocker; ☎ 383-6666 or 800-972-8343; $$-$$$). Looking for a lively mood of entertainment and games? Then try the **Wildcat Inn & Tavern** (chef/innkeepers Pam and Marty Sweeney, ☎ 383-4245 or 800-228-4245; $$-$$$).

Five minutes north of town on 300 acres is **The Dana Place**, a Colonial farmhouse retreat that's a well-appointed inn with a romantic country setting (☎ 383-6822 or 800-537-9276; $$$).

Pinkham Notch

The Appalachian Mountain Club offers the perfect base camp at Pinkham Notch: **Joe Dodge Lodge,** right next to the Visitor Center. There are small bunkrooms (up to five persons), and private rooms, plus fireside gathering rooms. Swap stories and information, meet new hiking and skiing partners, and enjoy breakfast and dinner. Reservations encouraged (☎ 466-2727; about $40 per person per night, with ups and downs for season and occupancy; lower prices for children).

Gorham & Shelburne

These are the lodging towns for visitors to Mt. Washington and the Presidentials. Shelburne, just east of Gorham on Route 2, offers the **Town & Country Motor Inn** (☎ 466-3315 or 800-325-4386; $$-$$$) plus some smaller inns: **Philbrook Farm Inn** with its simple country charm (☎ 466-3831; $$-$$$), and **Wildberry Inn**, a country bed and breakfast located at an Appalachian Trail crossing (☎ 466-5049; e-mail rec@moose.Ncia. net; $$). For a pub-and-parlor mood, try the **Inn at Shelburne** (innkeepers Mickey and Tina Doucette; ☎ 888-466-5969; $$-$$$).

In Gorham, there are comfortable lodgings at the **Libby House** at the east corner of the common (innkeepers Margaret and Paul Kuliga, ☎ 466-2271 or 800-453-0023; $$). Hikers have stayed at the Colonial Comfort Inn for so long that the Janicki family, which owns the inn, calls it the **Hikers Paradise** (370 Main Street, ☎ 466-2732 or 800-4224; $-$$).

There are also several motels: **Top of the Notch Motor Inn** (265 Main Street, ☎ 466-5496 or 800-228-5496; $$-$$$), **Royalty Inn** (130 Main Street, ☎ 466-3312 or 800-43-RELAX; $$-$$$); and **Gorham Motor Inn** (junction of Routes 2 and 16; ☎ 466-3381 or 800-445-0913; $$). The **Mt. Madison Motel** is also at Route 2 and 16 (☎ 466-3622 or 800-851-1136; $$).

Jefferson

Classic country inn relaxation with a touch of elegance is the hallmark of the **Jefferson Inn,** on Route 2. The gracious Victorian farmhouse is surrounded by spectacular mountain scenery; gourmet breakfasts are sumptuous. Ask for the Monticello room, with its turret and four-poster! Each room has more charm than the next... There's great swimming across the road with a beach and floating dock. Innkeepers are Marla Mason and Don Garretson; ☎ 586-7998; $$-$$$.

For a little less elegance but a friendly welcome, try the **Apple-brook Bed & Breakfast**, where there are 11 rooms plus dormitories and the fun of a hot tub under the stars (☎ 586-7713 or 800-545-6504; $$).

Franconia

This region offers elegant lodgings to guests; the problem is, picking which one suits you best. Consider the **Franconia Inn,** a "first-class, full-service, turn-of-the-century inn." Rooms are simple yet elegant, and the gracious front and back porches face sunrise and sunset over the nearby mountains. Elegant American cuisine complements the range of outdoor invitations, from ski trails that come to the door, bridle trails, hiking trails, and a small, tidy airfield just down the road. There are 35 guest rooms; ask for one with a fireplace. From Interstate 93, take Exit 38 and go south 2½ miles on Route 116. ☎ 823-5542 or 800-473-5299; closed March 30 to May 15; $$-$$$, depending on season and dining options).

The owners of the Franconia Inn also provide more casual lodging along the Gale River, two miles east of the village "crossroad" of Routes 116 and 18: **Hillwinds Lodge** is meant for family vacationing, and has its own steak-and-seafood restaurant (☎ 800-4-RELAXX; $$).

South of Franconia village on the Easton Valley Road (Route 116 south, 5½ miles) is the **Bungay Jar,** a whimsically furnished bed and breakfast with lovely garden walks and an enviable seclusion. Innkeepers are Kate Kerivan and Lee Steinbeck. (☎ 823-7775 or 800-421-0701; $$-$$$). Count on garden design workshops, English teas, and garden receptions.

If you take Route 116 north from the village, just past the interstate is the **Red Coach Inn**, with ample lodging, equipped with saunas, pool, restaurant, and support for business travel (☎ 800-262-2493; $$-$$$). Within two miles of the village center are the **Gale River Motel & Cottages** (☎ 823-5655 or 800-255-7989; $$); the **Inn at Forest Hills,** a romantic and historic 18-room Tudor manor house with its own walking trails (innkeepers Joanne and Gordon Hym; ☎ 823-9550 or 800-280-9550; e-mail InnFHills@ConnRiver.net; www.innfhills.com;

$$-$$$); **Stonybrook Motel & Lodge** (☎ 800-722-3552; $-$$);
and **Lovett's Inn,** which includes bungalows with fireplaces
and antique decor, right on cross-country or hiking trails
(☎ 823-7761 or 800-356-3802; $$-$$$). A little farther away is
the **Pinestead Farm Lodge**, serving vacationers since 1899
(hosts Bob and Kathleen Sherburn, Jr.; ☎ 823-8121; $). And if
you still can't decide, **Franconia Notch Vacations** (☎ 800-
247-5536) will find you a vacation home rental!

Sugar Hill

Route 18 west and then Route 117 take you up into Sugar Hill,
once a part of Franconia but now its own village. Here lodgings
follow a grand tradition of mountain resorts. For a luxurious
and well-tended vacation, indulge in a stay at **Sunset Hill
House**, where the views encompass both the Presidential
Range and the Kinsman Range, and history-laden trails ramble
beyond one of New Hampshire's oldest and most scenic golf
courses, disappearing into the woods. Hosts are the Coyle fam-
ily. (☎ 823-5522 or 800-786-4455; $$$-$$$$). More modest but
with a touch of the same appreciation for beauty are the **Sugar
Hill Inn**, with its romantic guest rooms and country cottage
rooms ($$$-$$$$ for two; ☎ 823-5621); the country inn called
Foxglove, located at Route 117 at Lovers Lane (☎ 823-8840);
and the comfortable, antique-filled atmosphere of the **Hilltop
Inn** (hosts Mike and Meri Hern; ☎ 823-5695 or 800-770-5695;
$$).

Along the Connecticut River Valley

Bethlehem's most elegant lodging is at the **Adair**, where in
summer and foliage season superb cuisine from the on-site
Tim-bir Alley restaurant complements the luxurious rooms.
Innkeepers are Patricia, Nancy, and Hardy Banfield (☎ 444-
2600 or 888-444-2600; $$$). Among the other choices are the
Grande Victorian Cottage, a bed and breakfast mansion in
the village (☎ 869-5755 and 401-333-6496; $$); the **Wayside
Inn** on the banks of the Ammonoosuc River, with a choice of ei-
ther country inn or motel lodging (☎ 800-448-9557; $-$$$); or
the 16 cottages of **Hearthside Village** (hosts Steve and
Rhonda Huggins; ☎ 444-1000; $-$$).

In neighboring Whitefield, after you've enjoyed a summer theatre performance at the Weathervane, you can snuggle into the North Country charm and elegance of either the **Inn at Whitefield** (next to the theater; ☎ 837-3049; $$-$$$) or the **Spalding Inn** just down the road, with cottages, golf course and putting green, tennis courts, and lawn bowling green (☎ 837-2572 or 800-368-VIEW; $$-$$$).

To the west of Bethlehem (or south of Whitefield) is Littleton, where the traditional lodging since 1843 has been **Thayer's Inn**, at the center of town on Main Street (☎ 444-6469; $-$$). More recent lodgings include the **Eastgate Motor Inn & Restaurant** (☎ 444-3971; $-$$) and the **Littleton Motel** (☎ 444-5780; $-$$), as well as the **Continental 93 Travellers Inn** at Exit 42 of Interstate 93 (☎ 444-5366 or 800-544-9366; $$).

Cozier options are the **Maple Leaf Motel** on West Main Street (☎ 444-5105; $-$$) and the **Beal House Inn** at the junction of Routes 18 and 10 (innkeepers Ted and Barbara Snell; ☎ 444-2661; e-mail NKRD98A@Prodigy.com; $$).

The **Rabbit Hill Inn** is actually across the town and state line from Littleton, in Lower Waterford, Vermont, but is worth a mention for its meticulous elegance and outstanding cuisine. From afternoon scones to profusely blooming gardens to candle-light dining, this inn adds luxurious touches to every aspect of lodging. Reserve well ahead (☎ 748-5168 or 800-76-BUNNY; $$$$).

■ Camping

Waterville Valley & Campton

 The White Mountain National Forest offers its **Campton Campground**, two miles east of Exit 28 of Interstate 93, on Mad River Road (Route 49). Open all year, with summer nature programs; 58 sites, each with picnic table, fire ring, tent pad, and parking. Reservations are encouraged in summer and fall (☎ 800-280-2267).

A second national forest site is the **Waterville Campground**, reached by taking Exit 28 from Interstate 93, then heading east on Route 49 for 10 miles to Tripoli Road. There are 27 wooded sites, each with picnic table, fire ring, tent pad, and parking (reservations, ☎ 800-280-2267; open all year). Or check out the **Pemi River Campground** (RFD1, Box 926, Campton, NH 03223; ☎ 726-7015; summer and fall), where kayak and tube rentals come with the river and swimming hole.

Woodstock & North Woodstock

Camp out with a view at the local KOA sites at **Broken Branch**, Box 6B, Woodstock, NH 03293; ☎ 745-8008 or 800-562-9736; $; open May 1 to October 15; or at **Lost River Valley Campground** on Route 112 in North Woodstock, which has a swimming beach, kayak and paddleboat rentals, and many recreation choices (☎ 745-8321 or 800-370-5678). The national forest offers back-to-basics with a wooded environment at **Wildwood Campground** off Route 112, about nine miles from North Woodstock and four miles before you reach Lost River Reservation. It has 26 sites with gravel pads, fire rings, and picnic tables. Closed in winter. No reservations; for information, ☎ 869-2626.

Kancamagus Highway

The national forest offers six campgrounds along the Kancamagus Highway that are great base locations for hikes and cross-country skiing. (Recall that there's no camping at all in the Pemigewasset Wilderness, but the rest of the nearby forest is open for primitive camping, provided you practice "no-trace" use.) Fees run $12 to $14 per night; a few sites can be reserved at the **Covered Bridge Campground** (☎ 800-280-CAMP), but all others are on a first-come, first-served basis. **Hancock** (56 sites, 35 trailer spaces) and **Big Rock** (28 campsites with fireplaces, trailer spaces) campgrounds are only five and seven miles east of Lincoln and are open year-round, with a swimming hole called Upper Lady's Bath just five minutes away. **Passaconaway** (33 sites, most suitable for RV's) is 15 miles west of Conway, and **Jigger Johnson** (75 sites, many suitable for RV's) is 12½ miles west of Conway; both have campground hosts at the sites and are closed in winter.

Closest to Conway are **Blackberry** (16 tent sites plus 20 suitable for RV's; historical site at campground) and **Covered Bridge** (49 tent and RV sites). Both have campground hosts. Blackberry is open all year (although you walk in during winter and spring), but Covered Bridge closes in winter. There are signs along the Kancamagus pointing out the sites. Good hiking and chances to watch wildlife are found around all six campgrounds. For more information, call the **Saco Ranger District Office** (the Conway end of the Kancamagus Highway) at ☎ 447-5448, or visit the Lincoln Woods Visitor Center, six miles west of Lincoln (no phone). There's also information at the White Mountain Attractions building just off Interstate 93 in Lincoln.

Bear Notch Road heads north from the Kancamagus to Bartlett. Near the Kancamagus end of this lovely route is **Wilderness Cabins** (Box 1289, Conway, NH 03818; ☎ 356-8899; $$; open year-round), which fits in well with the hiking mood.

Pinkham Notch

Toward the north end of the notch, five miles south of Gorham, is **Dolly Copp Campground**, a national forest facility open mid-May through mid-October with 177 sites and limited reservations (☎ 800-280-CAMP). This campground is a great base for hiking the Northern Presidentials as well as the Randolph trails.

Gorham & Shelburne

For camping, pick from the **White Birches Camping Park** two miles east of Gorham on Route 2 (family camping ranging from full hookups to wilderness; ☎ 466-3441) or **Moose Brook State Park** (RFD1, 30 Jimtown Road, Gorham, NH 03570; ☎ 466-3860), just around the corner from the village off Route 302 (good signs make it easy to find). Open late May through mid-October, weather permitting; two group camping areas, 40 tent sites, RVs welcome where they fit in; great swimming; reservations urged.

Jefferson

The **Israel River Campground** is reached from Route 115A, taking the marked turn onto "Old Route 115B." There are tables and fireplaces, water and electric at all sites, and a swimming pool; it's a family place, open May 1 to mid-October (☎ 586-7977).

Twin Mountain & Bretton Woods

This area also includes a trio of national forest campgrounds at Zealand (**Sugarloaf I**, 29 sites; **Sugarloaf II**, 32 sites; **Zealand**, 11 sites; ☎ 800-280-CAMP). **Beech Hill Campground** is on Route 302, two miles west of the junction with Route 3, and has 87 sites (☎ 846-5521). **Cherry Mountain KOA** is on Route 115 (☎ 846-5559 or 800-743-5819). Both are family campgrounds with swimming pools.

Franconia

In this area, try the **Franstead Family Campground** (☎ 823-5675), a casual place.

Along the Connecticut River Valley

A mile north of the center of Bethlehem is **Apple Hill Campground** (☎ 869-2238 or 800-284-2238; e-mail Apple.Hill@rr1. ConnRiver.net). **Mountain Lake Campground** (☎ 788-4500) is between Lancaster and Whitefield; **Crazy Horse Campground** (☎ 800-639-4107) is on the shore of Moore Lake outside Littleton; and there's **Littleton KOA** on the Ammonoosuc River (☎ 838-5525 or 800-779-5525).

Head farther south to East Haverhill on Route 25 to find the - **Oliverian Valley Wildlife Preserve and Campground** (☎ 989-3351), a 2,000-acre oasis with on-site mountain biking, hiking, and educational opportunities, including tours.

The White Mountains

Where To Eat

Woodstock & Lincoln

 There are many restaurants here, including the **Café Lafayette**, the dining car on the Hobo Railroad (Lincoln, ☎ 745-2135). The most elegant cuisine is surely found at the **Woodstock Inn** on Main Street in Woodstock (☎ 745-3951). The **Common Man** is a local favorite (at the Kancamagus Highway end of the town of Lincoln; ☎ 745-3463), with its very simple and fresh food prepared graciously. Only in summer, try **Govoni's Italian Restaurant** on the road to Lost River, Route 112 (☎ 745-8042). For more casual eating, the Chinese restaurant **Chieng Gardens** (☎ 745-8612) in Lincoln is good, and there's the adventure of a cookout on the summit of Loon Mountain in the summer (check schedules; the price includes the ride to the summit; ☎ 745-8111). Another summer treat is homemade ice cream at **Bishop's** in Lincoln.

Conway, North Conway, Intervale

You can nibble or dine from one end of this three-town segment to the other. So here are just a few highlights:

Just south of Conway village on Route 16 is the **Darby Field Inn** (☎ 447-2181), with a spectacular mountain view and creative country cuisine. Conway offers a casual taste of Maine seafood at **Jonathon's** (☎ 447-3838) on Route 16 across from the Reebok outlet. **Horsefeathers** (☎ 356-2687) in the center of North Conway village is the traditional place to relax, kick back, and enjoy pasta, sandwiches, and burgers.

Shalimar of India (☎ 356-0123 or 888-356-0123) is across from the train station in North Conway and offers vegetarian and non-vegetarian cuisine, including curries and vindaloos, with a specialty in Indian breads. On Seavey Street is **Bellini's** (☎ 356-7000), an energetic Italian restaurant with both southern and northern Italian cuisine and rich desserts.

Indulge yourself with dinner at **Stonehurst Manor** (☎ 356-3113), a mile north of North Conway village. There are great stone-oven pizzas, plus house specialties like grilled chicken with wood-roasted chicken sausage, or grilled vegetables and Asiago polenta.

Specialties of the **Scottish Lion Inn & Restaurant** (☎ 356-6381) just north of North Conway village include finnan haddie and Scottish Highland game pie, as well as traditional steak and seafood.

Be "in the know" for where local residents go when they slip out of town: to the **Oxford House Inn**, on Route 302 in Fryeburg (☎ 800-261-7206), eight miles to the east, to sample venison Hall, Maine lobster, scallops à l'orange, and champagne-poached salmon.

Bartlett

Familiar with the fun at the **Road Kill Café**? This isn't the only one in New England, but it's an adventure; we tell you no more but invite you to see for yourself on Route 302 (☎ 374-6116).

Attitash Bear Peak's Grand Summit Hotel now offers the **Alpine Garden Restaurant** (☎ 374-1900), with chef Brian Coffey's memorable cuisine (does grilled salmon with roasted red and yellow pepper purée give you a hint?).

Glen

Take the family for a fun breakfast at **Glen Junction** (junction of Routes 302 and 16; ☎ 383-9660) and check out the train at the same time.

Jackson

Relax at the **Red Fox Pub & Restaurant** (Route 16A, ☎ 383-6659) with steak and seafood or hearty sandwiches. On Sundays there's a jazz breakfast buffet.

Or savor romantic candlelight dining at the Inn at Thorn Hill, where brook trout and Atlantic salmon are treated with a delicate hand and perfect seasonings; the tournedos of beef are to die for (☎ 383-4242, reservations recommended).

The White Mountains

Find lunch at **As You Like It** (☎ 383-6425) in the center of the village, where handcrafted sandwiches and picnic lunches join cakes, cookies, and pastries.

And don't miss dinner at **Whitneys' Inn** (☎ 383-8916), at the foot of Black Mountain's slopes, where there's a tough choice between orchard stuffed chicken with cranberry, apple and raisin filling, or the inn's fettuccine laden with shrimp, mushrooms, spinach, garlic, and cream.

The long-time favorite in town remains **Wildcat Inn and Tavern** (☎ 383-4245), for flavorful seafood country gourmet dining.

Gorham

La Bottega Saladino at 152 Main Street (☎ 466-2520) offers fresh and delicious Italian specialties, and also has its own bakery. **Yokohama Restaurant** is a long-time favorite at 288 Main Street, with good Japanese food for hearty appetites (☎ 466-2501). For breakfast, a light lunch, or just a sweet snack, there's the **Loaf Around Bakery** on Exchange Street, just around the corner from Moriah Sports.

Twin Mountain

"Twin" is a place to recoup energy after hiking, with hearty barbecued ribs and chicken, ice cream, and pizza, at the **Big Red Store/Holy Cow Restaurant** on Route 302 just east of the junction of 302 and 3. Local residents acknowledge that dinner at **Paquette's Motor Inn** (☎ 846-5562) on Route 3, south of the junction, is reliably good. Also try **Munroe's Family Restaurant** next door on Route 3 (☎ 846-5547).

Bretton Woods

What could be more fun than riding the quad lift to the mountain top and dining with the valley and the White Mountains in front of you? That's the pleasure of **Top o' Quad** (☎ 278-5000) at Bretton Woods Resort on Route 302. There are lunches and sunset dinners through the summer; be sure to call ahead to check on which days and dates the meals are offered.

For an exquisite meal, call the **Mount Washington Hotel & Resort** and find out whether they have seating for non-staying guests that evening (☎ 278-1000); you'll enjoy the grand hotel ambiance as much as the fine cuisine.

Franconia & Sugar Hill

Count on the fine inns here to serve elegant dinners with innovative cuisine. The **Franconia Inn** (☎ 823-5542) offers an American and continental à la carte menu that changes often. **Lovett's Inn** (☎ 823-7761) provides five-course dinners likely to include novel and delicious combinations of herbs and fruits with the entrées. Do make reservations at both.

In Sugar Hill the seasonally changing menu at **Sunset Hill House** (☎ 823-5522) may include such distinctive appetizers as steamed mussels with Portuguese sausage, cherry peppers, and a cream sherry sauce; or grilled cod cakes served over sautéed calamari with a jalapeño and curry sauce. Wait until you see the entrées.

Just for fun, have breakfast at **Polly's Pancake Parlor** (☎ 823-5575) on the road between Sugar Hill and Laconia (Route 117). Pancakes are cooked to order; the walnut ones are especially good.

Along the Connecticut River Valley

Dining out at the **Inn at Whitefield** (☎ 837-2760) offers an entire evening of satisfaction: first a lovely meal, and then an hour or two in the adjacent lounge, listening on many Friday evenings to live music, often involving your hosts as jazz instrumentalists.

At the western edge of Bethlehem, **Tim-bir Alley** (at Adair, a fine inn) offers exquisite gourmet dining seasonally; call ahead to be sure it's open (☎ 444-6142). For less formal but still creative meals, **Lloyd Hills** at 311 Main Street is a good choice. At the other end of town, to the east, is **Rosa's Flamingo** (☎ 869-3111), where Rosa's flamingo wings (really chicken), pasta, and other hearty but casual suppers add to a bouncy atmosphere that includes live music on many weekends.

The White Mountains

Littleton offers a range of options starting with the tasty delicatessen offerings at **Porfido's** in the center of town. The **Littleton Diner** (145 Main Street, ☎ 444-3994) is a time-tested traditional spot for hearty breakfasts, quick lunches, or pie and coffee; so is the **Coffee Pot** (30 Main Street, ☎ 444-5722). Indulge in the ice cream at **Bishop's Homemade** on Cottage Street (the street that meets Main Street at the traffic light); the **Grand Depot Café** (☎ 444-5303) is also on Cottage Street and offers Continental cuisine with style.

Information Sources

Bethlehem Chamber of Commerce, Bethlehem, NH 03574; ☎ 869-2151.

Conway Village Chamber of Commerce, Conway, NH 03818; ☎ 447-2639.

Franconia/Easton/Sugar Hill Chamber of Commerce, Franconia, NH 03580; ☎ 823-5661 or 800-237-9007.

Lincoln-Woodstock Chamber of Commerce, PO Box 358, Kancamagus Scenic Byway, Lincoln, NH 03251; ☎ 745-6621 or 800-227-4191.

Littleton Chamber of Commerce, Littleton, NH 03561; ☎ 444-6561.

Plymouth Chamber of Commerce, PO Box 65, Plymouth, NH 03264; ☎ 536-1001 or 800-386-3678.

Mt. Washington Valley Chamber of Commerce, PO Box 2300, North Conway, NH 03860; ☎ 356-5701 or 356-3171.

Twin Mountain Chamber of Commerce, PO Box 194, Twin Mountain, NH 03595; ☎ 846-5520 or 800-245-TWIN for lodging referrals.

Waterville Valley Region Chamber of Commerce, Campton, NH 03223; ☎ 726-3804.

The Lakes

History & Geography

There are 273 lakes and ponds in New Hampshire's Lakes Region, so adventures range from swimming, boating, and diving to hiking the surrounding mountains for a view of the lakes, gliding on air over the sparkling waves, and skiing around and over the smooth hard ice of deep winter. Wildlife abounds, and not just underwater; there's some great moose habitat, the bogs are full of rare plants, and stands of old-growth timber that escaped the clearing axes of the early settlers wait silently in deep hollows.

Native Americans clearly camped in this region for fishing and hunting, and many of the place names reflect their presence. Winnipesaukee, the name of the largest lake in New Hampshire, has found two translations: "smile of the Great Spirit," and "beautiful water in a high place." Both are appropriate to this 72-square-mile lake with its hundreds of habitable islands (274 is the official count!) and its endlessly changing appearance, the blues and greens and dark threatening shadows that reflect the wind and skies.

In 1652 a surveying party from the Massachusetts Bay Colony claimed the region and marked its presence on a boulder still preserved at the west shore of Lake Winnipesaukee, at Endicott Rock Historical Site. Real development resulted later because the Royal Governor's nephew, John Wentworth, happened to own a large holding in today's town of Wolfeboro, at the south end of the lake. Wentworth began building a summer estate there in 1763, and by 1769 had completed a road to it all the way from Portsmouth, the center of business activity on the coast. Later he extended the road to Hanover on the west border of the state, where Dartmouth College had just been founded. Although Wentworth and his family fled the region at the beginning of the Revolutionary War in 1775, both a lake and town have been named Wentworth.

The Lakes Region

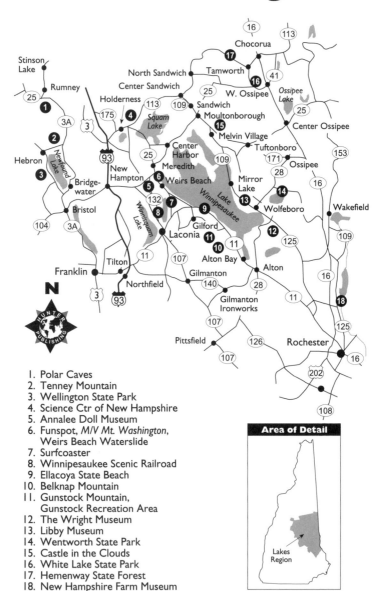

1. Polar Caves
2. Tenney Mountain
3. Wellington State Park
4. Science Ctr of New Hampshire
5. Annalee Doll Museum
6. Funspot, M/V Mt. Washington, Weirs Beach Waterslide
7. Surfcoaster
8. Winnipesaukee Scenic Railroad
9. Ellacoya State Beach
10. Belknap Mountain
11. Gunstock Mountain, Gunstock Recreation Area
12. The Wright Museum
13. Libby Museum
14. Wentworth State Park
15. Castle in the Clouds
16. White Lake State Park
17. Hemenway State Forest
18. New Hampshire Farm Museum

Area of Detail

Lakes Region

The resort towns around Lake Winnipesaukee developed quickly: Wolfeboro at the southeast, Alton and Alton Bay a little farther south, Weirs Beach (named for the Native American fishing weirs there) halfway up the west shore, and Meredith and Center Harbor to the north. Railroads brought visitors, and summer homes quickly surrounded the water. Steamboats plunged back and forth through the busy waterways. The most famous was the *Mount Washington,* a side-wheeler that caught fire and sank in December 1939 after 67 years of service. Even today, searching for her wreck and exploring nearly a dozen others provide high adventure under water. In the rush to make the most of the lakeshore, only a single large public beach was set aside, Ellacoya State Beach; but since those eager times of building and improving, a conservation ethic has taken hold of the region, and both islands and shore have now been set aside as preserves in generous portions.

Lake Winnipesaukee remains the centerpiece of the Lakes Region, but Squam Lake (where the movie *On Golden Pond* was filmed), Newfound Lake, and Ossipee Lake all have drawn their own communities. There are also smaller lakes to the northeast and along the Maine border, quieter and better suited to retreats where excellent inns and restaurants now thrive.

Getting Around

From the south, most first-time visitors enter the Lakes Region from **Interstate 93**, using Exit 20 to drive past first Silver Lake, then Winnisquam Lake, then Laconia, the bustling metropolis of the region. Take advantage of the way **Route 3** bends around the outside of Laconia to avoid the traffic congestion in town, and head directly toward Lake Winnipesaukee or beyond.

It makes sense to meet the towns and adventures of this region in connection with the lakes that tie them together, so here are the areas to explore: **Lake Winnipesaukee South & Lake Wentworth** (towns of Wolfeboro, Alton, and Gilford, including Ellacoya State Beach); **Lake Winnipesaukee North** (towns of

The Lakes

Weirs Beach, Meredith, and Center Harbor); **Mirror Lake & Moultonborough Bay** (Melvin Village and Moultonborough); **Squam Lakes** (Holderness, Sandwich, and Center Sandwich); **Newfound Lake & The Baker River Valley**; **Ossipee & The Northeast Lakes**; and **Along the Maine Border**.

Adventures

■ On Foot

Hiking around the Lakes Region is less strenuous than hiking in the White Mountains, and is an ideal way to start working up to the higher peaks. There's the added advantage that nearly every high hillside gives a great view of boats on a lake, or birds sailing the winds.

Lake Winnipesaukee South

Routes 3 and 11 together twist east around Laconia, then head north toward Weirs Beach. To explore the southern half of the lake first, watch for the turn onto Route 11A, marked Gilford and Gunstock (a state recreation and ski area). There's a scenic drive up Gunstock Mountain if you like, and an even better view if you climb Belknap Mountain. To find the trail for this 1½-mile round-trip with a lookout tower that views Lake Winnipesaukee, turn off Route 11A at Gilford and go right (south) through the village. You're in a residential area where the road makes a sharp left turn and then ascends a ridge, where it turns right and continues south under the mountain slopes. Signs may already be saying Belknap Mountain Road; this is the road you want, and about two miles from Gilford it forks to the left and heads into a steep valley. As it winds upward the paved surface changes to gravel and finally ends at a parking area. The trailhead is reached on foot by continuing up the road past a small garage. To the right is a service route called the Green Trail, marked with green blazes; skip it for now and look for the red blazes of the **Red Trail**, a few yards along the woods road on the right. The first vista is of **Mt. Kearsarge**; soon you'll see the fire lookout, with the summit directly beyond it. You get a direct view of Lake Winnipesaukee from here, and of the distant mountains beyond if the day is clear. For the return to the parking area, vary your route by picking green blazes instead.

Head back to Gilford and pick up Route 11A again. It will wind around the other side of Belknap Mountain, passing the Gunstock Recreation Area en route; if you'd like to look at maps of more trails up the mountain, stop at the recreation area. Otherwise, stay with Route 11A until it "Tees" into Route 11, which runs along the lakeshore here. A right turn takes you along a scenic stretch with parking areas to gaze out over Alton Bay. At 1.3 miles from where you pick up Route 11, on the right is the trailhead for **Mt. Major**. And you thought Belknap was great – here's another terrific place to view the lake, from the bare summit at 1,784 feet. That means a vertical rise of 1,000 feet from the trailhead, over the course of 1½ miles, so you're definitely going to get those lungs training for high peaks here. This is a flower-lover's trail in the first wooded section, with pink lady-slippers blooming in June; kids like the trail better in late July to early August for its blueberries (also found on Belknap). The trail is well marked with blue blazes, but if you like the reassurance of checking off turns and landmarks, take along David Doan's book, *50 Hikes in the White Mountains*. Doan warns that the ledges you'll scramble over should be taken cautiously; they don't require rock-climbing skills, but they can be slippery and worn. (Not a good rainy-day trail!) The lake and mountains view at the summit is worth the work, though. Descend by the same trail; there's no loop here.

Route 11 then takes you to Alton Bay and Alton, where a left onto Route 28 heads you into **Wolfeboro**. This is a good town for strolling with an ice cream or cup of coffee. A stop at the information booth in the old train station (visible from the main street) provides you with four brochures of **historic walking tours**, which will give you a good idea of how a 19th-century resort area developed.

Lake Winnipesaukee North

From the Laconia area, **Route 3** leads directly to the northern towns around Lake Winnipesaukee. Skip Weirs Beach for now (it's a classic "seaside" type resort town), and head up to Mere-

The Lakes

dith, where you turn right onto Route 25 to reach Center Harbor. Keep going another 1.7 miles northeast on Route 25 and note the blinker where Moultonborough Neck Road enters, but stay with Route 25 another 0.2 mile to the branch road on the left that was the old main highway. Take it, and after 0.1 mile go left again onto Red Hill Road. You are headed for Red Hill, a 3½-mile round-trip that will require about two hours, as it includes a vertical rise of 1,370 feet. When Red Hill Road turns to gravel at about two miles, watch for a farm on the left. Check mileage; at 0.2 miles past the farm is a parking area where the **Red Hill Trail** starts eastward up an old woods road with locked gate that keeps out cars but lets hikers through the turnstile. The first part of the trail is relaxing and woodsy, and eventually you pass a piped spring. There's still another uphill stretch, which comes out by a tower at the rocky summit. The tower should still be in climbable condition, although the top is closed; if you can reach the second landing you'll improve your view, but even on the ground it's a panoramic vista, southeast over Lake Winnipesaukee and around to the mountains to the Franconia, Sandwich, and Ossipee Ranges. Look for the rocky triangle of Mt. Chocorua to the north.

Stonedam Island Natural Area is a 112-acre portion of Lake Winnipesaukee's largest undeveloped island, and is just a stone's throw away from the Meredith shore. It's managed by the Lakes Region Conservation Trust and has pleasant walking trails. Access is by boat: on weekends via **Weirs Beach Boat Tours** (call the preserve at ☎ 279-3246 for fees and schedule), and also by private boats or rentals, allowed to dock at the 60-foot pier on the northeast side of the island. Nature programs especially designed for families are also offered on the island.

Mirror Lake & Moultonborough

On the back side of Lake Winnipesaukee, these small villages have hardly changed through the years. Preservation efforts have been mostly private and fortuitous, but in Tuftonboro there's a 60-acre **woodland preserve** donated by Sidney Butler Smith to the Society for the Preservation of New Hampshire Forests. If you'd like a quiet woodsy ramble there, from Wolfeboro take Route 109 north 4½ miles and turn left just past the Mirror Lake Chapel. Go 0.6 miles and turn right onto Windleblo Road. The preserve begins in 0.1 mile, and continues, mostly to the left of the road, for 0.6 mile more. Park at the woods road on the left just past the sign and walk in. The property is managed for forest products, wildlife, and watershed protection; look for signs of both change and preservation.

ABOUT PRESERVED LAND

Before the White Mountain National Forest had become a reality, New Hampshire residents were already taking steps to preserve wild and lovely landscapes and lakes. The **Society for the Protection of New Hampshire Forests** (the SPNHF, also called the Forest Society) helped secure the national forest in the early 1900s, but also began tending other parcels at the same time.

Today there are many preservation groups that accept responsibility for gifts of land or actively pursue ownership of very vulnerable spots. In addition to the SPNHF, the New Hampshire Audubon Society, the state of New Hampshire, and local groups like the Lakes Region Conservation Trust participate in the efforts, each with slightly varying goals.

The **Lakes Region Conservation Trust** offers a trail guide to its properties; contact the Trust at PO Box 1097, Meredith, NH 03253 (☎ 279-3246; e-mail lrct@ cyberportal.net). Maps to Audubon properties are available on site or by visiting the Audubon headquarters in Concord; the Audubon Society hesitates to send out large numbers of maps by mail, as it encourages gentle, limited use of its most vulnerable properties. Those well suited to public visits are described in this book.

For a lands map and guide to SPNHF properties (now over 100 of them), contact the SPNHF, 54 Portsmouth Street, Concord, NH 03301-5486 (☎ 224-9945); there is a fee. Better yet, visit their headquarters in person and catch up on recent efforts.

Another preserved area (200 acres) on the back side of the lake is the **Markus Wildlife Sanctuary**, cared for by the New

The Lakes

Hampshire Audubon Society. It's most easily reached from the north: Take Route 25 to Moultonborough and at the Moulton-borough Central School turn onto Blake Road; go one mile to the end and turn right onto Lees Mills Road. The sanctuary and the **Loon Center**, headquarters of the Audubon Society's Loon Preservation Committee, are on the left (open daily from 9 to 5, but Sundays are seasonal; confirm at ☎ 476-LOON). There are two well-marked trails, exploring the woods and 5,000 feet of undeveloped shoreline, with occasional rusted cans that are actually markers in honor of the original trail-blazing work.

> 🔥 **CAUTION:** *Beware of ticks in the high grasses here; be sure to wear socks and long pants.*

Squam Lakes

Looking for a gentle climb that will still give you a wide-area lake view? Here it is: **West Rattlesnake Mountain**. Don't worry about the name – there are probably no rattlesnakes this far north in New Hampshire! From Route 3 in Holderness take the right onto Route 113 and pass signs to Rockywold and Deephaven camps at five miles; after another half-mile there's a parking area on the left, which you can use for either this trail or the Mt. Morgan Trail. After you park, walk about 100 yards back along the highway to the **Old Bridle Path trailhead** on your left. The land is owned by the University of New Hampshire, and the Squam Lakes Association provides flyers about using it (e.g., no fires, no camping, no vehicles). The trail is wide and direct, and only near the top will you need to make a choice, opting for the arrow-marked trail to the left, not the unmarked one straight ahead. The summit view is famous, although the drop from the ledges in front of you is dangerous and should be treated with respect.

Across the road from the Old Bridle Path trailhead is the **Mt. Morgan Trail**, reached through an opening in a stone wall. Here's a more ambitious climb, for nearly six miles round-trip, approximately four hours of effort; you'll explore both **Mt. Morgan** and **Mt. Percival**. The Mt. Morgan Trail leaves northwest from the clearing and to the left of both the cellar hole and the rough logging trail. It follows an old road westward, and after 20 minutes turns right and begins to climb. When you reach the hairpin turn where the trail forks, more than a mile ahead, bear left for a ridge approach to Mt. Morgan, reaching a trail sign where you turn right onto the **Crawford-Ridgepole Trail**, which takes you along the base of a cliff. Stay to the left and climb to the summit (2,243 feet) for your reward.

From the summit of Mt. Morgan you can then take the Crawford-Ridgepole Trail to Mt. Percival by descending the short distance from the summit to the trail and turning left. Skip the old trail that branches right and follow the main trail's yellow blazes and arrow to the left. Your next summit is at 2,235 feet with a good south view of much more than just Lake Winnipesaukee. Make sure to look north, too, for the mountains. The trail down the mountain is southeast, down the ledges to the woods where there's a sign for the Mt. Percival Trail (you're leaving the yellow blazes now). There's a brief rough scramble over loose rocks, but the trail does ease, and returns you at last to Route 114; go west (right) half a mile to the parking area.

These trails are tended by the **Squam Lakes Association**, which protects more than 40 miles of trails north into the Squam Mountains. For a trail guide that lists them all, contact the Squam Lakes Association, PO Box 204, Holderness, NH 03245 (☎ 968-7336).

Newfound Lake & The Baker River Valley

Got your waterproof boots on? Actually, sneakers will do fine if you don't mind a little mud. The north shore of Newfound Lake has two lakesides for visitors to explore, one of which includes a stand of old-growth forest worth savoring. And in nearby Rumney there's a bog, with a few boardwalks added.

You might as well start with **Quincy Bog** in Rumney, as it is the most "tamed," then work your way south. From Route 25, take the right turn for Rumney Village and drive less than a mile to the village green, where you turn right onto Quincy road. Two miles takes you to stone pillars on the left marking the road you want; after 0.1 mile take another left to the bog entrance. Nature trails and a viewing deck let you see and get

The Lakes

closer to rare bog plants and ecosystems; visit in June for blossoms.

When you return to Route 25, go another mile north and turn left on Hall Brook Road for an impressive mountain-gap drive to the hamlet of North Groton, where a left onto the North Groton Road takes you gradually down to Groton. As soon as you enter the village, find the right turn for **Sculptured Rocks** and do some low-key climbing around the small river and the boulders; there's not much of a trail, but the rocks where the stream has cut through them are really interesting.

From Groton follow the signs (main road) to Hebron, and take the left turn along the north shore of Newfound Lake. Almost immediately on your right is the **Hebron Marsh Wildlife Sanctuary**; bring your field glasses. There are picnic tables where you can sit and watch the marsh for birds. When the naturalist is in residence, there's a small collection to see as well as tips on what and where to look for birds and amphibians in the refuge.

Sculptured Rocks at Groton.

Another mile along the north shore road brings you to another right turn, well-marked with state signage: **Paradise Point Nature Center**. If you're bringing kids or other restless folks, call ahead and find out when there's a nature program being offered (New Hampshire Audubon Society, ☎ 744-3516); the woods and trails by themselves are quiet and without explanations. But hidden here is a patch of old-growth spruce forest, as well as a lakeshore trail (caution: slippery ledges at the south point). The nature center includes hands-on exhibits, library, bird viewing, and naturalist activities.

Ossipee & The Northeast Lakes

There's a nice pair of trails at **Hemenway State Forest** in Tamworth, about eight miles from Ossipee. The forest is well-marked on Route 113A; trail brochures are left in boxes just up each trail. One is a **self-guided nature trail**, and the other a ramble to the **Great Hill** fire tower for a southward view. The **Big Pines Natural Area** includes 150-year-old conifers on a wild river, where the largest pine has a diameter of 42 inches. This is relaxed walking, a nice breather.

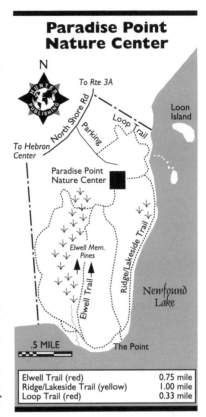

Paradise Point Nature Center

N

To Rte 3A

Loon Island

North Shore Rd

Parking

Loop Trail

To Hebron Center

Paradise Point Nature Center

Elwell Mem. Pines

Elwell Trail

Ridge/Lakeside Trail

Newfound Lake

.5 MILE

The Point

Elwell Trail (red)	0.75 mile
Ridge/Lakeside Trail (yellow)	1.00 mile
Loop Trail (red)	0.33 mile

Along the Maine Border

Here's another fire tower hike, only a mile long round trip but positioned for a view because **Blue Job** (pronounced Joh-b) **Mountain** is so much higher than the flat lakes country around it. Hike it when the day is clear for the most pleasure. From the town of Rochester take Route 202A west to Crown Point Road, which forks right as 202A bears left toward Center Strafford. On Crown Point Road, measure 5½ miles, passing through Strafford Corner and then past farms and woods. When you see the rounded top of Blue Job Mountain to the right, look for a farmhouse on the left, where there's parking in front of a locked gate that leads into a field of blueberries. Without signs, you need to look east from the gate to find the trail, which leads directly toward the hill. It goes into an oak woods, where a blueberry-picking trail heads to the left, and you stay right, walking up a slanting ledge until you see the trail to the top. Enjoy the tower and the view of the Belknap Mountains.

> **⊃ ROCKCLIMBERS TAKE NOTE:** *Rumney has some great rock outcrops to scramble up and over.* The Dartmouth Outing Guide, *available at the Dartmouth Bookstore on South Main Street in Hanover, gives the details that college students have been putting together about where the "bad" rock is and where safe routes have been located.*

If you drive into town – use Route 25 and turn north at the blinking light – make the left turn onto Buffalo Road by the white church and park half a mile down on the right. Now you can look the cliff over yourself; do get the book for details, though!

■ On Wheels

Road Biking

The gentle rolling terrain of the Lakes Region makes it ideal for road touring by bicycle. The handy guide *30 Bicycle Tours in New Hampshire* offers three routes to sample. The first is from **Wolfeboro** around the north shore of Lake Wentworth and out to the villages of Brookfield and Woodman, rounding the loop to Ossipee and back to Wolfeboro. This 38.4-mile loop uses Routes 28, then 109, then 153, then the Ballard Ridge/Brown Ridge Road, and back on Route 16 again. The second, which includes some challenging hilly terrain, is a 16.2-mile loop around the three villages of **Gilmanton Corner**, **Gilmanton Iron Works**, and **Lower Gilmanton**. It's fun to realize that these three little villages became the fictionalized setting for *Peyton Place*, the 1950s novel by Grace Metalious that suggested New England village life could be scandalous, rather than pastoral. The third trip is 23.2 miles long, starting in **Tamworth** and following the Swift River with Route 113A, passing through Wonalancet and North Sandwich and returning along Route 113 through South Tamworth and Whittier to the start.

But you can also determine to bike all the way around Lake Winnipesaukee (say, 35 miles), or to circle Newfound Lake, or to go all the way around Squam, or... you get the idea. There are general stores along each of the routes, although the loop around Squam has long stretches with only the woods and lakeshore for company.

Mountain Biking

Mountain bikers might as well head straight for **Belknap Mountain**, via the Gunstock Recreation Area (☎ 293-4341 or 800-GUNSTOCK; www.gunstock.com). The mountain bike center at Gunstock offers rentals, guided tours, repairs, and very reasonable day and season passes to the trails. Younger riders especially can have fun on the "Rad Rides." There are 18 trails for mountain bikers; four other trails are reserved for horseback traffic.

There's not a lot of mountain bike challenge otherwise in this region, except for the vibrations of a good rocky gravel road – try the back side of Belknap, as suggested in the *On Foot* section.

Support for both road and mountain biking comes from **Nordic Skier Sports**, located at the north end of Main Street in Wolfeboro (☎ 569-3151); rentals are available, as well as repairs and sales.

■ On Water

 Summers on the larger lakes are often filled with families who own or rent the same cottage year after year. Many area rentals include swimming access, dock space, and even boats on the property. If you do want to rent a boat from a local marina, you'll probably need reservations and, in the cases of motorboats, sometimes a considerable deposit. But there are lots of different options.

If this is your first time exploring the Lakes Region, or if you're looking for a relaxing day of it, consider a boat excursion trip. Not only will you see an entire lake (or half of Lake Winnipesaukee) at once, but you'll get lots of historical information and

The Lakes

some of the good stories about folks who've lived along the waterfront and on the islands. Squam Lakes tours will also include tidbits about the filming of *On Golden Pond*, the noted Katherine Hepburn movie set at the lake, as well as information about loons, the heavy fishing waterfowl whose rescue and rehabilitation as a state species have become important to so many people.

Lake Winnipesaukee South

In Wolfeboro, catch the *M/S* (motorship) *Mount Washington* for a lake cruise of over three hours, some 50 miles long. The ship is enormous, 230 feet long with space for 1,250 passengers (but rarely completely full). Check schedules, as they change seasonally (no winter cruises; ☎ 366-5531). You wait for the boat on the town dock (at PJ's Dockside Restaurant there are brochures and information), and buy tickets on board. Expect to pay about $15 per adult, a little less for children ages four to 12. There are also theme and dinner-dance cruises. Also boarded at the town dock is the *M/V Judge David Sewall*, which offers 1½-hour narrated cruises on a 65-foot vessel. ☎ 569-3016.

Lake Winnipesaukee.

Rent a smaller boat from one of the marinas: in Wolfeboro, **Goodhue and Hawkins Navy Yard** (☎ 569-2371), or **Wolfeboro Marina** (☎ 569-3200). In Alton Bay, there's **Castle Marine** (☎ 875-2777), and not far away is **West Alton Marina** (☎ 293-7788); farther north, into Gilford, are **Fay's Boat Yard** (☎ 293-8000) and **Smith Cover Marina** (☎ 293-2007). Fay's also rents canoes. On the quieter west side of the lake at Melvin Village is **KRB Marine** (☎ 544-3231).

Gadabout Golder offers guided fishing tours on Lake Winnipesaukee as well as on the Connecticut River. There are fly-fishing schools and individual lessons, too. Gadabout also offers non-fishing trips: canoe, nature, local history and New Hampshire folklore. Connect with Kurt "Gadabout" Golder at 79 Middleton Road (call ahead: ☎ 569-6426; e-mail cwg@worldpath. Net).

DIVING LAKE WINNIPESAUKEE

Why is it so important to have scuba gear and lessons at Winnipesaukee? Here's the fun part: There is missing wreck, the original *Mount Washington*, which was a wooden side-wheeler that burned during the off-season in 1939. There are easily a dozen other shipwrecks that make fascinating diving! Consider the *Lady of the Lake*, a steamboat in 30 feet of water in Smith Cove and an easy dive. Or the *Horseboat Barge*, 40 feet down by Bear Island. Three more wrecks are scattered on the east side of Ship Island. Other dives, not necessarily connected with wrecks, are Clark's Point where there's an underwater cliff, and Rum Point with its tremendous wall and rock formations and abundant marine life.

If you're staying in the Wolfeboro area and want to go swimming at a public beach, turn your back to Lake Winnipesaukee and skip over to Lake Wentworth, a mile up Route 109. Here's a state park open daily from mid-June to Labor Day, with swimming beach, play field, and picnic area; modest fee daily. Other options are smaller beaches offered by the local towns: Wolfeboro has Brewster Beach on Clark Road (off Route 28); Alton offers the Alton Town beach near the junction of Routes 28A and 11 with a small beach and swimming dock.

Outfitters

- **Winnipesaukee Kayak Company**, based in Wolfeboro, offers excursions on Squam, Wentworth, and Winnipesaukee lakes, as well as to the seacoast. Local rentals at the Wolfeboro store (☎ 569-9926) are at the Back Bay Marina. The variety of kayaks available is wide, and of course there's instruction too. The season is from mid-May to mid-October.

- **Sports & Marine Parafunalia** has two locations: in Gilford on Route 11B (look for the turnoff from the scenic shore road; ☎ 293-8998); the other is in Meredith. Open year-round, with kayak and paddleboat rentals, water-skis, wetsuits, tow tubes, and swimwear.

- For sailboards, kayaks, sailboats, pedal boats, and fishing boats, check with the **Winni Sailboarders' School and Outlet** at 687 Union Avenue in Laconia (☎ 528-4110).

- For water sports equipment like water-skis, wetsuits, inflatables, and even bathing suits and fishing gear, **Dive Winnipesaukee** at 4 North Main Street (☎ 569-8080) is the place to go. They offer lessons in water sports like water-skiing, snorkeling and windsurfing. Best of all, Dive Winnipesaukee is a scuba headquarters, with instructors and classes certified by the National Association of Scuba Diving Schools.

- For scuba and snorkeling equipment shop in Laconia: **Fathom Divers**, at 1002 Union Avenue, ☎ 528-4104.

- In Tilton, you'll find **Aquatic Adventure Center** at 24 Grange Rd., two miles east of Interstate 93 at Exit 20; ☎ 528-4901 or 800-728-2238; e-mail them at aquaticadventure@cyberportal.net.

Lake Winnipesaukee North

The *M/S Mount Washington* also makes port calls at Weirs Beach and Center Harbor, although not on the same route as the south lake cruise. Again, board at the town docks and purchase tickets on the ship; for schedules, ☎ 366-5531. The cruises are about 50 miles long, taking just over three hours each (round trip). The *M/S Mount Washington* is equipped with two levels of radar tracking, and sails in nearly any weather.

The *Doris E.* sails from Weirs Beach and Meredith. The 68-foot vessel gives cruises of one or two hours (☎ 366-5531).

For a different look at the lake, sail to the islands instead, on a US mailboat, the *Sophie C.* This 76-foot vessel leaves Weirs Beach daily to deliver mail to the islands (☎ 366-5531).

Or take a ride on a 46-foot sloop, the *Queen of Winnipesaukee*, which offers three cruises daily from Weirs Beach all summer. Ask about the special evening cruises, too (☎ 366-5531).

Marinas at Weirs Beach include **Anchor Marine** (☎ 366-4311) and **Thurston's Marina** (☎ 366-4811 or 800-834-4812). At Meredith there's **Meredith Marina** (☎ 279-7921), which also rents canoes.

If you're a paddler at heart, head for **Wild Meadow Canoes** (☎ 253-7536 or 800-427-7536) on Route 25 between Meredith and Center Harbor, where Tom and Sally Whalen have canoes, kayaks, and the paddles and accessories to go along with them. They also offer repair service.

Anglers take lake trout and salmon at Winnipesaukee; if you want to stay away from the summer boating activity and just set a hook, head for the **Moultonborough Bay** area of the lake. **Conway's Bait and Tackle** is a half-mile west of Center Harbor on Route 25 in Moultonborough; the shop offers bait and lures, as well as rowboat and canoe rentals by the hour or day or week, and kayak rentals by length.

In Meredith are two small sports shops catering to fishing, and you can pick up good maps of the lake; try **Waldron's Live**

The Lakes

Bait & Sport Shop for both bait and tackle as well as licenses (☎ 279-3152; e-mail waldroni@lr.net). Don't expect full and honest answers as to the best fishing spots, though – every angler has to keep some secrets!

Sports & Marine Parafunalia has one location in Meredith at the shopping center on Route 25 (☎ 279-8077) and another in Gilford. They are open year-round with kayak and paddleboat rentals as well as water-skis, wetsuits, tow tubes, and swimwear.

Looking for a swim? **Ellacoya State Beach** offers 600 feet of water frontage and is open daily from mid-June to Labor Day. There's a modest fee. Or take a quick cool-down at the **Surf Coaster** in Weirs Beach (see *Sightseeing*).

Squam Lakes

Now is a good time to realize that Squam consists of two lakes: Little Squam to the south of Route 3, and Big Squam to the north. You can just say "on Squam" and mean both!

There are two excursion boats that offer guided tours of this picturesque and largely undeveloped lake. The original **"Golden Pond" Tour** leaves from the Squam boat dock at the center of Holderness several times a day (call to confirm schedule, ☎ 279-4405). Half a mile south on Route 3 is Capt. Joe Nassar's **Squam Lakes Tours** on Golden Pond (☎ 968-7577; Capt. Joe Nassar, PO Box 185E, Holderness, NH 03245), which has a similar schedule at the same price ($10 for adults, $5 for children were recent rates) and uses a 32-foot canopy-topped pontoon boat. Capt. Nassar is also a fishing guide who offers half- and full-day trips and for the novice provides tackle, fish cleaning, and a photo of your catch!

For rentals of sailboats, sailboards, motorboats, and canoes, see the **Sailing Center** on Squam Lake (Holderness, ☎ 968-3654), which also offers instruction in sailing.

To explore the natural beauty and birdlife with trained naturalists and scientific equipment, take a cruise on one of the 28-foot pontoon boats provided by the **Science Center of New**

Hampshire. In July and August they offer frequent trips, and there are also foliage season outings. Advance reservations advised (☎ 968-7164; e-mail scnh@lr.net). You can even opt for a dawn or dusk or full moon trip!

Newfound Lake & Baker River Valley

There are seven daily cruises on the *M/V Moonlight Miss*, plus sunset cruises and breakfast or dinner packages; this can be a lot of fun! The boat leaves from the Pasquancy Inn Pier, halfway down the east shore of the lake. Private charters are also available (☎ 744-9254).

Ready to rent your own? Head to the north shore of the lake for **Newfound Lake Marina** for motorboats of all sizes (☎ 744-6307). If you're looking for a canoe or kayak instead, you'll find small boats at **Lone Wolf Canoe**, about two miles north of the lake on Route 3A (☎ 586-1885).

Wellington State Park is on the southwest side of the lake, on the West Shore Road. Here are excellent boat launch facilities, plus a half-mile-long beach on a peninsula that juts into the lake. Picnic under the pine trees. There's a modest fee (☎ 744-2197).

The **Baker River** makes a good run, with attractive riverbank scenery. There can be a lot of spring runoff at Warren, northwest of Rumney, where the first put-in is located. The bridge on Route 118 north of Warren is a good starting place. There are Class III rapids and a steep gradient in the first half-mile, but the river widens and the rapids ease up as you reach Warren. There's quick water through the rest of the six miles to Wentworth, where you take out above the old truss bridge to avoid the very turbulent Class IV drop. Then enjoy the 21 miles from Wentworth to Plymouth as a sort of rest: quick water turns to flat water and you have a leisurely float trip. Hazards are blowdowns and undercut banks; it's always good to scout first.

Ossipee & The Northeastern Lakes

Westward Shores Campground (PO Box 308, West Ossipee, NH 03890; ☎ 539-6445) has its own marina; stop by and ask about rentals, if the campers haven't got all the boats out on the lake. You may want to find a site yourself. There's also swimming, with 1,800 feet of frontage on Lake Ossipee.

In Tamworth, a resort town with a summer theater, **White Lake State Park** also offers a sandy beach for swimming, as well as trout fishing and hiking trails.

The lakes that chain through the area south from Tamworth, northeast of Winnipesaukee, invite paddlers to come and quietly explore. **Conway**, **Crystal**, **Hatch**, **Round**, and **Long** (the first two are lakes, the others ponds) all offer trout fishing, with brookies in the ponds. **Silver Lake** offers lake trout, too; **Ossipee** itself is brookies, as are **Shaw Pond** and **Trout Pond**.

A lovely spot for a swim is the small beach at the north shore of **Crystal Lake** in Eaton.

Along the Maine Border

If you're looking for an isolated lake with little development, the small ones along the Maine border offer pleasant canoeing, an informal swim, and good fishing.

■ With Llamas & On Horseback

Saddle up at **Gunstock Recreation Area** in Gilford, where five of the trails on Belknap Mountain are reserved for horseback traffic during the warm months. Ask about rates for trail rides, and times available (☎ 293-4341 or 800-GUNSTOCK; e-mail them at gunstock@gunstock.com; www.gunstock.com).

Castle in the Clouds on Route 171 in Moultonborough (see *Sightseeing*) also offers trail rides, on miles of trails. Open daily from mid-June to Labor Day and on May weekends. Reservations must be made in advance for horses; ☎ 476-2352.

At the northeastern end of Squam Lake is the village of Center Sandwich (see *Sightseeing*). Here Ken and Betty Alcock offer **Country Carriage Service**, with their own Belgian draft horses. Wedding carriage service, horse-drawn wagons, and special moments for photographers are among their specialties (277 Little Pond Road, Center Sandwich, NH 03227; ☎ 284-6210).

A trek with a llama is the perfect way to slow down and enjoy the day: **Llongneck Llamas** in Northfield can set up leisurely hikes for you, as well as farm tours, and educational tours – even birthday parties, with the soft-eyed, gentle beasts taking part! Use Exit 20 from Interstate 93 and take Route 3 to the right turn on Route 140; go right again on Shaker Road and turn left at the fork. Llongneck Llamas is at 321 Shaker Road; ☎ 286-7948. Call ahead for schedules and fees, mid-May to mid-October. You'll enjoy your chat with owner Carolyn Boeckman.

Snowvillage Inn also offers occasional llama treks; see *Where to Stay*.

■ On Snow & Ice

 Let's face it, the Lakes Region shuts down after Labor Day. Shops close their doors, lodging is hard to come by, and restaurants have short hours. The mountains aren't rugged enough for dramatic skiing, and Nordic is just barely catching on.

The silver lining of the cloud is that you won't be crowded on snow and ice in the Lakes Region. There are two alpine ski areas: Gunstock at the county-managed recreation area in Gilford, and Tenney Mountain north of Newfound Lake. A third, **King Pine** in East Madison (☎ 800-367-8897), is so small that it serves mostly as family entertainment for guests staying at Purity Spring Resort (see *Where To Stay*), but could be used a beginner slope (16 mostly gentle trails, as well as a snowboard park; 25 km of groomed cross-country trails adjacent; night skiing).

Tenney Mountain on Route 3A between Plymouth and Newfound Lake promotes affordable family skiing on a respectable but little-known mountain with a vertical drop of 1,400 feet. There are just four lifts, and 29 trails, with 90% snowmaking coverage. The ski area is entirely focused on the sports of skiing and snowboarding (lift-serviced halfpipe, park, slopes) so that there are no distractions, and prices are genuinely low (recent rates were adults $9 on weekends; weekdays $15 for all, an incredible bargain). Call for snow conditions and updated rates (☎ 888-TENNEY2).There's also slopeside lodging and a full-service ski and snowboard shop.

Gunstock (☎ 293-4341; ski conditions 800-486-7862; e-mail gunstock@lr.net; www.gunstock.com) offers both downhill and cross-country options. It's not hard to reach; take Route 11A between the Laconia area and Lake Winnipesaukee. A special treat is night skiing, offered Tuesday through Saturday from 4 to 10 pm (daily during holiday periods) on 15 trails with five lifts. Day skiing involves 45 trails, seven lifts, and lift tickets for about $40 on weekends, $30 on weekdays. The Nordic area has over 50 km of trails and a reputation for grooming excellence. There are rentals, lessons, track set and skating trails, telemark and back-country tours, and even candlelight events.

There's more cross-country energy at Wolfeboro, where **Nordic Skier Sports** at the north end of Main Street (☎ 569-3151) offers trail passes to the **X-C Ski Center of Wolfeboro**. Expect miles of trekking on old woods roads and on six well-frozen, snowcapped lakes and ponds, or take the 20 km of groomed trails, sorted as challenging in town, and family-oriented on the Lakeview segment. Much of the territory crossed is privately owned, so do respect the generous privilege of using the trails. The center also offers telemark lessons, as well as group and private cross-country ones.

One last twist on snow activities: Some years the weather has been perfect for world championship **sled dog races** in Laconia; check with the town's Chamber of Commerce for potential dates (☎ 524-5531 or 800-531-2347).

■ In The Air

 The **Moultonborough Airport** is at the intersection of Routes 171 and 25. Here you can find scenic flights for as little as $10 (☎ 476-8801). Better yet, try tandem skydiving at the **Winnipesaukee Skydiving Center** (☎ 569-2467). This is a nifty way to get a fledgling skydiver safely into the air after a half-hour lesson. The fee is $175 to $195 (weekends), including all equipment; for an additional fee, you can have your jump videotaped!

Ready to try parasailing? It's hard to say whether this is really a water sport or an air one – you're going to fly high, but as you land you might get wet! With an inflated parachute overhead, you rise on a tether behind a boat, lifting up to get a one-person flight over Lake Winnipesaukee. **Weirs Parasail** provides you with a moving raft system that's supposed to keep you dry as you settle back onto the lake at the end of your flight. It's a unique view of the lake and mountains! Reservations needed; ☎ 366-7723. Weirs Parasail is in the yellow building a quarter-mile west of Weirs Beach, next to the Mt. Washington cruise boat.

Sightseeing

Lake Winnipesaukee South

If you're a hiker, mountain biker, or skier or snowshoe tramper, you've already scoped out **Gunstock Recreation Area** in Gilford for your outdoor activities. But Gunstock, on Route 11A between Gilford village and Lake Winnipesaukee, is also the site of annual events like the **New Hampshire Crafts Festival** (first weekend of July), a **circus**, a **brewfest**, a **country jamboree**, an **Oktoberfest**, and winter treats like **skiing treasure hunts** and **full moon tours**. Contact the county-managed recreation area (☎ 293-4341 or 800-GUNSTOCK; e-mail gunstock@gunstock.com; www.gunstock.com).

On the other side of Belknap Mountain, in the village of Gilford, are two major musical festivals: the **New Hampshire Music Festival** draws brilliant young conductors and extraordinary musicians to its summer weekend performances and Tuesday chamber music series; check this year's schedule and specific locations (New Hampshire Music Festival, 88 Belknap Road, Gilford, NH 03246; ☎ 524-1000). **Meadowbrook Farm Musical Arts Center** has brought such stars as Ray Charles, Tom Jones, and Mary Chapin Carpenter; the center was building a

The Lakes

new facility recently, so confirm directions as well as schedule (☎ 528-5550 or 800-5MEADOW).

Wolfeboro is a classic lakeside summer town, not yet overgrown. It calls itself "America's oldest summer resort," and has a merry yet comfortable air. You can stroll the village with an ice cream in hand, gaze over Lake Winnipesaukee, ride a lake excursion boat (see *On Water*), and walk down Mill Street and Bay Street to the "Back Bay" where there's quieter boating. If you drive up from the Alton area on Route 28, you enter Wolfeboro on a small ridge where historic buildings still stand, including the **Clark House Museum Complex** offered by the Wolfeboro Historical Society at 337 South Main Street. These three historic buildings are authentically furnished: a 1778 home, an 1862 firehouse, and an 1805 one-room schoolhouse, which also houses genealogical reference materials. The museum is open July 5 to Labor Day (☎ 569-4997; may close on Sundays). A special twist for the kids: check out the hands-on 19th-century cooking experience offered at the **Farm at Frost Center** by Virginia Taylor (44 Stoddard Rd., ☎ 569-1773). Be sure to call ahead for available dates, hours, and directions.

A second museum, the **Wright Museum** (☎ 569-1212, open daily in summer and fall and some other weekends or by appointment), is outside the village on Routes 109 and 28, but you can walk there from the Chamber of Commerce (in the old train station) on a 200-yard footpath. The Wright Museum showcases the American homefront during World War II (don't miss the tanks, jeeps, command cars, and half tracks, too!).

A third museum in town displays Abenaki Indian relics, artifacts from the Governor Wentworth mansion (remains on Lake Wentworth nearby), and animal specimens: it's the **Libby Museum**, on North Main Street, open daily (except Mondays) all summer with a small fee (no phone). There are also free tours of a small handcraft studio in the village: the **Hampshire Pewter Company** at 43 Mill Street (☎ 569-4944, weekdays in summer and fall and by appointment in winter).

Pick up free **walking tour** brochures or check on summer events at the **Wolfeboro Chamber of Commerce** in the old train station (PO Box 547, Wolfeboro, NH 03894; ☎ 569-2200 or 800-516-5324). Music plays an especially big role here, with the **Great Waters Music Festival** and the **Lake Winnipesaukee Music Festival** nearby. Finally, to tour the town in style, take a 45-minute guided **trolley ride**, leaving the docks hourly on July and August days (☎ 569-5257 or 800-339-5257; small fee); the trolley will also take you to restaurants and professional summer theaters in Meredith and Tamworth.

Some of the towns south of Wolfeboro have summer events worth noting, too. For example, Laconia hosts a **motorcycle rally and race week** in early June that draws over 200,000 motorcyclists; call ☎ 366-2000 for a schedule of events (Laconia Motorcycle Week, PO Box 5399, Laconia, NH 03247). Or tour the farming country and stop in Pittsfield to see the miniature horses at the very small **White's Petting Farm** (Route 28 between Pittsfield and Epsom, turn on the Webster Mills Road; watch for signs; ☎ 435-8258). At nearby Bow Lake Village in late summer you can pick your own blueberries at **Berrybogg Farm** (call for directions and picking conditions, ☎ 664-2100), taking with you a true taste of New Hampshire.

One more adventure south of Wolfeboro deserves mention, although some people may have strong feelings about it: there's **greyhound racing** at Lakes Region Greyhound Park in Belmont on Route 106, six miles south of Laconia. Races are held from May to September at 7 pm; call for schedules (☎ 267-7778).

Lake Winnipesaukee North

Weirs Beach entertains water lovers and playful people with wild fun on two different water slides, on go-karts, and at a 500-game arcade. It's light-hearted fun that can last all day and evening. The **Surf Coaster Family Water Park** (☎ 366-4991) is on Route 3 and open daily from mid-June to Labor Day, with wave pool, kiddie slides, water slides, and action lagoon. **Weirs Beach Water Slide** (☎ 366-5161) varies the offerings with a pipeline express flume and an acceleration tube. It's a quarter-mile north of the Surf Coaster, and has a similar schedule.

The Lakes

Daytona Fun Park (☎ 366-5461; daily in summer to 11 pm and weekends in spring and fall), in between the two water slide parks, has go-karts, batting cages, miniature golf, and an arcade. And the big arcade is at the **Funspot**, on Route 3, a bit north of the other attractions. There's no admission charge, but come prepared to feed the slots of over 500 games, including videos, pinballs, and kiddie bumper cars. Bowling and miniature golf are on hand, too. You can even reserve for parties there (☎ 366-4377).

Weirs also has a new museum, the **New Hampshire Antique & Classic Boat Museum** on Route 11B at the Weirs Bridge in the Dexter Shoe complex. The collection is the work of avid boat enthusiasts and offers a look at the lake traffic over the past century (☎ 524-8989; open daily, summers).

Meredith has an active **historical society** with two museum sites, one in town at the corner of Main and Highland Streets and the other at a farm on Winona Road. Museum hours change by year and season, so call ahead (☎ 279-1190). To have your own **walking tour** of this always active town with its many 19th-century buildings, pick up the historic walking tour brochure at the information booth across the road from the town docks at the waterfront. Here you can also check on events like the annual art fair at the **Old Print Barn** (☎ 279-6479) in July, or the **fine arts and crafts festival** in late August (Chamber of Commerce: ☎ 279-6121). Savor the professional **Lakes Region Summer Theatre** on Route 25 northeast of town (☎ 279-9933).

Meredith is also home to the **Winnipesaukee Scenic Railroad**: catch a caboose ride, or ride the train on Wednesday or Saturday evening for dinner in July and August, catered by Hart's Turkey Farm Restaurant (reservations required: ☎ 279-5253 in summer and fall; 745-2135 year-round). Look for the ice cream parlor car on hot summer days! There's also fine dining on the Indian Waters dining car for the **Café Lafayette Dinner Train** (☎ 745-3500 for reservations). Ask about the fall foliage specials and the Christmas season Santa trains, too. Fares start from $6.50 per adult.

A treat for the young at heart is the **Zeeum**, a children's museum and toy shop at 28 Land Street (across from the town docks; take Lake Street to the first left, Lang; the Zeeum is on the left; ☎ 279-1007, open all year). It's a discovery museum and creative play center with hands-on exhibits. The town's other noted museum, the **Annalee Doll Museum**, is south of the village: take Route 3 to the right on Route 104 (well marked) and another right on Hemlock Drive. This museum is part of a "factory in the woods," where Annalee Thorndike creates dolls celebrating New England village and outdoor life, open daily from Memorial Day to the end of October. A playground, nature trail, and antique car display are also at the site.

Center Harbor is a smaller, more prosaic looking village at the top of the lake, and is a port for the excursion boats (see *On Water*). Best known of its shops is **Keepsake Quilting** (☎ 253-6618) in Senter's Marketplace on Route 25B, which even issues its own magazine of fabrics and patterns. The shop also has a large selection of knitting yarns. While you're in town, slip over to the **Bayswater Book Co.** (Main Street and Route 25, ☎ 253-8858) for a browse and a good cup of coffee.

Mirror Lake & Moultonborough

You'll have to leave the lakeshore for this one, but it's a scenic drive, and where else will you find a castle? Take Route 28 from Wolfeboro or Route 25 from Center Harbor to get to Route 171. **Castle in the Clouds** (☎ 476-2352) is just south of Moultonborough village; you drive up a long woodsy road to the top of the ridge and tour an eccentric millionaire's mansion. The grounds offer miles of hiking and horseback trails (reservations required for horses in advance), as well as a tour of the Castle Springs bottling plant and spring site, where one of the state's cool refreshers is collected. Admission with castle tour is about $10 (there are discounts), and less for just roaming the grounds. Looking out over the castle walls is a treat; so is exploring the lush residence, and there's a snack bar when you're ready to munch.

The Lakes

Squam Lakes

Touring the water on this relatively undeveloped lake with its many coves and islands is a treat (see *On Water*). When you want to try an activity on land, head for the **Science Center of New Hampshire**. From Route 25 just west of the town docks, take Route 113 north for 0.1 mile to the Science Center sign on the left. It's open daily from 9:30 to 4:30 in July and August, in September and October the weekend hours become just afternoons (☎ 968-7164; rates vary by season but top out around $5). Enjoy natural adventures like building a bat house or tracking wildlife; explore outdoor exhibits; tramp 200 acres of wildlife sanctuary on trails with informative notes alongside; and get close to a black bear, a deer, and a bald eagle in natural enclosures. Don't miss the trail talks and live animal presentations. Bring a picnic so you can stay all day.

The Squam Lakes Association exerts tremendous effort to keep Squam in a relatively natural state. The groups puts out a trail guide (see *On Foot*), and there are plans for a year-round headquarters with exhibits. Check for news at the shops in town and the village visitor center on Route 3, or stay in touch directly: **Squam Lakes Association**, PO Box 204, Holderness, NH 03245 (☎ 968-7336).

At the opposite end of Squam is the village of Center Sandwich, where 18th- and 19th-century buildings gather around a green common, and craftworkers and artisans find resources and inspiration. The **Corner House Inn** provides crafts (as well as lunch), and the historical society opens the **Elisha Marston House** from June through September (Tuesdays to Saturdays, and the first Sunday of each month; ☎ 284-6269). **Sandwich Home Industries**, the founding member of the League of NH Craftsmen, is on the green and offers a fascinating shop from mid-May to mid-October (☎ 284-6831).

Just west of Holderness is the busy town of Ashland, where you can take the kids to **Yogi Bear's Jellystone Park** for the daily activities involving Yogi, Cindy, and Boo Boo Bear. The easiest approach is from Exit 23 of Interstate 93; go east on Route 104 for 500 yards, then north (left) on Route 132 for four miles. The park is open from mid-June to Labor Day (☎ 968-9000).

Newfound Lake & Baker River Valley

At the south end of Newfound Lake, Route 3A meets the West Shore Road on the left. To reach the town of **Alexandria**, go two miles up the West Shore Road and take another left onto a road with various names but well marked for Alexandria. Small Appalachian Mountain Club signs lead you for eight miles to **Cardigan Lodge**, a rustic mountain inn owned by the AMC at the foot of Mt. Cardigan. Hiking and lodging facilities here are listed in *Where To Stay* for the Dartmouth and Lake Sunapee Region.

North of Newfound Lake is the Baker River Valley, where **Rumney** has many attractive sites to visit. Just before you get to Rumney on Route 25 is **Polar Caves**, where trails wind among glacial caves and passages that are cool year-round. The park charges an entry fee (check this year's rate at ☎ 536-1888 or 800-273-1886), and includes a herd of fallow deer to feed, as well as a flock of ducks, plus a gift shop, maple sugar museum, and mineral display.

Reach Rumney from the well-marked turn on Route 25, at the blinking light. It's a mile north to the village, with stunning flower gardens on the left, and a swimming hole to visit by the Baker River. At the village green you can turn right to visit the **Quincy Bog** (see *On Foot*), passing on the way a huge boulder on the right that nearly chokes off the road. Park here and cross the road to see an unusual old **town pound** (that's right, for stray animals) made of massive rocks.

If when you reach the village green you go straight ahead on Stinson Lake Road, the road starts uphill and the **Mary Baker Eddy House** is on your right, with parking across the street. It's open from May 1 to the end of October (closed Mondays; ☎ 786-9943) to give you a look into the amazing 19th-century life of the woman who founded the Church of Christ Scientist, better known as the Christian Science movement. There's a token admission and a small gift shop. It takes about 20 minutes to tour the house, and you can add another 45 minutes to go visit Mary Baker Eddy's later home in North Groton, six miles away. For a spectacularly scenic drive, continue up Stinson

The Lakes

Lake Road over the mountain (this is a summer-only route) and explore the lake.

It's handy to know about the **state rest area** in Rumney, another two miles up Route 25; from Memorial Day to Columbus Day it's open with restrooms, information, and a pleasant nature trail by the river.

Ossipee & The Northeastern Lakes

Drive beyond Ossipee to the village of **Tamworth** and sample the summer offerings of New Hampshire's oldest professional summer theater group, the **Barnstormers**. There's an Equity cast to stage plays through July and August; contact the Barnstormers for the season's schedule (PO Box 434, Tamworth, NH 03886; ☎ 323-8500 after July 1; www.theatre.com/bst.html). President Grover Cleveland's son Francis founded the theater in 1930. There's a brook nearby for swimming, and a good general store. **White Lake State Park** is on Route 16, worth a visit with its National Landmark stand of pitch pines and its lovely swimming beach. Rent a canoe or explore the hiking trails. Pay special attention to the 72-acre grove of pitch pines; without fire they can't reproduce, a quandary for those who want to "save" them. What would you do?

Along The Maine Border

To reach the town of Wakefield from Wolfeboro, take Route 25 to meet Route 109 as it curves around Lake Wentworth. Turn right on Route 109 (headed southeast) and go 10 miles to Route 16 north; take the right turn onto Route 153 (by Palmer's Motel) to enter the village. Bear right to find the **Museum of Childhood** (2784 Wakefield Rd., ☎ 522-8073). Savor an international collection of more than 3,000 dolls, 43 doll houses, puppets, trains, sleds, teddy bears, an 1890 child's room, and more. Collectors Marjorie G. Banks and Elizabeth B. MacRury are retired school administrators who say they're ready to pass the museum into fresh hands; you might want to volunteer once you've browsed through it! They'll also send you out into Wakefield to visit the town pound where stray animals were kept in the 1800s, the 1876 hay scales, a railroad turntable, and the stonework of the Newichawannock Canal. Museum hours are Monday and Wednesday through Saturday 11 to 4; Sunday 1-4 throughout the summer and foliage season (but call for special visits); adults enter for $3, children for less.

Farther south, in the border town of Milton, there's another museum to visit with the family (or indulge in by yourself): the **New Hampshire Farm Museum**, just north of the village center on Route 125. Open daily from mid-May to mid-October, the museum sets on two adjoining farms and offers a self-guided tour of the 100-foot Jones Great Barn, as well as the 1890s Plummer Homestead with its gardens, orchard, oxen, cow, sheep, pigs, geese, and chickens. There are major weekend events all summer, and these are the real gems to go for: planting week, llamas, children on the farm, spinners and weavers, forestry and logging, and taste treats like a soup tasting and a pig roast. Take your chances, or get the calendar for the season (New Hampshire Farm Museum, PO Box 644, Milton, NH 03851-0644; ☎ 652-7840).

New Hampshire Farm Museum, Milton.

The Lakes

ANTIQUING AROUND LAKE WINNIPESAUKEE

Meredith is an acknowledged center for antique shopping in the Lakes Region, with half a dozen shops in the village. Wolfeboro also has its share. For a day of delights, start in Meredith and drive around the far side of the lake, stopping in small villages, until you reach Wolfeboro. Look for:

- Center Harbor: **June's Junqtiques** (Fiesta ware, glass, china), ☎ 253-7794.

- Moultonboro: **Antiques at Moultonboro** (early 19th-century furniture, glass, pottery), ☎ 467-8863.

- Melvin Village (summers): **Colby's Collectibles** (watch for the moose), ☎ 544-3441; and **Dorian Antiques**, ☎ 544-8441.

- Center Tuftonboro: **The Ewings**, ☎ 569-3861 (furniture, folk art, textiles), and (summers) **Golden Past Antiques**, ☎ 569-4249 (group shop). **Log Cabin Antiques**, ☎ 569-1909 (general, plus postcards and buttons).

- Center Ossipee: **Grant Hill Antiques**, ☎ 539-2431 ("from the sublime to the ridiculous"); **John's Records**, ☎ 539-3708; in summer, **Kelley Wingate Shop**, ☎ 539-6047 (jewelry, glass, linens, vintage clothing, hats); and **Rita Nevins**, ☎ 539-4257 or 8260 (glass, china, Wedgewood, Majolica, more).

- Ossipee: **Gary R. Wallace Auction Gallery**, ☎ 539-5276; **Lakewood Station Antiques**, ☎ 539-7414; **Little Barn Antiques**, ☎ 539-2643 (including baseball cards and cut glass and old bottles); **Treasure Hunt**, ☎ 539-7877 (multi-dealer shop); and (summers) **The Stuff Shop**, ☎ 539-7715 (clocks).

Plan also for three regional shows: the **Wolfeboro Antiques fair** (last weekend of July, ☎ 539-1900), **NE Antiques and Collectibles Festival** in Center Sandwich at the fairgrounds (first weekend of August, ☎ 539-1900), and the **Altrusa Antiques Show and Sale** in mid-September in Meredith (☎ 279-6121).

Where To Stay

Lake Winnipesaukee South

Gilford

 Gilford offers a range of lodging. The **Misty Harbor Resort** on Route 11B (☎ 293-4500 or 800-33MISTY; $$) is open year-round and offers special winter packages that include skiing and sleigh rides. Camping in tents, RVs or cabins is available at **Gunstock Recreation Area** on Belknap Mountain (Route 11A; Gilford; ☎ 800-GUNSTOCK, ext. 191; www.gunstock.com). Within walking distance of a private beach and three marinas is **B-Mae's Resort Inn & Suites** on the Harris Shore Road at the junction of Routes 11 and 11B It's open from Memorial Day through mid-October. (☎ 293-7526 or 800-458-3877; $$-$$$.)

Wolfeboro

The **Wolfeboro Inn** is open year-round with a range of rooms from 1812 chambers with fireplaces to modern elegant country-style rooms and suites (44 North Main Street, ☎ 596-3016 or 800-451-2389; $$$-$$$$); it's just north of the shops of the village. The **Lakeview Inn** is also on North Main Street (200 North Main Street, ☎ 569-1335; $$) and includes a motor lodge. South of the shops on the ridge is the **Windrifter Resort**, also open year-round, specializing in week-long rentals and time shares. It sits next to the golf course and has its own pool and tennis court (South Main Street, ☎ 569-1323; $$). Another Main Street prize is the **Tuc'Me Inn Bed and Breakfast** (innkeepers Terry and Tina Foutz and Idabel Evans; ☎ 569-5702; $$-$$$), an early 1800s Federal/Colonial home (year-round).

For a place out of the village, consider **Brook & Bridle Summer Homes and Inn** (☎ 569-2707; $$$): from Wolfeboro, go four miles south on Route 28 and turn right on Roberts Cove Road. You'll be staying on the lake shore. Nearby cottages on other lakes include **Grey Shingles** on Rust Pond (rowboat and canoe rentals available; ☎ 569-6536; $$) and **King's Pine Lodges** on Crescent Lake (☎ 569-3556; $$).

The Lakes

Lake Winnipesaukee North

Weirs Beach

Weirs Beach offers abundant lodging. A quarter-mile from the beach is **Cedar Lodge at Brickyard Mountain**, with residential units and an entrance on Route 3 (☎ 366-4316 or 800-366-4883; $-$$). Look for more casual lodging at **Tower Hill Cottages** (☎ 366-5525; $$), **Abakee Cottages** (call for prices by the week; ☎ 366-4405), **Half Moon Hotel & Cottages** (☎ 366-4494; $$), and **Cozy Inn & Cottages** (on Maple Street, ☎ 366-4310; $$-$$$).

Meredith

In Meredith, right by the water and filled with light are the **Inn at Mill Falls** and the **Inn at Bay Point** (for both inns, ☎ 279-7006 or 800-622-6455; $$-$$$$). Others abound: try the **Tuckernuck Inn** (off Water Street on Red Gate Lane; ☎ 279-5521; $$), or the **Nutmeg Inn** on Pease Road (☎ 279-8811; $$). **Oliver Lodge** offers cabins and lodges on a private shoreline with canoes, paddleboats, rowboat, sailboat, and more; four miles out of town, call for directions. Host is Herb Oliver (☎ 279-4224; $$-$$$). **Olmec Motor Lodge** is on the bay (95 Pleasant Street; ☎ 279-8584; $$).

Center Harbor

In Center Harbor, the Victorian charm of the **Red Hill Inn** comes with views, fireplaces, balconies, and superb cuisine (Route 25B; ☎ 279-7001 or 800-5 RED HILL; $$-$$$). **Watch Hill Bed and Breakfast** is a village-edge retreat (☎ 253-4334; $$); there's also the **Meadows Lakeside Lodging** (motel-style, ☎ 253-4347; $$), **Lake Shore Motel and Cottages** (☎ 253-6244, in winter 941-439-6625; $-$$), and **Deepwood Lodges** with its sandy beach and boats (☎ 253-9210, in winter 407-743-3235; $$-$$$).

Mirror Lake & Moultonborough

There's a lovely resort located 4½ miles north of the center of Wolfeboro, on Route 109 in the community of Mirror Lake but actually on Lake Winnipesaukee. It's the **Heritage** (☎ 569-1533, nights and weekends, ☎ 569-5233; $$$). A little closer to town are **Mirror Lake Lodging** (boat dock, housekeeping units; ☎ 569-3846; $$) and **Pow-Wow Lodges** (private beaches with housekeeping lodges that accommodate two to six people; ☎ 569-2198; $$$).

Farther north, most easily reached from the north end of Lake Winnipesaukee, is the **Kona Mansion Inn**. Set on over 100 acres with its own golf course, this 1890 fieldstone and mock Tudor mansion borders the 700-acre Kona Wildlife Preserve. There are nine rooms, four cottages, and several chalets. Find the inn by taking Route 25 from Meredith nine miles to Moultonboro Neck Road, where you turn right and go another 2½ miles to Kona Road on the right (☎ 253-4900; $$-$$$).

Squam Lakes

Squam offers an especially gracious lodging: **The Manor on Golden Pond** is built in the style of an English country estate, with elegant bedrooms, most with fireplaces and views (Route 3, ☎ 800-545-2141; $$$-$$$$) and a 13-acre setting that includes water frontage. Don't confuse it with the **Inn on Golden Pond**, a more relaxed country-style home with welcoming front porch, also on Route 3 (☎ 968-7269; $$-$$$). Off Route 3, Shepard Hill Road leads to the **Pressed Petals Inn** (☎ 968-4417; $$$), where afternoon tea adds a special note. You might also consider the **White Oak Motel & Lakefront Cottages** at the junction of Routes 3 and 25 (☎ 968-3673; $$), with private beach and boats available.

Center Sandwich

In Center Sandwich, **Blanchard House** is an idyllic bed and breakfast in an 1822 home, where the canopied bed has an antique quilt with fresh flowers nearby. Proprietors are Catherine Hope and Roric Broderick; ☎ 284-6540; $$.

Ashland

Not far from the west end of Squam is the town of Ashland, at Exit 24 from Interstate 93. Here is the **Glynn House Inn**, a Victorian bed and breakfast in a restored inn with picture-perfect furnishings. Enjoy the fireplaces and Jacuzzis, as well as the gourmet breakfast (hosts Karol and Betsy Paterman; ☎ 968-3775 or 800-637-9599; $$-$$$).

The Lakes

Newfound Lake

The **Inn on Newfound Lake**, on Route 3A in Bridgewater, has welcomed guests since 1840, when it was a stage stop en route from Boston to Montreal. The four-story inn with its long veranda and painstakingly refurbished rooms offers an enchanting retreat (innkeepers Larry DeLangis and Phelps C. Boyce II; ☎ 744-9111 or 800-745-7990; $$-$$$). There are more casual choices too: **Bungalo Village Cottages** on West Shore Road in Bristol (mid-May to mid-October; $$; ☎ 744-2220), and **Lakeside Cottages** at 68 Lake Street, also in Bristol; ask about weekly packages (☎ 744-3075; $$).

North of the lake, on the way to Rumney if you take Route 3A north and then Route 25, is the **Crab Apple Inn** (four miles west of Interstate 93 using Exit 26). Savor the 1835 brick Federal country inn and its cozy comforts (innkeeper Christine DeCamp; ☎ 536-4476; $$-$$$).

Ossipee & The Northeastern Lakes

Tamworth

The delicate beauty of the small lakes northeast of Winnipesaukee has drawn a handful of truly gracious and lovely inns. In the village of Tamworth is the authentic 1883 **Tamworth Inn** (innkeepers Phil and Kathy Bender; $$-$$$; ☎ 800-NH2-RELAX; www.tamworth.com). Don't let the Main Street address fool you; the village is quiet and secluded. Relax by the four fireplaces, by the pool, or in the gazebo by the Swift River. You'll be across the road from New England's oldest summer theater, the Barnstormers, so you might as well get tickets to a show.

Snowville

From the **Snowvillage Inn** in Snowville there's a "heartstopping" view across the lawn, over the forest, to Crystal Lake, with the White Mountains in the background. The inn is charming and recognized for its elegant cuisine served in the romantic candlelit dining room. Touches like secluded hammocks and garden chairs add to the deep relaxation of a true vacation. In winter the inn offers 10 km of cross-country ski trails.

Hosts are Kevin and Barbara Flynn (☎ 447-2818 or 800-447-4345; $$$-$$$$).

> ❷ **BIKING FUN:** *Snowvillage Inn and Tamworth Inn are two of the three inns linked by **Bike the Whites**, a self-guided bicycle tour (the third is The Forest in Intervale, north of North Conway); for more information, see* On Wheels, *page 117.*

Eaton Center

In Eaton Center, also on Crystal Lake, is the **Inn at Crystal Lake**. Hosts Richard and Janice Octeau provide a chance for guests to savor romance ($$-$$$; ☎ 447-2120 or 800-343-7336). **Rockhouse Mountain Farm Inn** is a summer retreat in Eaton Center, offering 450 acres to ramble and photograph, including wildflowers and animals from piglets to peacocks. Hosts are the Edge family (☎ 447-2880; $$, with reduced rates for children).

Purity Lake

At Purity Lake is the **Purity Spring Resort** (near the junction of Route 153 and 113), a four-season vacation resort owned by the Hoyt family; swimming, boating, fishing, water-skiing and, in winter cross-country and downhill skiing (at King Pine, right at the resort) entertain visitors. The resort is especially family-friendly (☎ 367-8896 or 800-367-8897; $-$$).

■ Camping

 Camping choices are numerous in this area. Outside of Wolfeboro, try the **Wolfeboro Campground** at 61 Haines Hill Road, which is a right turn off Route 28 beyond Lake Wentworth, 4½ miles from the center of Wolfeboro (☎ 569-9881).

There's RV camping at a great beach at **Ellacoya State RV Park** in Gilford, bypassing the entrance to the state beach. Open mid-May to mid-October, the campground has 38 full hook-up sites and accepts reservations from January to October (☎ 271-3628 and 293-7821; no pets).

Outside of Meredith, camp at **Harbor Hill**, which is on Route 25, 11½ miles east from the Meredith traffic light, (☎ 279-6910).

Four miles from Center Harbor is **Camp Iroquois Campground**, where there are 90 tent and trailer sites, a beach, and boat ramp (PO Box 150, Center Harbor, NH 03226; ☎ 253-4287).

In the Moultonborough area is **Pine Woods Campground** (on Moultonboro Neck Road, four miles from Route 25), with 92 tent and trailer sites, all wooded (PO Box 776, Moultonborough, NH 03254; ☎ 253-6251).

Primitive camping (tents and a gentle regard for the surroundings) on land owned or managed by the Squam Lakes Association is a wonderful way to get to know Squam. At present there are sites on **Moon and Bowman Islands**, as well as in the **Chamberlain-Reynolds Forest**. Reservations must be made well in advance, by contacting Squam Lakes Association, PO Box 204, Holderness, NH 03245 (☎ 968-7336). A more commercial, well-known campground is the **Meredith Woods 4-Season Camping Area** (☎ 279-5549) on Route 104, halfway between Meredith and Interstate 91. It has an RV park and shares the beach with **Clearwater Campground** (☎ 279-7761), just across Route 104, where there are tent and trailer sites and boat rentals.

In the Baker River Valley, there are two campgrounds in Bristol: **Pine's Acres** on Wulamat Road (☎ 744-3097), and **Newfound Hills** off West Shore Road on Lunn Ave., (☎ 744-2830 and 744-2184). Rumney offers the **Baker River Campground**; from Interstate 93 at Exit 26, take Route 25 three miles to Smith Bridge Road on the right; cross the bridge and go two miles down Quincy Road to the campground entrance on the left. There are 40 large wooded and grassy sites along the river, with swimming, tubing, canoeing, and fishing (56 Campground Rd., Rumney, NH 03266, ☎ 786-9707; after October 15, 813-755-5222).

Center Ossipee offers **Deer Cap Campground** with its own cross-country ski center (PO Box 332, Center, Ossipee, NH

03814; ☎ 539-6030) and **Ossipee Lake Campground** with a 1,200-foot beach (☎ 539-6631). In West Ossipee there's the **Bearcamp River Campground** off Route 25 on Newman Drew Road, set on the Bearcamp River with swimming, canoeing, and cottage rentals (PO Box 104, W. Ossipee, NH 03890; ☎ 539-4898), and **Chocorua Camping Village** on Route 16 with 200 acres on Moore's Pond for fishing, boat rentals, and swimming (Box 118N, W. Ossipee, NH 03890; ☎ 323-8536 or 800-462-2426).

In Tamworth, there are 200 tent sites at **White Lake State Park**, where canoe rentals, trout fishing, and swimming keep you busy until the evening theater shows at the Barnstormers in the village (☎ 323-7350; January to October, reservations, ☎ 271-3628).

Visiting the Museum of Childhood in Wakefield and the New Hampshire Farm Museum in Milton along the Maine border? Here are three nearby campgrounds: **Beachwood Shores Campground** (take Route 16 to Route 153 and go north 12 miles, turn left onto Berryman Road and go two miles). It has 89 sites, a beach, and boats; HC Box 228, E. Wakefield, NH 03830; ☎ 539-4272 or 800-371-4282). **Lake Forest Resort** is a good spot for RVs but not tents (call for directions, ☎ 522-3306; off-season, 569-6186). **Mi-Te-Jo Campground** in Milton on Townhouse Road off Route 125 has two beaches, boat docks and ramp (☎ 652-9022).

Where To Eat

Lake Winnipesaukee South

Wolfeboro

For fine dining, Wolfeboro offers the **Lakeview Inn** at 200 North Main Street (☎ 569-1335). The **Wolfeboro Inn** serves an extensive pub menu in its tavern, and seafood and prime rib in the 1812 Room for more formal dining. Try the newer **Loves' Quay** for Continental offerings, on Mill Street in the Bay Village on Lake Winnipesaukee (☎ 569-3303). Family suppers, as well as mid-day ice creams, are enjoyable at

Bailey's on South Main Street (☎ 569-3662); save room for the sundaes with special sauces. And "dine Asian" at **West Lake** on Route 28 (☎ 569-6700).

Alton Bay & Gilford

Around the lake a bit on Alton Bay is the **Sandy Point Restaurant**, a local seafood tradition; go for the lobster (☎ 875-6001). Farther northwest in Gilford, the **Victorian House** offers consistently elegant dining, on Route 11 a half-mile before Ellacoya State Beach (☎ 293-8155). Also in Gilford, where Route 11B meets Route 11, is **Patrick's Pub & Eatery**, a spot for fun and entertainment in the evenings (☎ 293-0841).

Lake Winnipesaukee North

Meredith

When you reach Meredith, there's reliably tasty lunch and dinner at **Mame's** on Plymouth Street; look for the tall brick end of the building, set behind True's at the light. This is a traditional place to relax with friends (☎ 279-4631). **Hart's Turkey Farm** is a family spot, specializing in turkey but also serving prime rib, steaks, and seafood, at the junction of Routes 3 and 104 (☎ 279-6212). Hart's also caters the turkey dinner on the **Winnipesaukee Scenic Railroad**, where you're served family-style (make reservations; ☎ 279-5253) on your route along the lake. You can also opt for the more elegant dining car on the **Café Lafayette Dinner Train** (reservations ☎ 745-3500; mention Meredith departure).

Meredith also has comfortable coffee shops and a bakery for munching as you stroll among the shops. It is the antique center of the lakeshore towns, too.

Center Harbor

Between Meredith and Center Harbor on Route 25B, dining is a prime focus at the **Red Hill Inn**, where you gaze at the White Mountains from a restored mansion and savor scrumptious food, highly recommended (☎ 279-7001; also a Sunday brunch buffet). In Center Harbor itself, local residents recommend **Chequers Harbor** on Route 25 just south of the village, especially for the Italian specialties (☎ 253-8613).

Squam Lakes

When you drive up to Squam Lakes, visit the **Manor on Golden Pond**, an inn that opens its award-winning dining room to the public (reservations advised; ☎ 968-3348). **The Corner House Inn**, at Center Sandwich, offers delicious candlelight dining and is also noted for its lunches (☎ 284-6219 or 800-832-7829). Continue back toward the far side of Lake Winnipesaukee to Moultonborough for the superb fresh pasta at **Sweetwater Inn** (☎ 476-5079); don't miss the Belgian chocolate dessert specialty! You can also dine at the **Kona Mansion** in Continental style (☎ 253-4900), on Moultonboro Neck Road, or at the **Woodshed**, an excellent steak and seafood restaurant in a refurbished farmhouse and barn on Lee's Mill Road (☎ 476-2311).

Newfound Lake

At Newfound Lake, the south end of the shore is the water-view spot for **Cliff Lodge** (☎ 744-8660) on Route 3A. Dinner entrées range from "Gruyèred chicken" to wiener schnitzel, with some lovely Italian dishes. Prowl the east shore to see what's new in seafood take-out stands.

Plymouth & Rumney

If you're headed to the Baker River Valley, stop in Plymouth to enjoy a comfortable Italian meal at the **Italian Farmhouse** (a mile south of Plymouth on Route 3; ☎ 536-4536). Or drive all the way to Rumney for a relaxing family supper at **Steve's Restaurant**, a local spot to relax. On the way, on Route 25, you'll see the neon sign and gleaming chrome of **Glory Jean's Diner** (☎ 786-2352), a good spot for breakfast or a light lunch. The decor is great fun!

Ossipee & The Northeastern Lakes

In the Ossipee and Northeastern Lakes area, plan to dine at one of the inns like the **Tamworth** (☎ 323-7721), or stop at **Stafford's in the Field** in Chocorua off Route 113, where the entrées change regularly, the vegetables are deftly different and the desserts worth saving room for (☎ 323-7766).

The Lakes

Information Sources

Center Harbor/Moultonboro Chamber of Commerce, Center Harbor, NH 03226; ☎ 253-4582.

Franklin Chamber of Commerce, Franklin, NH 03235; ☎ 934-6909.

Greater Laconia/Weirs Beach Chamber of Commerce, Laconia, NH 03246; ☎ 524-5531 or 800-531-2347.

Greater Ossipee Area Chamber of Commerce, W. Ossipee, NH 03864; ☎ 539-6201 or 800-382-2371.

Greater Rochester Chamber of Commerce, Wakefield, NH 03872; ☎ 522-6106.

Lakes Region Association, PO Box 589, Center Harbor, NH 03226; ☎ 253-8555.

Meredith Chamber of Commerce, Meredith, NH 03253; ☎ 279-6121.

Newfound Region Chamber of Commerce, Bristol, NH 03222; ☎ 744-2150.

Squam Lake Chamber of Commerce, Holderness, NH 03217; ☎ 968-4494.

Wolfeboro Chamber of Commerce, Wolfeboro, NH 03894; ☎ 569-2200 or 800-516-5324.

Dartmouth-Lake Sunapee Region

Vacationing in this region has become a fine art, with summer colonies around Lake Sunapee, gracious dining in New London, and the endless cultural activities that surround Dartmouth College in Hanover, a college town with gentle "class." But there are also wild mountains to climb, great mountain biking routes on back roads and wooded slopes, and ski slopes that offer a good winter workout. Newly established to lead hikers, bikers, and snow travelers through the regions many parks and forests is the Monadnock-Sunapee Greenway, a 50-mile trail from Mt. Monadnock to the summit of Mt. Sunapee. The trail is not yet very "discovered," so you'll meet few others, especially on weekdays, and can savor the wildness and solitude that hide behind the tourist-available surface of the region.

Getting Around

There are two principal routes into the area: on Interstate 89 as it forges across the highlands northwest from Concord, or along the Connecticut River Valley roads, especially Routes 12 and 10, and where Vermont's section of Interstate 91 north-south gives good access to bridges across the Connecticut River into the White Mountain state. The spine of alluring mountains up the center of this region is where the best hiking, skiing, and mountain biking tend to be. From the south, the mountains to note are **Mt. Sunapee**, **Mt. Kearsarge**, **Mt. Cardigan**, and then **Smarts Mountain** and **Mt. Cube**. In the midst of the mountains is **Lake Sunapee**, so long that cruise ships ply its waters. To the west of this center ridge are the rich history and arts of the college town of Hanover, the "mall city" of West Lebanon, and a fascinating history-laden series of villages north and south. To the east of these mountain peaks are small towns like Bradford, Henniker, Grafton, Andover, Wilmot, and Warner; look here for the Mt. Kearsarge Indian Museum, interesting shops and restaurants, and old mine towns – you can tramp down into an old mine near Grafton and take home your own samples of minerals.

Adventures

■ On Foot

Hiking the Mountains

Connect with the **Monadnock-Sunapee Greenway** in the tiny town of Washington, New Hampshire's most elevated village, the first in the country to be named in honor of George Washington. It's a classic village with white-clapboard buildings and a pleasant general store where you can get last-minute hiking nibbles. If you want to hike the Greenway from here, parking is available behind the town hall or on Symonds Lane, a quarter-mile south of Route 31. But if you're looking for a good day hike over **Lovewell Mountain**, there's a 7½-mile loop that starts at a parking area a bit farther north: at the common, take the road on the church side, where the historic society signs are, for 0.6 miles and turn left on the Half Moon Pond Road. The parking area is on your left, 0.8 miles in (don't block access to the pond, please). You'll walk another half-mile down the road, then take the right-hand path up the mountain (this may be muddy). Follow the blazes and then the stone cairns to hike right up to the 2,473-foot summit, where there are fine views, and a side overlook to Mt. Kearsarge and Mt. Sunapee. You can see why trailblazers had an urge to connect these highlands! The trail goes down the other side of the mountain more gently, crosses a small brook, turns right to cross overgrown fields, and descends to connect with the gravel road that you walked on at the beginning – but you are now 2.4 miles from where you parked, so turn left and hike the gravel road back to the Half Moon Pond access.

Dartmouth-Lake Sunapee Region

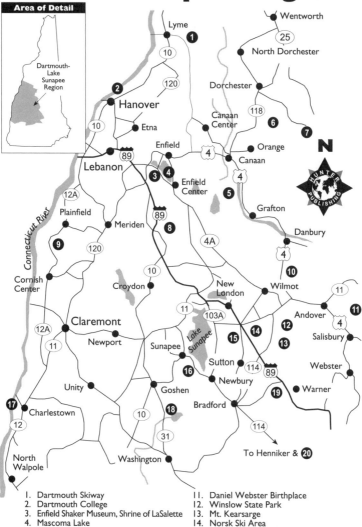

1. Dartmouth Skiway
2. Dartmouth College
3. Enfield Shaker Museum, Shrine of LaSalette
4. Mascoma Lake
5. Ruggles Mine
6. Mt. Cardigan, Cardigan State Park
7. Wellington State Park
8. Eastman Cross Country Center
9. Saint Gaudens Nat'l Historical Site
10. Ragged Mtn Ski Area
11. Daniel Webster Birthplace
12. Winslow State Park
13. Mt. Kearsarge
14. Norsk Ski Area
15. Wadleigh State Park
16. Mt. Sunapee, Mt. Sunapee State Park
17. The Fort at No. 4
18. Pillsbury State Park
19. Mt. Kearsarge Indian Museum
20. Pat's Peak Ski Area

Pillsbury State Park

If you hiked over Lovewell Mountain, you entered part of Pillsbury State Park (☎ 863-2860). From Washington, Route 31 leads up to the park, a 9,000-acre near wilderness of beaver ponds and a handful of well-marked trails. The ranger station at the park entrance is staffed from early May to Labor Day and has trail maps showing a seven-mile tramp around three ponds, an 8½-mile one that uses parts of the Greenway Trail, and a five-mile loop with some stiff changes in elevation. See *Camping* for the unusual campsites here.

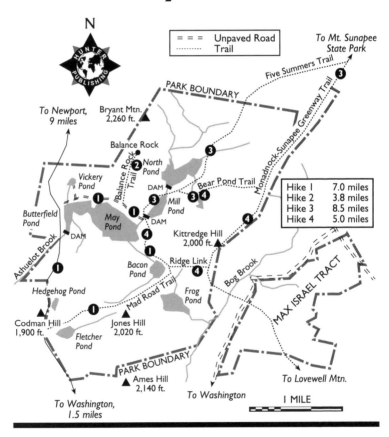

Pillsbury State Park

N

Hike 1	7.0 miles
Hike 2	3.8 miles
Hike 3	8.5 miles
Hike 4	5.0 miles

= = = Unpaved Road
·········· Trail

To Mt. Sunapee State Park

Five Summers Trail

PARK BOUNDARY

To Newport, 9 miles

Bryant Mtn. 2,260 ft.

Balance Rock

Monadnock-Sunapee Greenway Trail

Vickery Pond

North Pond

Balance Rock Trail

Bear Pond Trail

DAM

Mill Pond

Butterfield Pond

May Pond

DAM

Kittredge Hill 2,000 ft.

Ashuelot Brook

DAM

Bacon Pond

Ridge Link

Bog Brook

MAX ISRAEL TRACT

Hedgehog Pond

Mad Road Trail

Frog Pond

Codman Hill 1,900 ft.

Jones Hill 2,020 ft.

Fletcher Pond

PARK BOUNDARY

Ames Hill 2,140 ft.

To Lovewell Mtn.

To Washington

1 MILE

To Washington, 1.5 miles

Mt. Sunapee State Park

Pillsbury State Park stretches northward to meet **Mt. Sunapee State Park** (☎ 763-2356); the Greenway uses the connection between the two to reach Mt. Sunapee. Many first-time hikers on this 2,743-foot mountain start with a gondola lift to the summit and hike the **Solitude Trail** across to a small mountain pond, Lake Solitude, elevation 2,510 feet. It's a wonderful way to get away from the busy ski resort on the north side of the mountain. The gondola operates in winter, and from late June to Labor Day; it costs about $5 (children about $2.50) and makes the walking easy.

But if you'd rather climb the mountain more strenuously, there are several other routes. You can get a well-marked trail map from the state park office during its winter and summer seasons, but it tends to shut down at other times. So here's a description of the route up the **Andrew Brook Trail**, a hike of just over seven miles round-trip. You should allow five hours for this hike because of the 1,550-foot elevation rise. Lake Sunapee is ringed by Routes 11 (west and north), 103A (east), and 103 (south shore); the town of Sunapee is on the west shore, and the town of Newbury at the southern tip. Head for Newbury and look one mile south of town for the Mountain Road going right. Take this road 1.2 miles to the trailhead. There's room for several cars to park along the shoulder of the road. The Andrew Brook Trail begins at an opening in the woods just before a bridge over the brook. It follows an old logging road and crosses the brook three times. The logging road then heads off to the left and the trail goes straight ahead, marked with orange paint blazes. When the trail gets close to Lake Solitude it climbs over the ridge that holds the water in place and through spruces to a grassy area by the lake. White Ledge rises from the shore hundreds of feet upward. Here the trail turns right to go around the shore and at the north end of the lake meets a trail junction; take the right trail, the **Lake Solitude Trail**, uphill, now marked with white blazes to show that it's part of the Monadnock-Sunapee Greenway. The trail takes you above the cliffs to the top of White Ledge and a panoramic view. Then it drops into a wooded col, or lower sheltered area, where birds sing and flowers bloom, especially in June. When the trail crosses the ski slope and passes under the chair lift it crosses another ski trail and reaches the gondola access path, where you turn left and climb to the summit. There's a lodge that's open during the resort peak seasons (winter and summer). Return by the same route, watching carefully for blazes as you enter the woods, taking the left back onto the Andrew Brook Trail, and returning to where you parked.

Mt. Kearsarge

Once someone points out **Mt. Kearsarge** to you, you'll realize you've been seeing it nearly every time the road has opened in front of you in this region. It has a peak elevation of 2,931 feet and literally looms over the countryside. It's not shown clearly on the state highway map, and the state lands around it are also missing, but the location is north of Warner, south of Andover. From Interstate 89, take Exit 10 and pick up the Warner Road to **Winslow State Park**, following signs into the park. Pay a small day-use fee at the ranger's cottage and drive to the picnic area, where you park for the **Northside Trail** that leaves the southeast corner of the picnic area. Your round trip will be two miles, with a rise of 1,105 feet, a steep climb at times; allow an hour and a half for the round trip, and wear your hiking boots for clambering up the smooth rock ledges. In fair summer weather you may get to watch hang gliders descend from the summit to the picnic area; if you don't want much company, climb on weekdays and in cooler weather. The view is worth the effort, as it includes Lake Sunapee and Mt. Sunapee (see the ski trails?), the rocky top of Mt. Cardigan, Mt. Moosilauke in the distance, and to the northeast the Sandwich Range with Mt. Washington beyond it. As you circle further around, the Ossipee range and the Belknap Mountains come into view.

Mt. Cardigan

There are two ways to approach **Mt. Cardigan**: from the west, through the town of Canaan not far from Hanover, along trails maintained by the Dartmouth Outing Club. Or from the east on a very steep trail that reaches the mountain from the Appalachian Mountain Club lodge at the foot of the mountain on the Alexandria side, Cardigan Lodge. Most sensible people try it from the west. But if you want a little extra adventure, contact the lodge folks and stay there for a night or two, exploring not only Cardigan but also Welton Falls, Mt. Gilman, and Fire-screw Mountain with its cave and hanging ledges. Contact: Manager, AMC Cardigan Lodge, RFD1, Box 712, Bristol, NH 03222 (☎ 744-8011).

The west approach from Canaan is not especially steep, but it is rocky, so hiking boots are a good idea. From Interstate 89 take Exit 17 and follow Route 4 east to Canaan, bearing left onto Route 118. After 0.5 mile, turn right just after the fairgrounds (by the sign for the state park) and go 2.8 miles to where the road becomes gravel; when it becomes pavement again, stay to the left and continue uphill to the end of the road, where there's parking. Select the **West Ridge Trail** by its orange blazes, and keep a close eye out because there are other trails crossing yours. When you pass the old shelter, stay to its left in order to keep with the trail, looking for blazes marked on the rocks. Above the treeline, rock cairns mark the trail, and there's a lookout tower at the top (elevation 3,121 feet). The round trip is 2.6 miles and will take about 2½ hours.

Smarts Mountain & Mt. Cube

If you have a copy of the DeLorme *New Hampshire Atlas & Gazetteer*, look at the map on page 38 to see the **Appalachian Trail** winding over the peaks of Smarts Mountain and Mt. Cube. It's not easy to get to a trailhead for **Smarts**, and the hike is 6½ miles; your best guide to it is the description in Daniel Doan's new edition of his book *50 Hikes in the White Mountains*. He takes you to the peak from the north, from an area of old farms. Or if you shop at the Dartmouth Bookstore in Hanover (and who can resist it?), pick up the *DOG* – that is, the *Dartmouth Outing Guide*, an entertaining mix of chapters by Dartmouth students and alumni who've scrambled up these trails a lot. The *DOG* takes the southern approach to the mountain, for a round trip of 7½ miles. Either way, it's a day's worth of challenging hiking.

Mt. Cube isn't going to enter any record books for height, especially in New Hampshire, but the wide granite ledges at the summit provide excellent views, and it's fun to hike the Appalachian Trail and be part of the great north-south hikers' conduit. Expect to spend 4½ hours on the 6.6-mile round trip. Try to set your climb for early August to appreciate the blueberries along the way! From the Hanover area, take Route 10 north to Orford, and just before the village green, turn right onto Route 25A and check your odometer: you want the 10.2-mile point, when you will have passed over the "height of the land" and descended to Upper Baker Pond. Look for the brown-and-white metal Appalachian Trail sign (it may be only a picture of hikers), and park on the far side of the steel highway bridge. The trail leaves the road on the other side of the bridge, headed south. You're on the Appalachian Trail (AT), whose rectangular, white-painted blazes run from Georgia to Mt. Katahdin in Maine. Cross a gravel road and go uphill; when you drop down to a bridge across Brackett Brook (1.6 miles), enjoy knowing that it's the longest log bridge on the 70 miles of AT maintained by the Dartmouth Outing Club. The trail rises again, and at 3.1 miles reaches a T-junction; turn right to the summit (the left turn is the AT going on toward Smarts Mountain, seven miles away). After you've feasted on the view and whatever you hauled up in your lunch pack, descend by the same route.

Walking In & Around Town

Hanover, west of the mountains, offers a wide variety of shorter hikes. Most of them can be done comfortably in sneakers rather than hiking boots. For example, the **Hanover Mink Brook Natural Area** is almost in town: From the Hanover Inn, take South Main Street 0.6 mile to a right turn onto a gravel road with parking area, just before the power substation and bridge over Mink Brook. Walk past the chains onto the trail, which winds along the Mink Brook for about two-thirds of a mile. Pleasant views are occasionally enriched by wildlife sightings: waterfowl, kingfishers, herons, and otters.

It's also worth wandering through **Pine Park**, where the Civil War-era pine trees were saved from the Diamond Match Company through a community effort in 1900. To reach the park, from the Hanover Inn go north on North Main Street, which turns into Rope Ferry Road. Go to the end of the parking lot above the Hanover Country Club clubhouse (beware of flying golf balls, seriously!) and follow the wide path for about 100 feet until the small trail sign sends you to the right onto a narrow trail. Soon the path crosses a brook, then turns left and follows it to the Connecticut River. You are now walking among the pines, along the riverbank. In another half-mile the trail leaves the river to return to the country club, where you can carefully go around the green to your right and see the clubhouse where you parked your car.

If it's not summer (the crowded season), a 1½-mile walk around **Storrs Pond** may bring you much peace. From the center of town follow signs to Route 10 north, which you take for two miles to a right turn onto Reservoir Road. Follow it to the end and turn left into Storrs Pond area; the trail begins on the dirt road just past the brook. Take every left turn until the path returns by the tennis courts.

The **Hanover Trails Association** (Box 106, Hanover, NH 03755, ☎ 643-2408) encourages use of these trails, along with the ones at **Balch Hill**, which is close to Storrs Pond. To reach the Balch Hill parking area, again take Route 10 north to the right turn onto Reservoir Road, and watch for Hemlock Road on your right; take it to the end, but don't drive up the driveway. The trails are obvious and wind around pleasantly; watch for the old oak trees. One just north of the summit of the hill is at least 200 years old and has a trunk measuring almost 17 feet in diameter.

Ready to explore a bog? The **Philbrick-Cricenti Bog** is just west of New London. As you approach the town from the Lake Sunapee direction, on the outskirts you'll find a large grocery store, called Cricenti's; when you see it, you've just passed the bog trail. Now turn the car around and head the other way, measuring 0.25 mile on your right; see the little pull-off that you never would have noticed otherwise? Park here and look for a descriptive leaflet at the trailhead; then start on the trail, which uses wooden walkways to protect the fragile plants. Watch the red maples give way to cinnamon ferns, and then to black spruce. When the woods open and you're stepping on peat-based soils, you can feel the bounce underfoot. The board-walk is set on a literally floating mat of sphagnum. Bend down and look hard at the unusual plants around you.

For a woodsy ramble, head to the south end of Lake Sunapee and the town of Newbury, then take Route 103A north up the east side of the lake for 1.3 miles. Turn right onto Rollins Road (gravel) and go 0.3 mile to the parking area for the **Hay For-**

estry and Wildlife Management Area, managed by the Society for the Protection of New Hampshire Forests. There are miles of woods roads and trails in the 675 acres, which are managed as a productive woodlot. Climb Sunset Hill for a view and to savor what the family of US Secretary of State John Hay considered a perfect picnic spot in the 1800s. If you return to Route 103A for another 1.3 miles, you find an entrance into another part of the Hay estate, this section managed by the U.S. Fish and Wildlife Service as a migratory bird and wildlife refuge. In the estate home, **The Fells**, is a library that includes Hay's books. Be sure to visit the gardens, too, where more than 400 species were planted. The Fells is open from 10 am to 6 pm on weekends, from Memorial Day to Labor Day. It is operated by the NH Division of Parks and Recreation (☎ 763-2452).

Just one more place on Route 103A, please? A half-mile farther north is a right turn onto Chalk Pond Road, with trails into the **Stoney Brook Wildlife Sanctuary** starting at 1.3 and at two miles down this road. The sanctuary is a good place to hear and maybe see the pileated woodpecker; look for evidence of its insect hunting as it leaves large rectangular holes in the trunks of dead trees. This is Audubon Society turf. By now, you should have a good idea of how great a portion of New Hampshire land is becoming protected in one way or another.

Another interesting ramble in this region is detailed in the *Sightseeing* section (see page 248) with a description of the **Saint-Gaudens National Historic Site** in Cornish.

> ➡ **ROCK CLIMBERS TAKE NOTE:** *The* DOG, *more respectfully known as the* Dartmouth Outing Guide, *lists ledges and cliffs with tried-and-true routes. Among them are Pickledish Hollow in Lyme, and Holt's Ledge just up the road from Pickledish. Do get the book for the detailed observations of crumbling, weathered rock areas that you'll want to avoid. The* DOG *also lists the classic White Mountain climbs at Cathedral and White Horse Ledges.*

OUTDOOR ADVENTURES FOR WOMEN

A special note for women and girls: If you've always wanted to try rock climbing, or even hiking, biking, kayaking, canoeing, or back-country skiing, but didn't know how to get started or thought it would be too hard, consider getting in touch with **Women's Outdoor Challenges** (400 Will Hill Road, Sunapee, NH 03782; ☎ 763-5400; e-mail jgoldbo@mail.tds.net). This group intends to empower girls and women through experiential outdoor programs, many of them in New Hampshire. Recent offerings included an intro to telemark skiing, a women's snow adventure weekend, snowboarding for women, and some terrific hikes.

▪ On Wheels

Road Biking

Road bikers, rejoice! You can get exactly the mix you want of rolling to level roads and short stiff ascents by playing with routes in this region. The **river valley regions** – both along the Connecticut River and to the east around Wilmot Flat and Andover – are smooth and swift, although there's a challenging loop around Lake Sunapee with some hilly ups and downs. You can cover a lot of ground and see a lot of lake and valley terrain, speckled with wildlife and forest preserves, as you roll the roads. It's pleasant to ride among the farms along Route 12A by the Connecticut River, heading south from the Lebanon area. The return north on Route 120 is even more rural, and covered bridges help you cross back and forth between the two parallel roads.

The book *30 Bicycle Tours in New Hampshire* maps out five different loops to get you started. First is the 23½-mile loop around **Lake Sunapee**, starting at the Mt. Sunapee State Park off Route 103 where there's plenty of parking space. Pedal it in early fall or late spring – the off-seasons for the lake and ski resort area – to avoid traffic. When you roll down the slope from the parking area, go three-quarters around the rotary to pick up Route 103 headed northwest (signs will suggest Newport). After four miles of smooth road and wide shoulder, go right onto Route 11 and cover another 7.7 miles, this time with some hills, including a steep grade just beyond the turn to Sunapee Harbor. Just before the Interstate 89 underpass, turn right onto Route 103A (sign suggests Blodgett Landing and Newbury), which you ride for 7.9 miles to Newbury. On the way, at 0.8 mile south on Route 103A, check out Herrick Cove, where boat passengers used to arrive to catch the stage to New London's lodgings. When you arrive in Newbury, turn right onto Route 103 again and stop for an ice cream at the Newbury Harbor Restaurant or the Lake Sunapee Trading Post General Store on your left. Finally, finish the 2½ miles on Route 103 to the park entrance where you began.

For a full day of cycling with challenging hills, try the 54.7 miles from **Canaan** up Route 118 and along the **Baker River** to the right that leads to the Dorchester General Store, then right again up toward **North Groton** and down into **Groton** (respectable hills!), where there's an interesting short side trip to the right to Sculptured Rocks. Otherwise, scoot into Hebron, then right down the west shore of Newfound Lake (on west Shore Road, of course), turning right in Alexandria to shunt over to Route 104 and then Route 4 back through Grafton to Canaan. Parts of this route may have heavy traffic, especially in summer and foliage season; beware.

Another recommended ride is the 24.1-mile double loop around **Little Lake Sunapee** in **New London** and nearby **Pleasant Lake**. Bucklin Beach on Little Lake Sunapee offers good swimming; Elkins Beach at the far end of Pleasant Lake offers a view of Mt. Kearsarge, a popular hiking peak. Detour into town and swap stories at **Village Sports**, 140 Main Street (☎ 526-4948), in the same building as the New London Inn; owner John Kiernan will swap routes with you.

Mountain Biking

Mountain bikers may also benefit from checking in at Village Sports – owner John Kiernan keeps a topo map on the wall marked with good routes he and others have already explored, and invites riders to add their own.

⊃ **PEDAL POWER:** *When a new student at the local Colby-Sawyer College stopped in at Village Sports to ask about routes, bike shop owner John Kiernan asked how long the young man planned to stay at the college. "Four years," the puzzled student replied. Straight-faced, Kiernan told him, "Then you won't have time to ride them all."*

There are woods roads around **Little Lake Sunapee**, and more back roads around **Pleasant Lake** and en route to Andover through Wilmot Flat. **New London** is a good center for hitting the trails; so is **Hanover**, believe it or not, despite the cultured center of the college town by the Connecticut River. The **Storrs Hill Trails**, described in *On Foot*, are open to mountain bikers as long as the ground isn't too wet. And the power line clearings near **Sachem Village** in West Lebanon are considered fair game by Dartmouth riders; head south of campus on Route 10 1.2 miles, and turn left on the Sachem Village Road, also known as Gould Road, following it to the back of the complex. Trails are rough, rutted, and muddy – single or double track, your choice. A third opportunity is in **Lyme**, 10 miles north of Dartmouth College on Route 10: when you reach the village, just past the general store go straight ahead onto Dorchester Road, also known as Grafton Turnpike. In three miles, the Dartmouth Skiway turn is on the right, but you bear left on the gravel road, which climbs 3½ miles to Reservoir Pond and two more to Cummins Pond. (You may notice that the Appalachian Trail cuts across near the Skiway; sorry, bikes are not allowed on that trail, but the scenery where you are is just as good.)

A pleasant place to take those fat tires is **Pillsbury State Park**, the southern end of the green stretch that's topped by Mt. Sunapee. The park entrance on Route 31 is well marked; all trails are bikeable except the Balance Rock Trail, and the terrain has plenty of variety.

Eighteen miles of trails with many tough stretches have been laid out at the **Hopkinton-Everett Reservoir**. This is in the Merrimack Valley Region, but it's really not far off; check *On Wheels* on page 296 in that region for suggestions on a good workout.

Of course, mountain bikers get a "lift" in the sport at ski areas that open their trails in summer and are willing to bring those wheels up the hill. Of the ski resorts in this region, only **Mt. Sunapee** is open to lift-served mountain biking so far. The state park is open daily from late May to Labor Day. An unlimited day fee recently was $15, and a single ride $8.

Outfitters

Sunapee area support and rental shops for bicyclists include the following shops:

- **Bob Skinner's Ski & Sports** (☎ 763-9880) in Sunapee Harbor, halfway down the west shore of the lake.

- **Outspokin'** (☎ 763-9500) in Newbury on Route 103, at the southeastern corner of the lake.

- **Tom Mowatt Cycles** in Lebanon, at 213 Mechanic Street (☎ 448-5556).

- **Olde Nugget Alley** in Hanover (☎ 643-5522).

▪ On Water

 Lake Sunapee is the center of water action just because of its size; it's 10 miles long, with 25 miles of coastline. But don't underestimate the smaller lakes and ponds, and the rivers, in this region. There is easy access to nearly every one, and even a taste of wilderness for those willing to head up to Grafton Pond.

For a pleasant afternoon or evening on Lake Sunapee, take either of two boat cruises. You can also rent your own vessel, whether motored or not, from the marinas. Some of the resources are listed below.

Guided Cruises on Lake Sunapee

The first large passenger boat on Lake Sunapee was actually a horse-powered one, carrying 100 passengers, and built in 1854 (for a detailed explanation, take the *M/V Mt. Sunapee II* cruise). Vacationers used to come for the summer then; by 1885

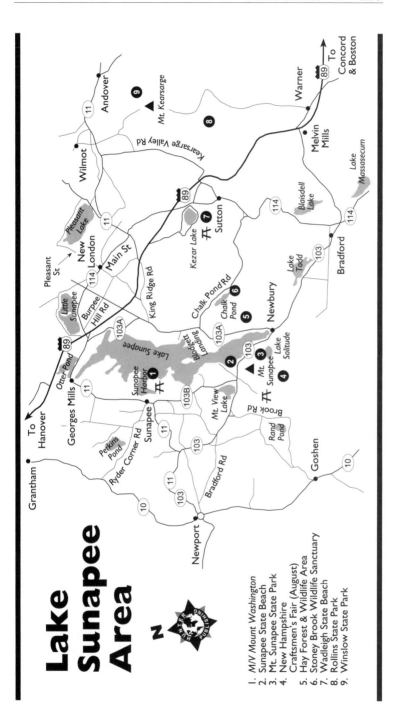

Lake
Sunapee
Area

1. M/V Mount Washington
2. Sunapee State Beach
3. Mt. Sunapee State Park
4. New Hampshire
   Craftsmen's Fair (August)
5. Hay Forest & Wildlife Area
6. Stoney Brook Wildlife Sanctuary
7. Wadleigh State Beach
8. Rollins State Park
9. Winslow State Park

All aboard to cruise Lake Sunapee!

the tourist traffic was so busy that a really big ship, the *Edmund Burke*, was built, followed in 1897 by the *Kearsarge* to carry 250 passengers. The original ships are long gone, scuttled or burned years ago.

Now the *M/V Kearsarge* plies the lake, a re-creation of a 19th-century steamer, taking passengers back into the Victorian era for their dinners. The buffet supper cruises run all summer, with reservations advised (☎ 763-5477).

The *M/V Mt. Sunapee II* offers public cruises twice daily in the summer, and once a day during fall foliage season. Captain Dave Hargboll offers lake history and stories for an hour and a half; the boat is also available for private parties (*M/V Mt. Sunapee II* Excursions, PO Box 345, Sunapee, NH 03782; ☎ 763-4030).

Fishing

Headed out to go fishing? Sunapee offers land-locked salmon and lake trout, as well as smallmouth bass and pickerel; Little Sunapee has rainbows. **Dickie's Outdoor Sports & Power Equipment** (☎ 938-5393, 800-640-5393) on Route 103 between Newbury and Bradford offers bait and gear, including trout flies. (Don't forget to stop at Sargent's Marina in Georges Mills for more fish talk.) Over near Enfield, at **Mascoma Lake**, there are both brown trout and rainbows. If you swing into Hanover, visit **Lyme Anglers** at 8 South Main Street

(☎ 643-1263); the store is an Orvis dealer and also offers guide services and a fly-fishing school.

Grafton Pond doesn't have trout despite its 234 acres, but is highly regarded as a smallmouth bass fishery. It is a paddler's haven, quiet and almost wild. The 935 acres surrounding the pond's seven-mile shoreline are now a reservation managed by the Society for the Protection of New Hampshire Forests, which is aiming to preserve the local wildlife habitats while improving commercial timber stands in the forest. There are many small islands and inlets where loons nest and other wildlife can quietly thrive. Visit with tenderness. From Wilmot go 13.2 miles west on Route 4A and turn right onto Grafton Pond Road, going 0.9 mile and then bearing right and going another 0.9 mile. Turn right and go 0.2 mile to the dam, and park at the boat ramp. (You can also get here from Canaan on Route 118, then Route 4 west, going left after 0.2 mile on Potato Road. It's then 5.1 miles to the dam.) If you want to walk around on land, bring a topographical map and compass; there are few trails.

Canoeing

Over on the Connecticut River, **North Star Canoes** (☎ 542-5802) on Route 12A in Cornish not only rents canoes but also provides a shuttle to put-ins either three or 12 miles above the covered bridge in Cornish. They've developed family outings with island picnic, provide support for overnight canoe camping, and have six-person rafts for river float trips. Call ahead, as the livery reserves a few days a week to do farm and other business!

There's a wonderful taste of Dartmouth outdoor adventure at the **Ledyard Canoe Club** in Hanover. It's the oldest collegiate canoe club in America, on the shore of the Connecticut, reached by the right turn just before the river as you come from Hanover on Wheelock Street. (After you make the turn, stay to the left, and drive past the elegant Friends of Dartmouth boathouse to the rough path leading down to the much less formal Ledyard Clubhouse.) Open to anyone with an enthusiasm for the river, Ledyard provides a clubhouse, boat shed, and repair shop, as well as renting out a secluded cabin a mile down the river on an island. Membership in the club entitles one to club trips and to some free rentals, but nonmembers can also rent some of the boats: canoes and whitewater kayaks. Make reservations to be on the safe side, and check hours, which change seasonally (Ledyard Canoe Club, PO Box 9, Robinson Hall, Hanover, NH 03755; ☎ 643-6709).

The **Connecticut River** is practically a flatwater sport along this stretch; the current can be strong, but the river is wide enough to let paddlers stay out of most entanglements. At Orford, to the north, there's a municipal boat-launching area. Six miles farther down the river there's an old bridge abutment visible in midstream, and another two miles later. The **Opompanoosuc River** enters after another five miles, and five miles more brings you to the dock at the Ledyard Canoe Club followed by the Hanover Bridge. Now you are two miles from the dam at Wilder, and need to think about getting out of the river for the quarter-mile portage. There's a visitor center at the dam that lets you watch the fish using their "ladder" in spring. The two miles after the dam can have sudden changes of water level from the power generators; they are also relatively wild and deserted, a good spot for seeing an osprey or eagle, as well as Atlantic salmon and water birds. It is absolutely essential to portage around the dangerously changeable falls at the next power dam, at North Hartland, Vermont. Then you get a nice eight miles down to the covered bridge at Cornish, and steady paddling all the way to Bellows Falls, where the next portage is required (try the east bank for an easier time).

If you're up for some Class II and III **rapids**, try the **Mascoma River**, which drains the area west of Mt. Cardigan and flows to the Connecticut. The upper section of the river is small, but once the Indian River joins it, the four miles between Mascoma Lake and the dam outside Lebanon are active and challenging; in fact, each April one of America's oldest slalom and whitewater races takes place here. As you take Route 4 from Lebanon toward Enfield, watch for the split to the right of Route 4A, which traces the southern shore of Mascoma Lake. Here's the boat put-in, on Route 4A, just past the split. There's a parking lot, and a good eddy under the dam to make things easy. Around the first turn is the USGS water gauge (2.3-2.8, medium water; 3.0 and up, high water; over 3.5, flood stage), and rapids begin immediately. You'll want to have walked the shore to check for blowdowns, as immediately after the Route 4 bridge an island splits the river into left and right channels, both often blocked by trees. You can stop in the eddy on the left before entering. And the next half-mile is the slalom course, where the wires and gates, if up, should not be disturbed please. You'll speed under two more railroad bridges before there's time to catch your breath. Where the main course turns right is another area often made hazardous by trees. Pass under the high Interstate 89 bridge (you've gone three miles) and prepare for the next race course, as you drop under a small metal and stone bridge. You can take out on the right under the bridge if you choose. Otherwise, follow the river bend left (rest on the sand to the left if you like), then enter an S-turn and take the middle course to avoid a ledge. There's a 100-yard run to a right turn under a railroad bridge, where again you'll want to pause and scout before entering **Excelsior Rapids** (Class III, sometimes close to Class IV in high water). Double-check the runout of Excelsior to the dam, which is very dangerous. You'll need to portage (on the right in low water, on the left in high) before the 100-yard stretch below the dam, and the take-out by the city pool and water treatment facility. A few more details (and more emphasis on the risky parts of this run) can be found in the *AMC River Guide to New Hampshire and Vermont*.

The nearly 10 miles of runnable water on the **Sugar River** is good to know about because the water level stays high longer in the season, thanks to dam control. It's not runnable close to Lake Sunapee, which it drains, so put in at North Newport and plan to take out in Claremont, well above the Route 11 bridge, where retaining walls and a gorge to follow make the route impassable. There are some nice Class II rapids; you can judge the water before you start from the level at the Route 11 bridge in Kellyville, three miles west of Newport.

Swimming

Swimming at Lake Sunapee is a vacation sport at **Lake Sunapee State Beach** (☎ 763-2356), across the rotary from the state park entrance on Route 103, three miles west of Newbury. The beach is open daily from mid-June to Labor Day, and weekends before and after. There's a small fee for access to the 900-foot beach, bathhouse, picnic tables, and snack bar. Another local favorite is the **Wadleigh State Beach** at Kezar Lake in Sutton, east of Sunapee; from Route 114 the entrance is marked. It's open daily from mid-June to Labor Day and is less well known and less crowded than Sunapee; small fee here, too (☎ 927-4724).

In the Hanover area, plan to swim at **Storrs Pond Recreation Area** (see directions in *On Foot*, page 229; ☎ 643-2134), open from June through Labor Day, with lifeguards for both a pool and 15-acre pond with its two sandy beaches. Non-members pay a fee.

Outfitters

- Rent a boat for yourself at **Sargent's Marina** on Route 11 in Georges Mills, at the top of the lake (canoes, motorboats; ☎ 763-5036) and receive suggestions on where to fish!

- In Sunapee Harbor, halfway down the west shore of the lake, **Bob Skinner's Ski & Sports** (☎ 763-2303) offers canoes and paddleboats.

- Also in Sunapee Harbor, at the waterfront, is **Alden of Sunapee Rentals** (☎ 763-5190), with kayaks, canoes, hydro-bikes, and pedal boats.

- Get a lesson in kayaking, plus professional guide service not just on Sunapee but on other lakes and rivers too, even as far away as Umbagog up north, from **Shoreline Kayaking** (PO Box 462, Goshen, NH 03752; ☎ 863-4017).

Scuba & Snorkeling

How about scuba and snorkeling? The waters of Lake Sunapee offer intriguing exploration. The wreck of the scuttled steamship the *Weetamoo* has been found and marked off Pinecliff, and you can explore it as well as the rest of the lake. In Newbury the LaPortes have been diving and giving lessons since 1957; get in touch at **LaPorte's Skin-diving**, Route 103, Box 53, Newbury, NH 03255 (☎ 763-5353). Or visit **Lebanon** (not the mall area of "West Leb," but the small city reached by taking Exit 19 off Interstate 89 and heading west on Route 4). The

New England Dive Center (☎ 448-1222) is just off Route 4 on Mascoma Street, a right-hand turn from this direction. If you reach the downtown area, you've gone too far. The shop is well-equipped and specializes in sport dives, with plenty of classes, and year-round activity, including ocean dives.

■ With Llamas

 Visit a llama farm with plenty of other animals to pet, and take part in the children's and family educational sessions that Mary and Jim Mitchell put together at **Mini Meadow Llamas** in Bradford, southeast of Lake Sunapee (☎ 938-5268). The farm also offers llama treks, those incredibly relaxing hikes where you keep the gentle pace of the llama while it carries the baggage, and you get to really look and listen to the woods and fields around you because you're not hurrying or huffing.

■ On Snow & Ice

 Mt. Sunapee offers the most impressive downhill skiing in this region, with a 1,500-foot vertical drop, 38 trails, 95% snowmaking coverage, and six lifts. You'll find a ski shop, ski and snowboard rentals, and children's programs. Most trails are intermediate, and the resort emphasizes family fun. The season is strongly weather dependent, so check first (☎ 763-2356). You can also sign up for free guided mountain tours (sign up on Saturdays for Sunday tours; ☎ 763-4642). The NE Handicapped Sportsman's Association also offers programs here.

Nearby cross-country opportunities include **Eastman Ski Touring Center** (Exit 13 off Interstate 89, 30 km of groomed trails; ☎ 863-4500) and **Norsk Ski Touring Center** (Exit 11 off Interstate 89, east on Route 11, 85 km of groomed trails; moonlight tours, too!; ☎ 526-4685).

Smaller ski areas can be a great place to get the kids started, or just unwind, away from performance pressure. **Pat's Peak** on Route 114 in Henniker (☎ 428-3245; ski school, ☎ 428-7653; www.patspeak.com) draws loyal fans for its 20 trails, and the combination packages of lift ticket and lesson are very reasonably priced. Count on homemade food and a rustic lodge, as well as short lift lines and plenty of beginner and intermediate trails. Both skis and snowboards are rented and repaired.

Danbury's **Ragged Mountain** is just getting discovered by skiers looking for the dip and roll of wide open cruising trails; there's also glade skiing. Vertical drop is 1,250 feet, with a summit elevation of 2,250; there are 150 skiable acres, 32 trails, and six lifts. Snowmaking coverage is 98%. The resort often provides a "learn to ski free" week in early December; check dates (☎ 768-3971; www.ragged-mt.com/ski). To reach the slopes, get to Danbury and start east on Route 104; follow signs on the right. Lift tickets are priced lower than most, and the scenery is superb.

Two Dartmouth ski resources are open to the public at terrific prices: The **Dartmouth Skiway** (☎ 795-2143), reached by taking Route 10 north to Lyme and bearing right just before the church (four miles more to the slope), has a 928-foot vertical drop, three lifts, and 16 trails, and a lift ticket costs less than $30 even on holidays. **Occom Touring Center** in Hanover (☎ 646-2440) has 35 km of groomed Nordic trails and is located near the golf course (see Pine Park directions in *On Foot*, page 228).

In Enfield, just east of Lebanon at Exit 16 from Interstate 89, there's one more small ski slope: **Whaleback** (☎ 448-1489). The vertical drop is a snug 700 feet, which keeps the 26 trails in the gentle range; it's a good learning slope, especially for kids, and midweek lift rates are very low. They offer night skiing from 4 pm on, for some evening fun.

■ In The Air

Hang Gliding

Longing for a chance to feel your own wings? **Morningside Flight Park** in North Charlestown can get you started on hang gliding. Owner Jeff Nicolay established the flight park on part of a farm, where the trimmed slopes are perfectly angled to catch the breezes and stiffer winds. He's also close to Vermont's Mt. Ascutney, just across the Connecticut River, where long-distance hang-glide flights often begin. (How about a 93-mile flight to the ocean? No kidding, one of the fliers did it once! But most flights are much shorter!) There are lessons and rentals for hang gliding, paragliding, and a complete repair shop to fabricate custom parts along with on-site sail-making. Flight fees are low enough to let you do this a lot; call ahead for an appointment and to check the winds at the last minute (☎ 542-4416). To reach the flight park, coming south from Claremont on Route 12, watch for the yellow garage on the left, across from the miniature golf park; make the left turn, and you'll see the big blue silos behind the flight park, not to mention the windsocks all around.

Scenic Flights

In nearby Newport at Parlin Field, **Carl's Flying Service** offers scenic flights (☎ 543-0770).

Hang gliding over North Charlestown.

Sightseeing

Washington

Washington is a village to fall in love with, photogenic and historic, with its white clapboard buildings, Congregational church, soldiers' memorial, and active if small **historical society museum** (hours are Saturday from 10-3 and Sunday from 1-4, but call for an appointment, ☎ 495-3097 or 495-3941). And it's just a few miles from Goshen to the north where Route 31 meets Route 10; in the center of Goshen a big sign points you east to **Nelson's Rare Books**, just two miles off the main road, which is crammed with 70,000 pre-loved volumes. The bookstore is open daily in the summer, but only on weekends in the off-season, when you should call ahead in case the owners take off on a book-buying spree (☎ 863-4394).

Newport

North of Goshen is Newport, a gateway town to the Lake Sunapee region. The **Newport Opera House** offers a year-round series of shows (☎ 863-2412).

Lake Sunapee

When you leave Newport, head for Lake Sunapee. Take Route 11 and 103, combined here, to the east, and watch on the right for the **Dorr Woolen Company**, which has a stunning inventory of wool fabrics and yarns (☎ 863-6377). Then Route 11 and Route 103 split; if you want to go to the north half of the lake, where Sunapee Harbor and Georges Mills are, stay with Route 11. **Sunapee Harbor** is a charming waterfront section, with good food and great views across the lake; board the *M/V Mt. Kearsarge* for an excursion (☎ 763-5477), or rent a small craft next door. **Georges Mills** offers some antique shopping, and is on the way to **New London**, a "must visit" town with historic buildings, good restaurants, and lovely roads for summer walking. While you're in New London be sure to stop at **Baynham's New England Mercantile**, an emporium of merchandise from around the world, in a dramatic setting from the past (☎ 526-8070).

Theater lovers may want to visit New London for a show: the **New London Barn Playhouse Summer Theatre** performs from mid-June through Labor Day at 209 Main Street (☎ 800-633-2276).

If you want to go to the Sunapee south shore, which includes **Mt. Sunapee State Park** and **State Beach** (☎ 763-2356), as well as the town of Newbury, watch for the right turn onto Route 103 from Route 11. Route 103 leads you directly to the rotary where both the park (hiking and skiing) and the swimming beach have entrances. Not only is the park a resource for outdoors explorers; it hosts annual events like the Craftsmen's Fair, a 10-day festival of handmade art and elegance in early August. If you stay with Route 11 past the state parks, you pass many motel and cottage lodgings and come into Newbury, where the marina busily serves lake traffic. Here Route 103A turns left (north) up the east shore of the lake, to the string of preserved parcels described in *On Foot*.

ANTIQUING AROUND LAKE SUNAPEE

New London offers the fun of shopping in Baynham's New England Mercantile, which in a way lets you shop as if you were in a past era. But there are also bona fide antiques to be found in town, at **George Turgeon Furniture, Antiques and Refinishing**, on Main Street at the village green (☎ 526-4177; refinishing, 768-3882) and at **Priscilla Drake Antiques**, 33 Main Street (☎ 526-2151, open Memorial Day to Columbus Day).

Travel a loop around Lake Sunapee and find more:

- Georges Mills: **Mill Pond Antiques**, ☎ 763-2905, and **Prospect Hill Antiques**, ☎ 763-9676 (special collection of country pine and Victorian furniture).

- Sunapee: **Young & Olde Antiques**, ☎ 863-1330 (specializing in restored antique furniture), and **Herbert's Clock & Watch Repair Shop**, ☎ 863-0986.

- Mt. Sunapee Park Entrance: **Windhorse Farm**, ☎ 763-9788 (country antiques for house and garden).

- Newbury: **Newbury Antique Center**, ☎ 763-9777 (group shop), and **The Andrew Brook** (on Route 103; ☎ 938-5333).

- Bradford: **Sunshine Farm** (☎ 938-2716).

- Sutton Mills: **Sutton Mills Antiques**, ☎ 927-4557 (furniture, jewelry, glass, tools, ephemera, coins).

- Wilmot (at the base of Mt. Kearsarge): **Kearsarge Lodge Antiques**, ☎ 927-4594 (group shop, Americana and folk art).

Henniker

Continue east from Newbury on Route 103 about seven miles until Route 114 branches to the right, and take Route 114 another eight miles to **Henniker**, which describes itself as "the only Henniker on earth." It's a 200-year-old village with covered bridge, family ski area, shops, art gallery, and the **New Hampshire Winery**, which offers tours (during May and June, Wednesday-Sunday from noon to 5; July to December, daily 10-noon and 1-6 pm; ☎ 428-9463). Walk all over the village and make sure you get to the stone bridge, the covered bridge, and the developing historic park at the site of the first sawmill in town (take Main Street east for 1.3 miles to Amey Brook Park).

Warner

Backtracking from Henniker to Route 103 and heading toward Interstate 89 will bring you to Warner, home of an **annual fall foliage festival** during Columbus Day weekend, and also of the **Mt. Kearsarge Indian Museum** on Kearsarge Mountain Road. The museum is open daily from May through October, 10-5 (noon to 5 on Sundays) and hosts numerous special events. The museum's holdings began as a personal collection, which now has an amazing breadth. There are trained guides to take you through 15,000 years of history. The brochure sums it up: "A visit to Mt. Kearsarge Indian Museum will help you to understand the beliefs that allowed Native Americans to live in harmony with the land for thousands of years. Following their example may help us heal the land and preserve it for future generations." Be sure to call ahead and check on dates for the

Strawberry Moon Festival (fourth Sunday in June), **Harvest Moon Festival** (Sunday after Labor Day), and **holiday celebration** on the Saturday and Sunday after Thanksgiving (☎ 456-2600; admission charged).

Grafton

From Warner, you might as well take the interstate north to Exit 10, which gives you access to three **state parks**: **Wadleigh** for swimming, **Winslow** for climbing Mt. Kearsarge, and **Rollins** for the **scenic auto route** up the other side of Kearsarge. Beyond the state parks, Route 11 continues north to meet Route 4. You'll pass the turn for Ragged Mtn. ski area (nice rambling in summer, when it's deserted), and arrive in Danbury. Here a left turn (west) with Route 4 brings you to Grafton, home of **Ruggles Mine**, which you've probably already seen advertised on billboards since you arrived in New Hampshire. Don't let the aggressive publicity for the mine make you skip the visit! There's a phenomenal view from the top of Isinglass Mountain, where the mine entrance is located. And the mine itself is plain fun to go through, with caves and passages, and places to collect minerals (if you buy a mine visit ticket, you get to keep whatever you collect!). Famous for its mica, the mine also yields feldspar, beryl, and about 150 more minerals, including amethyst and garnet. It's open weekends from mid-May to mid-June, then daily until mid-October (☎ 448-6911).

Canaan

Canaan is on Route 4 on the way from Grafton to the west side of New Hampshire. There's an interesting historic stretch if you take the right turn at the light through Canaan Street to Canaan Center; some antique shops also flourish here, including **American Decorative Arts** (early Americana, Shaker, and English "bits," according to owner Richard E. Vandall; open by appointment only, ☎ 523-4276).

Enfield

Beyond Canaan on Route 4 is Enfield, on the shore of Lake Mascoma. Be sure to cross the lake on the Shaker Bridge to reach **Lower Shaker Village** on Route 4A (turn left as you leave the bridge), where the **Enfield Shaker Museum** opens its riches to the public year-round (from mid-October to mid-May it's open only Saturday and Sunday, but the rest of the year it's open daily). The museum's recent efforts to buy more of the historic buildings from the peaceable village of believers that once thrived here may mean dramatic expansion of its holdings; keep in touch with changes (☎ 632-4346). Also in Enfield is the **LaSalette Shrine**, an impressive celebration of the Catholic faith; visit the landscaped gardens, or come at Christmas to enjoy the illuminations. To enjoy a retreat here with the outdoor Stations of the Cross and the Peace Walk, contact the Reverend Director, LaSalette Shrine, PO Box 420, Enfield, NH 03748-0420; ☎ 632-7087).

West Lebanon, Cornish

The highways whisk you past the town of Lebanon and into its mall-covered neighbor, West Lebanon. The malls have brought enthusiastic shopping to this area and, as a result, restaurants have multiplied; you can find a wide variety of food. When you've eaten, choose either Route 12A south to the historically fascinating towns of **Cornish** and **Charlestown**, or take a drive north on Route 10 to savor the college town of **Hanover** where Dartmouth College stands, and the very rural environment of the villages of **Lyme** and **Orford** (an architecturally rich village of Federal homes).

If you opt to go south on Route 12A, you'll soon arrive at the **Saint-Gaudens National Historic Site** in Cornish, 12 miles south of West Lebanon. Augustine Saint-Gaudens, born in Dublin, Ireland, in 1848, to a French shoemaker and his Irish wife, became one of America's most noted immigrants, a pioneer in architecture, landscape design, and sculpture. His public monuments still grace American cities: the Sherman monument in New York's Central Park, the "Standing Lincoln" in Chicago. He designed coins for the American Mint, including the standing Liberty from the obverse of the twenty-dollar gold piece. When he began to summer in Cornish, and then to live there year-round, he drew a colony of artists with him, including painter Maxfield Parrish. His estate, Aspet, has become a fitting monument, with its lovely gardens and overwhelming collection of sculpture and other art. The site is open daily from late May through late October. Many buildings and areas are wheelchair accessible, and interpretive information is offered in Braille, on closed-caption videos, audio tapes, and laserdiscs. There are Sunday concerts, woodland walks, and picnic areas. By the way, a stage set designed by Saint-Gaudens' friend Maxfield Parrish, known for his romantic paintings of New England, still can be viewed at the Town Hall in Plainfield, just north of the historic site, on summer Sunday afternoons; your dollar admission will also show you a movie about Parrish (☎ 675-6866).

Claremont & Charlestown

Just south of the Saint-Gaudens site, there are signs for several side roads with **old covered bridges** in the Cornish Center region. Then Route 12A passes the west edge of Claremont, which you might want to detour into on Route 103 to see the old mills and the early churches and cemeteries (Revolutionary War era). There's a **historical society museum** open on summer Sunday afternoons or by appointment (Claremont Historical Society, 26 Mulberry Street, Claremont, NH 03742; ☎ 543-1400; free admission, but donations welcome).

If you're a fan of Colonial history, Charlestown, the next town south on Route 12A as it becomes Route 12, is going to be quite a treat. Not only does the town have lovely old houses; it has a living history museum, **The Fort at No. 4**, where you can get a taste of the fortified settlement here in the 1740s and 1750s. Here is life of the eastern frontier during the French and Indian War. Furnished province houses, stockade, and demonstrations of "skills of the times" make the museum fascinating. It's open from Memorial Day to Labor Day except Tuesdays, and reopens from the third week of September to Columbus Day (☎ 826-5700; admission charge).

Hanover

North of West Lebanon on Route 10 is Hanover, a town that mixes pastoral beauty with college-town energy. Brick buildings and ample sidewalks make the downtown pleasant, and it blends smoothly with the adjoining campus. The elegant **Hanover Inn**, where the American orator Daniel Webster often stayed, is at the junction of Main Street and Wheelock Street. It makes a good central meeting place and location for starting to give directions around town. If you stand at the front of the inn, you are looking into the main part of the college campus. **Wheelock Street** runs west and east in front of you, and Main Street is to your left, divided into North and South by this traffic light. Look across the green and spot the small white information booth, open in summer and foliage season, where you can get a map of the town, the campus, or even of the Dartmouth-Hitchcock Medical Center, on Route 120 south of town. At other seasons, stop at the **Dartmouth Chamber of Commerce** office (☎ 643-3115) upstairs in the Nugget Building on South Main Street.

NOT TO SCALE

Hanover

1. Storr's Pond Recreation Area
2. Pine Park
3. Hanover Country Club
4. Occum Pond
5. Ledyard Canoe Club
6. Information Booth, Baker Library
7. Hanover Inn
8. Hopkins Center
9. Hanover Mink Brook Natural Area

Stand in front of the Hanover Inn again, with the inn at your back. Turn right and walk less than a block to the entrance of the **Hopkins Center**, where Dartmouth's theatrical life takes place. Just beyond the "Hop" and accessible from within it is the

Hood Museum of Art, where collections change often and range from Asian and Egyptian artifacts and art to dramatic modern sculptures of neon and chrome. There are many Old Master paintings, and a collection of American artists' work: picture Frederic Remington and Thomas Eakins, for example. Admission is free; the museum is closed Mondays, and has evening hours on Wednesdays (☎ 646-2808). To see the museum's other startling artwork, head across the green, staying to the right and walking down College Street. The Rollins Chapel (where there are good concerts) is on your right, and Webster on the left; then on the left is **Baker Library** (☎ 646-2560), where in the downstairs rooms you can find an incredible set of murals by Mexican artist José Clemente Orozco, condemning the white invasion of Latin America, celebrating the triumph of the industrial worker, and incidentally criticizing the side effects of "diploma mills" rather than true education. Don't miss it; even kids will be stunned by the intense color and images.

Downtown Hanover also includes the **Dartmouth Bookstore** (☎ 643-3616; 800-624-8800 outside NH); pick up a map and guide when you walk in at 33 South Main Street, as the rooms are specialized. This is a good spot to browse through the latest local hiking, fishing, biking, and snow sports guides; the *Dartmouth Outing Guide* is sold here, and you'll want a copy for its range of trail and paddling options, some as far away as Canada. Farther down South Main Street, take a left onto Lebanon Street and visit the showroom of the **League of NH Craftsmen** (☎ 643-5050), where you may find anything from a hand-carved, near-life-size moose to elegant necklaces, formal paintings, and handmade pottery and glass.

> ❷ **TOWN TRANSPORTATION:** *Hanover buses operated by Advanced Transit are free from Monday through Friday in the "free zone" that goes from the Cold Regions lab north of town, to the Dartmouth Medical School, to the Hanover Inn, down Main Street and stopping by the bookstore, to the Thompson parking lot at the south end of town, to the Dartmouth-Hitchcock Medical Center, and all the way to Lebanon. There are even bike racks.*

By the way, not open to visitors but interesting to know about is the **Cold Regions Research & Engineering Laboratory** of the U.S. Army Corps of Engineers, located north of town. There's an ice engineering facility, plus permafrost tunnel, sea ice ponds, and 24 labs with temperatures 35° below zero! Something to think about when you're hoping for snow.

Where To Stay

Hanover

 There are comfortable bed and breakfast homes and small inns scattered among the towns and back roads of this region. Two locations for more elegant lodging are Hanover and New London. Hanover offers the **Hanover Inn** (Main and Wheelock Street; ☎ 643-4300 or 800-443-7024; www.dartmouth.edu/inn; $$$$), a 92-room neo-Georgian building owned and operated by Dartmouth College. The front terrace, the sitting rooms with comfortable armchairs, and the Ivy Grill are meeting places for local residents and guests alike. Or enjoy bed and breakfast at the **Trumbull House** on 40 Etna Road, east of town (Wheelock Road tees into Etna Road to the east, then you go right for 0.3 mile), a refurbished 1919 cape with college history to share (☎ 643-2370 or 800-651-5141; e-mail bnb@valley.net; $$-$$$); or at **Two Mile Farm**, a 1790 home on a sunny ridge, also on Etna Road, north of the Hanover Center Green (☎ 643-6462; $$).

New London

New London's gracious streets are flower-lined in summer, festive in winter. The **New London Inn** is a classic country inn dating to 1792, warmly welcoming, with 29 rooms and a delightful restaurant (innkeepers Kimberley and Terance O'Mahoney; ☎ 526-2791 or 800-526-2791; e-mail nlinn@srnet.com; $$-$$$). Outside the Main Street area of the village is the **Inn at Pleasant Lake**, with 12 guest rooms that share a view of either the woods or Pleasant Lake. There's a chef-prepared menu in the dining room (innkeepers Brian and Linda MacKenzie; ☎ 526-6271 or 800-626-4907; $$-$$$).

Lake Sunapee Area

Other area options include the **Sunapee Lake Lodge Best Western** at Sunapee (☎ 763-2010 or 800-606-5253; $$-$$$), **Follansbee Inn** at North Sutton (☎ 927-4221; $$), **Hide-Away Inn** at New London (☎ 526-4861 or 800-457-0589; $$), **Lake Sunapee Country Club Inn and Motel** at New London (☎ 526-6040; $$), **Hospitality Motel** at Newbury (☎ 763-2701, $$), **Lamplighter Motel** at New London (☎ 526-6484; $$), and **Mt. Sunapee Motel** at Sunapee (☎ 763-5592; $$).

For very small and intimate bed-and-breakfast type lodgings, consider the **Village House** in Sutton Mills (☎ 927-4765; $), **Schoolhouse Corner B&B** at Danbury (☎ 768-3467; $-$$), **Thistle & Shamrock Inn** at Bradford (☎ 938-5553; $$), **Sleeper Inn** at Sunapee (☎ 863-1144 or 800-484-1144; $$), and **Potter Place Inn** at Andover (☎ 735-5141; $$). **Rosewood** in Bradford (☎ 938-5253; $$) is especially charming, with lovely gardens, candlelight and crystal breakfasts on the porches, and dining room with fireplace.

Henniker

If you love dogs, meet Bertha among the friendly hosts at **Colby Hill Inn**, Henniker (innkeepers Ellen and John Day and Laurel Day; ☎ 428-3281 or 800-531-0330; $$), where the cookie jar is always full.

Newport & Goshen

Just a few miles away from the summer busy-ness of Lake Sunapee are the towns of Newport and Goshen, which offer interesting lodging. In Newport, there's a 1760 Georgian home at the north end of town that has become the **Eagle Inn** (523 North Main Street; ☎ 863-3583 or 800-367-2364; $$-$$$). With Newport addresses but actually out on the back roads are the **Soo Nipi Lodge** (☎ 863-7509 or 800-760-8477, ask about weekly and group rates) and the country charm of the **Back Side Inn** (innkeepers Bruce and Mackie Hefka, ☎ 863-5161, e-mail BsideInn@aol.com, $$), which is across the road from Goshen's amazing used book shop, Nelson's Rare Books (see *Sightseeing*).

Claremont

If you're planning to explore the historically rich towns of Claremont and Charlestown, why not sleep and dine in another era too? The **Goddard Mansion** dates from 1905 and offers a range of very different rooms, from French country mood to Victorian; common rooms include a fireplace, baby grand piano, and 1939 Wurlitzer jukebox. It's in Claremont (call for directions from the hosts, the Albee family; ☎ 543-0603 or 800-736-0603; $$-$$$).

Lyme

If you've gone north instead along the Connecticut River, Lyme offers two small inns with New England charm: the **Alden Country Inn and Tavern & Grille** on Route 10 at the far end of the green (☎ 795-2222 or 800-794-2296; $$) and the **Dowds' Country Inn** on the left side of the common (innkeeper Tami Dowd; ☎ 795-4712 or 800-482-4712; $$$-$$$$). The main attraction of staying in Lyme is being able to visit its out-of-the-way antique shops. Half a mile north of the Lyme common on Route 10 is **Lyme Creamery Antiques** (☎ 795-4204), which you might want to visit while you stay in the area. In the next village north, Orford, make the right turn to Orfordville to find **Dame Hill Nostalgia** (☎ 353-4717), a shop specializing in Amish quilts as well as antiques and collectibles.

■ Camping

 Camping out? Try **Mascoma Lake Campground** with its swimming beach (Route 4A; RR2, Box 331, Enfield, NH 03748; ☎ 448-5076 or 800-769-7861), or in New London, **Otter Lake Campground** (beach, boats, swimming; 55 Otterville Rd., New London, NH 03257; ☎ 763-5600). In Bradford, **Lake Massasecum Campground** is also on the water (Route 114, four miles south of Route 103; RR1 Box 499, Bradford, NH 03221; ☎ 938-2571 or, in winter, 668-8060). At **Pillsbury State Park** in Washington there are 38 tent sites and three remote access sites for primitive camping; you may need to canoe in! Reservations accepted from January to October at ☎ 271-3638; campground open from early May to mid-October. Finally, don't forget that the AMC provides a lodge at

Cardigan Mountain where you can stay as you explore the trails; contact Manager, **AMC Cardigan Lodge**, RFD1, Box 712, Bristol, NH 03222 (☎ 744-8011). There are also 11 well-spaced campsites near the lodge, and a high cabin two miles up the trail. Lodge reservations include sheets, blankets, and meals; meals can also be added to other arrangements.

Where To Eat

Hanover

 Gracious dining in Hanover traditionally means the Daniel Webster Room in the **Hanover Inn**, open daily for all three meals, with flavorful continental and New England cuisine served elegantly (☎ 643-4300 or 800-443-7024). Another local tradition is lunch at **Lou's** (30 South Main Street, ☎ 643-3321), across the road from the Dartmouth Bookstore (great sandwiches). South of town near the Dartmouth Medical Center on Route 120 is **Jesse's** (☎ 643-4111), which has good steak and seafood and maybe the best salad bar around.

West Lebanon & Lebanon

Slip down to West Lebanon and go "ethnic" at **Lui Lui** (☎ 298-7070) at the Power House Mall for a good Italian meal, or try the **Seven Barrel Brewery** (☎ 298-5566), just south of Interstate 89, for a lively brew pub with tavern fare. In Lebanon, **Sweet Tomatoes Trattoria** is a local favorite, with outrageous pasta creations and amazing pizzas (One Court Street, ☎ 448-1711).

Newport

If you're in Newport, try the Green Room at the **Eagle Inn** (523 North Main Street, ☎ 863-3583).

Claremont

On the way to "parts south," slip into **Shirley's Restaurant & Donut Shop** on Route 11 in Claremont (official address 162 Pleasant Street, ☎ 542-6413). These are the donuts your great-aunt made and that you haven't had since – better hike an extra hour afterward, but they are so good.

New London

In New London, **Peter Christian's Tavern** (186 Main Street, ☎ 526-4042) offers a meal with innovative sandwiches (try the Fourth Musketeer Puff if you get a chance) and rich desserts. Experience the gentle sophistication of dinner at the **New London Inn** (☎ 526-2791). For a light lunch, drop into **Gourmet Garden** (☎ 526-6656), also on Main Street in New London, or else slip down the west shore of the lake to Sunapee Harbor and enjoy lakeside dining with specialty sandwiches at **The Anchorage** (☎ 763-4021).

Wilmot

Probably the best food in this region is at **La Meridiana** (☎ 526-2033), on Route 11 in Wilmot. The Northern Italian food is delicious, with outstanding pastas to pastries.

Information Sources

Claremont Chamber of Commerce, Claremont, NH 03743; ☎ 543-1296.

Hanover Chamber of Commerce, Hanover, NH 03755; ☎ 643-3115.

Lake Sunapee Business Association, PO Box 400, Sunapee, NH 03782; ☎ 800-258-3530.

Lebanon Chamber of Commerce, Lebanon, NH 03766; ☎ 448-1203.

New London Chamber of Commerce, New London, NH 03257; ☎ 526-6575.

Newport Chamber of Commerce, Newport, NH 03773; ☎ 863-1510.

The Monadnock Region

Keene is the principal city of the Monadnock Region, the southwestern corner of New Hampshire. It's a college town grown into a restaurant and coffee shop haven, with plenty of music, especially live jazz. Just 24 miles east, **Peterborough** also attracts musicians, as well as artists and writers, focused at the noted **MacDowell Colony** and spilling joyfully into the rest of the town. Around these two busy centers the gentle mountains rise up, unexpectedly wild and lovely. Farms extend green pastures, which in winter become rolling snowfields. Relatively undiscovered, the area gives sweet rewards to visitors.

Getting Around

Route 101 crosses New Hampshire from east to west, and visitors driving in from the Concord and Manchester areas are likely to arrive this way. From the corridor of these larger cities, the towns you enter are first **Peterborough**, then **Dublin**, the home of *Yankee Magazine*; **Marlborough**; and **Keene**, where Route 101 ends. **Route 9** links Keene to the Connecticut River to the west, and sets a diagonal northeast to the very scenic cluster of the Hillsborough villages. **Routes 10 and 12**, the major north-south highways (usually two-lane) for southwestern New Hampshire, converge in Keene. Boston residents may take the cross-country drive and come into New Hampshire from south of Keene, also on Route 12. One more north-south route, **Route 202**, links Peterborough to **Jaffrey** to the south, and **Hillsborough** to the north. These are the routes to which most directions refer.

In terms of adventure for hikers, bikers, and snow travelers, this region ties in strongly with the Dartmouth/Lake Sunapee region, thanks to the recently established **Monadnock-Sunapee Greenway**, nearly 50 miles of north-south trail link-

ing Mt. Monadnock to Mt. Sunapee along the Monadnock Highlands. What a great idea! There are also vast tracts of state
parkland and acreage preserved by private groups, and attractive small villages with special summer events that lure yearly
visitors.

Adventures

■ On Foot

Monadnock & Pack Monadnock

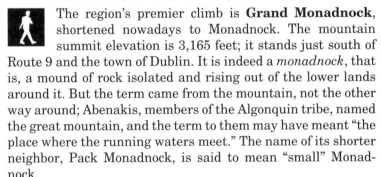

The region's premier climb is **Grand Monadnock**,
shortened nowadays to Monadnock. The mountain
summit elevation is 3,165 feet; it stands just south of
Route 9 and the town of Dublin. It is indeed a *monadnock*, that
is, a mound of rock isolated and rising out of the lower lands
around it. But the term came from the mountain, not the other
way around; Abenakis, members of the Algonquin tribe, named
the great mountain, and the term to them may have meant "the
place where the running waters meet." The name of its shorter
neighbor, Pack Monadnock, is said to mean "small" Monadnock.

> ● **DID YOU KNOW?** *By reputation, Mt. Monad-*
> *nock is the second most climbed mountain in the*
> *world – only Mt. Fuji in Japan gets more climb-*
> *ers!*

Today Mt. Monadnock is the center of an enormous reserve of
nearly 6,000 acres of land. Part of it is a state park with headquarters in Jaffrey. The park visitor center (☎ 532-8862) is located off Dublin Road, which in turn is off Route 124, in Jaffrey
Center. More than half of the reserve is protected by the Society
for the Preservation of New Hampshire Forests, better known
as the SPNHF or just the Forest Society (54 Portsmouth St,
Concord, NH 03301-5486; ☎ 224-9945). The Forest Society bal-
ances land use, combining high-quality hiking trails with carefully planned timber harvests and habitat wildlife protection.

Monadnock Region

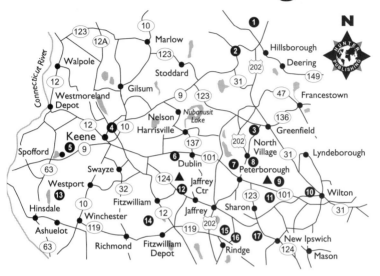

1. Fox Forest
2. Franklin Pierce Homestead
3. Greenfield State Park
4. Monadnock Children's Museum
5. Chesterfield Gorge
6. Friendly Farm
7. MacDowell Colony
8. Sheiling Forest
9. Pack Monadnock, Miller State Park
10. Frye's Measure Mill
11. Temple Mountain Ski Area
12. Monadnock State Park, Mt. Monadnock
13. Pisgah State Park
14. Rhododendron State Park
15. Windblown Ski Touring
16. Cathedral of the Pines
17. Annett State Forest

Area of Detail

Monadnock
Region

Monadnock climbers savor the views from the peak, which has a manmade timberline created by farmers burning the mountain over in the early 19th century, at first for pasture and later to drive out wolves. From the south, the **Metacomet-Monadnock Trail** arrives here after crossing central Massachusetts; north from the summit the newly formed **Monadnock-Sunapee Greenway** heads north toward **Love-**

Monadnock-Sunapee Greenway

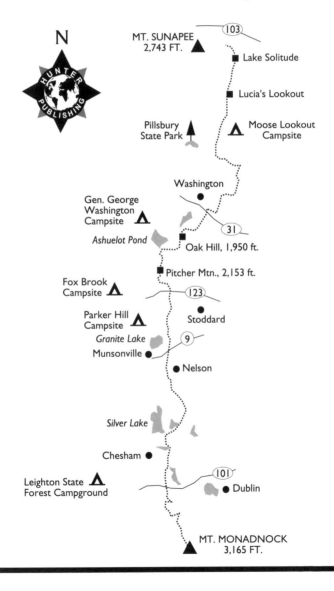

well **Mountain** and eventually for the peak of **Mt. Sunapee**, 49 miles away. Much of the Greenway passes over private land, with owners consenting to hiking and winter snow travel; your careful protection of the land and of its sense of quiet rural life and in places of wilderness will help convince landowners to continue to agree to the Greenway's existence. It is a wonderful trail, a great example of long-distance freedom to move through the mountains. You can purchase a *Monadnock-Sunapee Greenway Guide* from the SPNHF or at the Pinkham Notch Base Camp of the Appalachian Mountain Club.

New Hampshire hiker and author Daniel Doan recommended in his *50 More Hikes in New Hampshire* an approach to the mountain from the northern side on the **Pumpelly Trail**. It's a nine-mile round trip, with a rise of 2,670 feet, so it takes about seven hours. You'll want to bring along at least two quarts of water per person (plus lunch) for this long, dry hike! Also bring rain gear and warm clothes for the cold winds above treeline – this isn't as rough as the weather on Mt. Washington to the north, but you can still count on a 10° drop in temperature and a chance of fog or rain. Why have to cut the hike short because you're cold?

Start from Route 101 at the east end of Dublin Lake and turn (south) onto the Lake Road. In less than a half-mile the trailhead appears on the left, a woods road and bridle path opposite a shorefront log cabin. You'll probably have to park on the shoulder of the road a bit farther down, and walk back to the trail. Its first section is through private land, but a sharp right turn after some 350 feet takes you up through a stone wall and in about five minutes to another woods road, where you turn left, uphill. There's a spring, and beyond it the route goes up Oak Hill and down to a small valley. As you climb out of the valley, watch for a right-hand turn onto a more typical mountain trail, a winding footpath named for the trail's 1884 creator, Dublin resident Ralph Pumpelly. As the trail rises, there are lookouts from ledges on spur trails. Finally the terrain becomes barren, as you crest a slanting ledge and follow rock cairns. There's a long shoulder to cross to the summit, and a rounded knob on the left for wide vistas. Stay with the cairns to the top of Dublin Ridge, and follow the trail left for a short drop into woods, then right, back into the turf of mountain cranberry.

Monadnock Region

Skip the white-blazed trail on your left, the Spellman Trail, and follow the Pumpelly sharply right into a small wooded ravine. Again skip a leftward trail, this time marked with red; the summit is three-fourths of a mile ahead of you, in sight. You'll be glad to have hiking boots on for the last stretch, and will probably stand in amazement like so many other hikers before you, soaking up the views of lowlands and mountains. This isolated mountain towers some 2,000 feet above the countryside, so you get great rewards for your climb! When you descend, get your thoughts back out of the clouds and watch closely for the arrow painted on the rocks and for the first few cairns to be sure you've found the Pumpelly Trail again.

For easier and more often used trails to the summit, head to the state park office and park your car. You can make a round-trip on either the **White Dot** or **White Cross Trail** from here; the former will take four miles, and the latter 4.4 miles, each about a two-hour climb (up). The drawback is that so many other hikers take these trails, so try to go on a a weekday. Using the *AMC White Mountain Guide* you can pick from several other less used trails that are not as long or as strenuous as the Pumpelly. Another option is the **south side circuit** recommended by Eastern Mountain Sports, an outdoor supply store with an shop in Peterborough. Plan five or six hours for the trip, and take plenty of water and warm and rainproof summit clothing. Park at the Old Toll Road parking area, which is on Route 124 between Jaffrey and Marlborough. The first half-mile of hike is directly up the **Old Toll Road**, but then you turn right onto the **Parker Trail** and left onto the **Cliff Trail** (yellow C blazes). When you reach Bald Rock you pick up the Smith Connecting Trail (yellow S blazes) and hike to the popular White Cross Trail for the last half-mile to the summit. Look back to Bald Rock, where you switched trails earlier; to the right of it is a small peak with a weathervane, called **Monta Rose**. You're headed toward it. Look at the summit signs and find the **Dublin Trail**, which in less than a hundred yards brings you to the **Smith Summit Trail** on your left. Take it past Monta Rosa to the **Fairy Spring Trail**, which in turn goes to the halfway house and the toll road, a mile above the parking lot.

Hiking up nearby **Pack Monadnock** lets you look across and view Monadnock! The easiest access is from Route 101, Miller

State Park, five miles east of Peterborough. There's a modest day fee for use of the park. From the parking area there are two good routes (not counting the auto road, which you can take when you're simply sightseeing). The "old" route has blue blazes, and the "new" one is more challenging and is blazed with yellow, with a sign: **Wapack Trail**. This is the last part of a 21-mile ridgeline trail from the base of Mt. Watatic in Ashburnham, Massachusetts, to the northern slope of North Pack Monadnock. There are actually two peaks of Pack: the south peak at 2,310 feet, very civilized (relay towers, fire tower, shelter, tables), and the north peak, wild and 2,278 feet up. You'll probably enjoy the old trail more (the one on the right with blue blazes), now called the **Marion Davis Trail**. From Route 101 to the south peak is 1.6 miles and takes about 1½ hours; if you follow the **Wapack Trail** from the south to the north peak you'll have some tough climbing with a descent of 500 feet before you go uphill again, and you'll be hiking another two hours for the added 2.4 miles. Figure the same for the return on each trail, as the descent even from the south peak is not easy. A little surprise: the view from Pack Monadnock on a clear day stretches to Boston!

More Mountains and Other Hikes

Other New Hampshire mountains along the Wapack Trail are **Barrett**, **Kidder**, and **Temple**. Eastern Mountain Sports recommends **Bald Mountain** for a "lively three-hour round-trip with great views." For this hike, start from the Willard Pond sanctuary off Route 123, three miles northwest of Hancock, where Willard Pond Road is on the right (gravel), leading in one mile to a left at the parking area and trail (to the left of the beach). There's also abundant hiking in the thousands of acres of preserved land that makes this region so forested: state parks, and acreage managed by the Forest Society and the Audubon Society. Here are some of them (yes, there are even more!):

Bear Den Natural Area, Gilsum: On Route 10 south of town. Short walk to ancient glacial potholes and a bit farther to ledges that may once have been a bear denning area.

Pisgah State Park: Wilderness area of 13,500 acres stretching from Chesterfield, Hinsdale, and Winchester, with marked entrances from Routes 9, 10, 63, and 119. We're talking 21 square miles here, the largest in the NH State Park system – always leave word with a friend where you're planning to hike and when you expect to return. There should be trail maps in the mailboxes at each entrance. (If you prefer, you may write and request one in advance from the Bureau of Trails, PO Box 1856, Concord, NH 03302-1856.) Pick your own loop; you can easily tramp 10 miles through this engaging former pastureland that has grown up in woods and bogs. Take plenty of drinking water. And keep an eye out for tracks and scat as well as scratched tree trunks – Pisgah is home to beaver, bobcat, coyote, red fox, porcupine, raccoon, deer, and plenty of birds including herons, waterfowl, hawks and owls.

Sheiling State Forest, Peterborough: Tamer, with 45 acres of ridges and valleys including a wildflower preserve and Forest Learning Center. On Old Street Road in Peterborough.

Fox State Forest, Hillsborough: A woodland of 1,432 acres with 20 miles of day-hiking trails and a forestry center. Includes old-growth forest. If you'd like an eco-center tour, make an appointment (☎ 464-3453). Get here from the town of Hillsborough by going north on the Hillsborough Center Road from the very center of town (at the location of the post office and Chamber of Commerce).

Harris Center for Conservation Education, Hancock (north of Peterborough): More trails (seven miles), two mountains with summit views and a conservation center, in the midst of 7,000 preserved acres. Free weekend programs in the summer and fall; snowshoe treks in winter (☎ 525-3394). Take Route 202 from Peterborough to Hancock, and at the bandstand go left on Route 123 for 2.4 miles to find the left turn for the center.

MacDowell Lake, West Peterborough: To get here, take Route 101 west of town to the right turn onto Union Street, followed by a left on Wilder Street. Calling this 1,198 acres is a tad deceptive, as a lot of the space is taken up by the lake! But there are some short hiking trails, a picnic shelter, and a chance to see plenty of waterfowl. Interpretive programs are offered all summer, starting at 2 pm, and include dam tours, wildlife tracking, the insect world, botany and tree identification, and a junior rangers program for kids age six to 12; call ahead to find out what's happening and when (☎ 924-3431). All programs are free.

Rhododendron blossoms at Rhododendron State Park, Fitzwilliam.

Annett State Park, Rindge: You may well visit Rindge to see the Cathedral of the Pines, a scenic and often deeply spiritual area. But people don't always realize that practically next door is Annett State Park, with 1,336 acres of woodland and trails (☎ 532-8862). When you visit the Pines you're one mile north of Route 119 on Cathedral Road; go another mile north to get to the state park.

Rhododendron State Park, Fitzwilliam: This is partly ancient woodlands, 494 acres total, with 15 acres crowded with a jungle of rhododendrons up to 20 feet tall, which flower impressively in early to mid-July. It's a National Nature Landmark, and when staffed may charge a day-use fee. There are several trails, including a connection with the Metacomet Trail and Monadnock approach, all well marked. Follow signs from the village of Fitzwilliam; the approach road is only a mile out of town, but it's long.

Thurston V. Williams Family Forest (379 acres) and **Charles L. Peirce Wildlife and Forest Reservation** (3,461 acres): These two parcels adjoin each other and are managed by the SPNHF. The Peirce Reservation has more than 10 miles of hiking trails and woods roads; look for the **Trout-n-Bacon Trail** with its views from Bacon Ledge and its destination of Bacon Pond. From Route 9 in Stoddard, go west on Route 123 for two miles, and turn right at the fire station. Cross the bridge and immediately turn right onto the dirt road; go one mile and park on the left. Bring a topo map and compass for this relatively wild property. The Williams Forest includes a stand of old-growth forest with impressive birch, white pine, sugar and red maple, beech, hemlock, and white ash; trees range from 20 to 44 inches in diameter and 70 to 100 feet high. To get to the trail, take Route 9 west from Hillsborough to Route 31 north and go 7.2 miles; turn left onto the gravel Bailey Road, go 0.4 mile, bear left, and go uphill 0.5 mile. Turn right at the cluster of signs and go 0.6 mile to another cluster of signs, where you turn left, go 0.3 mile, and turn left again. From there, proceed 0.5 mile, turn right, go 0.2 mile, and park in the open area; if these last two roads are too wet, park and walk the last bit. (You deserve orienteering credit just for getting here.) From the parking area go another 1,000 feet to the end of the dirt road and bear right onto the grassy logging road; after 900 feet go right again on a footpath among young trees. Finally you'll get confirmation that you're in the right place – an SPNHF sign 250 feet later. The trail divides up ahead to form a loop through the old-growth stands; do take a topo map and compass along so you'll be able to roam confidently.

Gap Mountain Reservation in Troy and Jaffrey: Try to visit in blueberry season (late July). The SPNHF manages 1,142 acres here, crossed by the Metacomet-Monadnock Trail, and with superb views. From the north, start with Route 202 in Jaffrey and take Route 124 west 6.3 miles. Turn left onto Old County Road (gravel) and go 0.6 mile, then park. (Please don't block Old Mill Road to the right.) Walk 700 feet up the unimproved Old County Road to the Metacomet-Monadnock Trail crossing and turn right to head for the summit. The mountain is relatively easy to climb. If you explore the land around it, you'll find two bogs and a rich variety of plants and wildlife; try late May to early June for wildflowers.

If long-distance hiking with overnight backpacking interests you, hiking the length of the **Monadnock-Sunapee Greenway** is a great idea. Some 80 landowners are voluntarily hosting the trail, which also crosses three state parks. Starting at Mt. Monadnock, it goes north through Leighton State Forest, to Silver lake, through Nelson and Munsonville, past Granite Lake, and into Stoddard, where there's camping at Parker Hill Campsite. When it climbs Pitcher Mountain it's about halfway to Sunapee. Jackson Hill, Ashuelot Pond, and Washington (with Gen. Geo. Washington Campsite) are ahead before the trail enters Pillsbury State Park and then Mt. Sunapee State Park (northern section described in *Dartmouth/Lake Sunapee Region*, page 225). The entire trip takes four or five days. Get more details from the Monadnock-Sunapee Greenway Club, PO Box 164, Marlow, NH 03456.

A short but fascinating trail in **Chesterfield Gorge** is mentioned in *Sightseeing*, page 276.

Support and route planning for hikers and other outdoor trekkers can be found at **Eastern Mountain Sports** in Peterborough (two miles north of town on Route 202; ☎ 924-7231). EMS will also direct rock climbers and discuss the condition of local routes; rock conditions do change.

Speaking of climbing, how about going underground? The little town of **Gilsum**, eight miles north of Keene on Route 10, holds an **annual rock swap and show** that's attended by some 8,000 people (truly!). It's the last weekend of June, at the elementary school off Route 10 (plenty of signs; ☎ 353-2472). Why here? Gilsum is a former mining center. The show annually provides maps and material on over 60 inactive mines in New Hampshire, and some of the people trading and selling minerals at the show actually own their own mine shafts. For instance, exhibitor Jim Tovey owns the Wise Mine near Westmoreland, where discoveries include quartz and fluorite crystals; if you join the **Keene Mineral Club**, you can get in on the restricted trips to it (recent annual membership cost $10; Dave Redfield, treasurer, Keene Mineral Club, PO Box 627, Marlborough, NH 03455; more questions, contact Dick Homes, President, ☎ 352-5932). There are still several mine shafts in the Gilsum area to explore, but all are on private land; stop at the show for a list, then visit the town clerk's office to develop contacts with the owners. If you're experienced in cave spelunking, you may be able to convince a few to let you go below ground and explore.

■ On Wheels

Road Biking

 This is a tough region for road touring because the roads tend to be narrow and hilly. Route 101 and Route 9 are especially dangerous because of fast car traffic. So choose loops that head away from these main route; in *30 Bicycle Tours in New Hampshire* there are nine suggested paths to start with. One of them, the 18.3-mile easy cycling loop around **Swanzey** and extending to Winchester, includes five covered bridges! The 27½-mile challenging loop from **Alstead** on Route 123 to Marlow and then on Route 123A through South Acworth back to Alstead leads through truly charming, unspoiled countryside with a lake, a pond, and the late 18th-century Mill Village with its standing grist mill. Roads are still narrow here, but not as heavily traveled. If you take the 27.2-mile easy to moderate tour from **Hancock** to Peterborough and around through Dublin and Harrisville, you run the risk of being distracted by the great sightseeing, from a 1788 meeting house to a games museum to a mill village. Allow extra time! By the way, the **Keene Chamber of Commerce** provides its own maps and route suggestions for biking, an unusual service for a town office – open Monday through Friday, 9-5, at 48 Central Square (☎ 352-1303).

Mountain Biking

Mountain bikers, rejoice: **Pisgah State Forest** welcomes your wheels. This is a rough forested range of 13,500 acres in the towns of Winchester, Chesterfield, and Hinsdale, off Route 63, with 21 square miles of trails. Call the park to request maps if you like (☎ 239-8153) or write to the **Bureau of Trails** (PO Box 1856, Concord, NH 03302-1856); you can usually get a map at the mailboxes just inside each of the park entrances, which are located on Routes 9, 10, 63, and 119. Bring a topo map and compass too, and plenty of drinking water.

Outfitters

There are several support shops for bikers in this area; just a few are listed here.

- **Summers' Back Country Outfitters** (☎ 357-5107) off West Street in Keene, across from the Colony Mill Marketplace. You can see the canoes stacked up from West Street. They offer enthusiastic route planning.

- Also in Keene is **Banagan's Cycling Co.** (41 Central Street on the square in the middle of town; ☎ 357-2331). Banagan's and Summers' are both very experienced with repairs.

- Also well recommended: **Spokes and Slopes** on School Street in Peterborough (☎ 924-9961); they've been known to stay open late to help out a cyclist in trouble.

- If you're in the Hillsboro area, try **Ped'ling Fool** at 77 Main Street (☎ 464-5286).

■ On Water

Canoeing

In Greenfield, five miles north of Peterborough, is **Greenfield State Park**, located off Route 136. The park includes the east shore of Otter Lake, a pleasant paddling spot. In New Ipswich there's another acreage with water frontage, the **Nussdorfer Nature Area**, where canoeing and fishing are encouraged at Hoar Pond. Brook and rainbow trout are the catch at **Otter Brook** in Roxbury; good access is offered from the **Taves Reservation**, 571 acres managed by the SPNHF. From Keene, take Route 101 east for 2.3 miles, then turn left at the flashing light and go 1½ miles to find the right turn onto Middletown Road. Go out this road 3.1 miles and park near the granite historical marker. When you walk another 500 feet you'll find a road to the left going down to the brook.

If you don't mind a few portages over beaver dams, you can get an intimate look at **Tophet Swamp**, the central feature of the 509-acre **Perry Reservation** managed by the SPNHF in New Ipswich, Sharon, and Rindge. From Route 202 in Jaffrey, take Route 124 east 4½ miles and park on the right at the Gridley River bridge; the river is the best access into the swamp.

If you're willing to tote your boat some distance, there's wilderness flatwater in **Pisgah State Park**. For starters, take Route 119 from Route 63, going east to the village of Ashuelot and then heading north on Fullam Road. This should take you right into Chesterfield Road, which in two miles enters the park. A gate (open 9 am to dusk from mid-May until snow blockage) lets you proceed another 3.8 miles to the two parking areas at the south end of **Fullam Pond**. Make sure to leave before the gate closes (probably at dusk, but check on your way in). The **Pisgah Reservoir** is larger, and also approached from Route 119, but this time east of Ashuelot, about two miles from Route 63. Look for the turn north onto Reservoir Road, which is also gated, and head 1.8 miles into the preserve for a parking area close to the south end of the reservoir. There's a steep half-mile carry to the water. It's worth the trouble, with many islands, deep inlets, and hidden coves. Look for blueberry bushes on shore. **Tufts Pond** is connected by a stream to the south of the reservoir. If you've got a lightweight inflatable or other easy option, try it; you'll be nearly solitary as a paddler, although a few anglers on foot may join you. Four more ponds are north of the reservoir. (Sorry, no trout here.)

Whitewater paddlers have one main attraction: the **Ashuelot River** (pronounced Ash-WEE-lot), which runs from Marlow down to the Connecticut, with rapid rough upper stretches, a winding and placid middle section, and utterly wild paddling for the lower section. Only the middle section stays runnable most of the year; the upper part is for spring whitewater, and the lower for summer or fall. Check the *AMC River Guide for New Hampshire and Vermont* to get the skinny on the Class III and IV rapids and how to run them. Remember to scout before running; trees fall, banks move, and the wild stretch from Lower Stillwater to Gilsum Gorge includes **Surprise Rapids**, a tricky bit of water.

And there's always the **Connecticut River**, which in this area is wide and flat. The most interesting section is from the Vernon Dam (near the Hinsdale Greyhound Park), past the mouth of the Ashuelot entering from the east, and through another 3½ miles to the Massachusetts border – swift and rocky if the river is low. Of course, you might cross the state line and find the first 10 miles of Massachusetts water to the gorge at French King irresistible for its pastoral surroundings and good camping spots. Come back north before you get spoiled!

Other good paddling waters include the **Contoocook River** and its **Powdermill Pond** north of Peterborough; **Willard Pond**, three miles northwest of Hancock off Route 123; and, on the other side of Route 123 from the Willard Pond Sanctuary, **Nubanusit Lake** and its close neighbor **Spoonwood Pond**. For pointers on these locations and others, stop in Wilton at **Monadnock Canoe and Kayak**, where you can rent, get lessons, arrange tours, arrange waterfront delivery and pickup of a boat, and plan routes (call for directions: ☎ 654-5198).

Outfitters

- For a chance to try out a kayak or canoe, or do some water route planning, stop at **Summers' Backcountry Outfitters**, just west of the center of Keene and visible from West Street, across from the Colony Mill Marketplace (the town's classiest shopping block). You'll see the stacks of canoes. In this unusual shop, there are experts on specific sports, and Pat Manion, the manager, is likely to be out at the Ashuelot River with a bunch of boats (☎ 357-5107, year-round).

Scenic Cruises

If you'd like to see the Connecticut River in relaxed fashion, **Peacemaker Cruises** departs from North Walpole, some 20 miles north of Keene, with **pontoon boats** that offer a leisurely approach to the wide water. Captain Bill Gallagher encourages guests to bring picnics along, as well as camera and binoculars. He also puts fishing charters at a higher priority than daily cruises – not surprising when you're after salmon and trout!

The 20-foot boat can take up to 14 passengers; an average cruise lasts two to 2½ hours. Peacemaker Cruises, 22 West Street, North Walpole, NH 03609; ☎ 445-2371; e-mail pcbwhu@ cyberportal.net.

Fishing

Edward MacDowell Lake west of Peterborough on Route 101 is not exactly isolated, but there's still good boating and excellent fishing (largemouth bass, pickerel, yellow perch, horned pout). To get to the boat ramp, turn right off Route 101 onto Union Street, pass by the turn to the dam, and take the next left on Windy Row; a left gain on Spring Road will take you past a parking area for hikers, and on to the sharp left for Richardson Road, where there's boat ramp parking.

Visiting in winter? **Ice fishing** is a great sport; to get equipped, visit the **Sportsmen's Den** (☎ 242-6651 or 242-3639) on Route 12 in Troy, where Buzz Bowers not only has all the gear but also can point you toward local ponds where you'll get a bite.

Swimming

Most of the little lakes here are too small for good sailing, let alone windsurfing. However, almost all have swimming beaches; check out the town beach at **Spofford Lake** on Route 9, and **Greenfield State Park** (north of Peterborough), the only notable public beach in the region (plan on it being crowded on summer weekends especially). You can also swim at **Pillsbury State Park** in Washington. Hancock's **Norway Pond** and Antrim's **Gregg Lake** are good local swimming spots.

■ On Horseback

In Peterborough, see **Pixel Acres** for ring riding on registered Morgan horses. This may not be the trail ride through the mountains you were picturing, but how often are you going to get a chance to ride such gorgeous horseflesh? (You might as well ask about trails, too, though.) The riding facility is open year-round: Pixel Acres, 468 Greenfield Road, Peterborough, NH 03458 (☎ 924-3341). You can also write for information from **N.E.A.T.S. Equestrian Riding Center**, 127 Goldmine Road, Dublin, NH 03444.

Horse-Drawn Excursions

In Jaffrey, **Silver Ranch Stables** on Route 124, one mile east of the village, puts together sleigh rides, hayrides, and carriages (☎ 532-7363).

Combine a horse-drawn hayride or sleigh ride, drawn by Belgian draft horses, with farm animal displays and a campfire for roasting marshmallows, and in early spring a tour of the sugar house as maple syrup is made. That's what **Stonewall Farm** puts together. The horses are the centerpiece, but the frills are just as much fun. Rides must be scheduled in advance. The farm is outside Keene, three miles west toward Brattleboro, Vermont, on Route 9. Turn right onto Chesterfield Road and the farm is just 0.8 mile more. Stonewall Farm, 243 Chesterfield Rd., Keene, NH 03431; ☎ 357-7278.

■ On Snow & Ice

There is only one alpine resort here, and cross-country skiing is less commercially offered than in other regions of the state. However, every hiking area mentioned in *On Foot* is open to cross-country skiers and snowshoe travelers, which means there are hundreds of miles of wooded trails, with a good likelihood of seeing wildlife tracks in the snow all winter long. New Hampshire even offers a free *Pocket Guide to Animal Tracks*; write to New Hampshire Fish and Game Department, 2 Hazen Drive, Concord, NH 03301.

Temple Mountain Ski Area in Peterborough (☎ 924-6949; e-mail templemtn@monad.net) is the only Monadnock region alpine slope. Although it's small, you'll need plenty of energy, as it includes a snowboard park with halfpipe and night skiing. Temple also offers 50 km of cross-country trails and a Friday night telemarking clinic, plus sleigh rides and a new tubing park. Other cross-country areas are **Windblown Ski Touring**, New Ipswich, with 35 km of trails, a rustic lodge, ski shop, and good lunches (☎ 878-2869); **Fitzwilliam Inn**, Fitzwilliam (☎ 585-9000); **Franklin Pierce College**, Rindge (☎ 899-4000);

Greenfield State Park, Greenfield (☎ 547-3373); the Inn at East Hill Farm, Troy (☎ 242-6495); Monadnock State Park, Jaffrey (☎ 532-8862); Sargent Camp, Peterborough (☎ 525-3311); and Woodbound Inn, Jaffrey (☎ 532-8341).

■ In The Air

Jaffrey offers Silver Ranch Airpark on Route 124 with scenic flights that range from a $10 "local" to a grand tour of the Monadnock Region for about $100 per flight, including two or three passengers (☎ 532-8870).

■ Eco-Travel

The Harris Center for Outdoor Education is mentioned in On Foot. With 2,000 acres surrounding the center, and 5,000 more adjoining, the "supersanctuary" here results from efforts of the Harris Center, the New Hampshire Audubon Society, the SPNHF, and NH Fish and Game Department, and the town of Hancock, as well as private individuals. Setting aside so much space helps large predators like the bobcat, fisher, and bear survive, as well as the huge and gangling moose. Environmental education programs here are held year-round; contact the Harris Center at King's Highway, Hancock, NH 03449 (☎ 525-3394).

Both the Harris Center and NH Audubon (Concord office: ☎ 224-9909) have information on hawk watching, which can be done from the north peak of Pack Monadnock between September 10 and 20 each year. Not just one or two hawks pass by – there are hundreds, even thousands. Contact either preservation group for scheduled hikes and bird watches.

More migratory birds find a way station in the Wapack National Wildlife Refuge that covers the north part of Pack Monadnock (1,672 acres). From Peterborough, take Route 202 north to Sand Hill Road; in 4.3 miles you come to the trailhead at the northern end of the Wapack Trail. Park on the gravel shoulder. If you want to do more than just walk the one trail, prepare ahead of time with the map and the Wapack Trail

Guide, both from **Friends of the Wapack**, PO Box 115, West Peterborough, NH 03468.

Finally, what would a New Hampshire summer be without **picking blueberries**? Here's a hot tip: **Pitcher Mountain**, **Bald Mountain**, and **Gap Mountain** are great places to pick and eat in late July. Bald Mountain and Gap are described in *On Foot*; to reach Pitcher, go to Stoddard and pick up Route 123 west for 1½ miles to the parking area on the right. Follow either the fire road or the Monadnock-Sunapee Greenway Trail there. Don't forget your pail.

Sightseeing

Keene Area

Either **Keene** or **Peterborough** makes a good start for sightseeing. Keene is the large of the two, a bona fide city of about 25,000 with a strip shopping mall to its west and an all-weather airport. Nourished by Keene State College at the south end of town, the city actually centers on a picturesque Central Square with the elegant white-spired Fourth Meetinghouse of the United Church of Christ at its head. The **Chamber of Commerce** (☎ 352-1303) is also on Central Square and offers an abundantly illustrated brochure of a historical walking tour of the "shire town" (county seat). Walk around the common and down **Main Street** to get the flavor of the town, and then stroll the streets north of the common for more **Victorian homes**. Keene also has a **bus system**, CityExpress, that extends out to the college and the shopping areas (recent fare $1).

Two very different museums are in Keene: The **Wyman Tavern** is at 339 Main Street, just beyond the Historical Society of Cheshire County archive center. It's a 1762 tavern where trustees of Dartmouth College held their first meeting in 1770. Keene's Minutemen assembled here at dawn on April 22, 1775, to march to Lexington and Concord for the opening hostilities of the American Revolution. It's now a period house museum, open summers from Thursday to Saturday, 11 to 4, or by appointment (☎ 357-3855). The **Monadnock Children's Mu-**

seum (☎ 357-5161) is north of the common at 147 Washington Street, offering a place where young children can play and not realize how much they are learning!

The **Colonial Theatre** at 95 Main Street was recently restored and is a grand movie house from Hollywood's golden years. In those days you could see Lon Chaney on the silver screen, hear an aria from opera star Rosa Ponselle, and listen to famed aviatrix Amelia Earhart. Later, Thornton Wilder read his work, and in the 1980s EmmyLou Harris and Holly Near arrived. The community united to support efforts to give the building new life, and the restored theater's first new season included 300 nights of performances, including shows like *Fiddler on the Roof* by the local Lion's Club and appearances by Ani DiFranco and Tom Chapin. Reservations are advised (☎ 352-2033).

Another performance delight is northeast of Keene in the small town of East Sullivan, where the **Apple Hill Center for Chamber Music** offers a summer festival. There are public concerts every Tuesday evening from mid-June to mid-August. At the end of each school session there are participant concerts, also open to the public; for tickets and schedules, inquire in advance (☎ 847-3371 or 800-472-6677; e-mail ahkstu@aol.com; www.applehill.org).

Nightlife in Keene focuses on music, with impromptu and scheduled jazz and folk performances. Drop in at **BrewBakers** at 97 Main Street, one jazz center, where the daytime mood is peaceful (espresso and lattes, soups and sandwiches, reading at your table) and the night is hot. Here you'll also find information on who's playing where.

When you've had enough of town life, drive five miles west on Route 9 to **Chesterfield Gorge**, on the right-hand side. There's a half-mile walking trail that descends into a natural rock-walled gorge, cool and shady, with massive hemlock trees around it. Five miles west of the Gorge, Route 63 crosses Route 9; Spofford Lake, which can be best accessed by renting a cottage on the shore, is to your right, and the road to Pisgah State Forest is to the left. Take the left turn into Chesterfield and go south to Hinsdale, where another left turn, onto Route 119, leads to Winchester, Richmond, and Fitzwilliam. If you want to visit the **Swanzey Historical Society** (☎ 352-4579), open mid-May through fall foliage season in the afternoons, or the **Cheshire County Fair** in Swanzey at the end of July, you'll have to backtrack north on Route 10.

Richmond

Stop by **Lambs & Thyme** in **Richmond** for a mix of antiques, herbs, dried flowers, culinaries, gardens, and herbal crafts and remedies. From Route 119 take Route 32 north and turn left on Bullock Road; the shop is 1.2 miles west and is open from April through December on weekend afternoons (☎ 239-8621).

Fitzwilliam

Fitzwilliam is the New England town of dreams: white homes with porches and gardens around a green common, a Civil War memorial, a lovely church. Nearby **Rhododendron State Park** is impressive even if the 20-foot-tall shrubs are not blooming (peak bloom usually mid-July); it's a dark and lovely jungle with paths and benches. This is also an antique center, and shops abound.

ANTIQUING IN FITZWILLIAM & RICHMOND

- **Randallane Antiques** and **Lambs & Thyme Herbs**, 240 Bullock Road off Route 32, Richmond. Open weekend afternoons from April through December; ☎ 239-8621.

- **John D. Wahl Antiques**, Route 32 (135 Old Homestead Highway), Richmond. Country furniture with emphasis on painted and original surfaces, folk art. Open year-round by chance or by appointment; ☎ 239-7200.

- **Yankee Smuggler Antiques**, Route 119 (122 Fitzwilliam Road), Richmond. American country and original painted furniture. Open daily year-round; ☎ 239-4188.

- **Bob Jessen/Jim Hohnwald**, one mile from the common in Fitzwilliam; call for directions. American country furniture in paint and old surfaces, treenware (wooden dishes and utensils), 18th- and 19th-century accessories, including baskets, homespuns, lighting. Open by appointment; ☎ 585-9188.

- **Dennis & Dad Antiques**, Route 119 in Fitzwilliam, four houses east of Route 12 on left. Features 18th and 19th-century English pottery, glass, china, and furniture of New England. Closed Sundays; ☎ 585-9479.

- **Fitzwilliam Antiques**, junction of Routes 12 and 119, Fitzwilliam. Multi-dealer shop, open year-round; ☎ 585-9092.

- **Rainy Day Books**, Route 119 between Route 12 and the common, Fitzwilliam. Antiquarian books and prints. Open May to mid-November, closed Tuesdays and Wednesdays, winter appointments; ☎ 585-3448.

- **Macreay Landy Antiques**, Route 119 on the common next to the Common Market, Fitzwilliam. General antiques. Open May to December Thursday to Monday; ☎ 585-9202.

- **Bloomin' Antiques**, on the common in Fitzwilliam. Country and formal furniture. Open Monday through Thursday 10 to 5, closed winters, appointments welcome; ☎ 585-6688.

- **Clocks on the Common**, on the common in Fitzwilliam. Antique clocks bought, sold, and repaired. Open most afternoons, but call ahead; ☎ 585-3321.

- **Red Barn Antiques**, in back of the Fitzwilliam Inn on Richmond Road, Fitzwilliam. Country and decorative items. Open daily all year by chance; appointments welcome; ☎ 585-3134.

- **William Lewan Antiques**, Route 119, 4½ miles west of Fitzwilliam village. Early country and painted furniture. Open year-round by chance or appointment; ☎ 585-3365.

Troy

Between Fitzwilliam and Keene is Troy, where there are great roadside views of Mt. Monadnock. On Route 12 in Troy is the **Sportsmen's Den** (☎ 242-6651), stocking archery, fishing, and hunting gear; Buzz Bowers offers "everything for the sportsman," including an indoor archery range across the road.

Troy also has a pick-your-own blueberries farm, **Monadnock Berries**, open from mid-July to the first frost in October, daily 8 to 8. For picking conditions and directions call ahead (545 West Hill Road; ☎ 242-6417).

Dublin
Back on Route 101, 12 miles east of Keene is Dublin, a town noted for being the home of *Yankee Magazine*, located on Route 101. Visitors can check the blackboard out front for odds and ends of information. Also on Route 101 is the **Friendly Farm** (late April through Labor Day daily, and weekends during the fall; ☎ 563-8444), five acres of agreeable animals from sheep to goats to turkeys to pigs. Admission is about $5 for adults and less for children; buy feed and let the animals eat out of your hand. When you're done, go half a mile farther east and visit Dublin Lake.

Harrisville
At the center of the village of Dublin, a road heads north. This is Dublin Road, which leads to Harrisville, an entire town center designated as a National Historic Landmark. The village is a cluster of brick buildings and attractive homes around a small millpond, and was once the home of water-powered textile mills. For dates of special programs in town, inquire at the **historic center** (☎ 827-3431) and at **Harrisville Design & Weaving Center** (☎ 827-3996).

Peterborough
Dublin actually preceded Peterborough as an arts colony, with writers Willa Cather and Samuel Clemens visiting or living nearby. But in 1907 the MacDowell Colony opened north of Peterborough, one of the first American retreats specifically for musicians, artists, and writers. Now the town reflects this influence strongly, melding the arts with the old brick buildings of the mills that once used the power of the Contoocook River.

Monadnock Region

To reach the center of town, first pause on Route 101 at the **Peterborough Chamber of Commerce** (☎ 924-7234) for a fistful of information, including the comprehensive *Guide to the Monadnock Region*, updated yearly. Don't enter town on Route 202; instead, use the turn north onto Grove Street and see the old mills, now shops, and the historic society's **Peterborough Museum** (open year-round, but hours change; ☎ 924-3235). At the end of the street is the **Unitarian Church**, home of the **Monadnock Summer Lyceum**, a lecture series featuring nationally known speakers on summer Sunday mornings at 11 am. (Write for a schedule: Monadnock Summer Lyceum, 25 Main Street, Peterborough, NH 03458.) The Lyceum was founded in 1828 and revived in the 1960s; it often issues a call to social conscience, with speakers like prize-winning journalist Roger Wilkins.

Turning right on Main Street means the **New England Marionette Opera** is on the right, half a block down. This is a marionette theater devoted primarily to opera, a great way to turn on kids or other new opera guests; performances are on weekends, and reservations are advised. The music and action of the 32-inch-tall figures sweep the audience away, and people end up commenting, "It felt like they were real."

Turning left on Main Street instead is the way to get to High Street and the **MacDowell Colony**, where 200 exceptional writers, composers, visual artists, filmmakers, photographers, and others live in an intensely stimulating community each summer. Here Edward Arlington Robinson wrote, long before his work was known. Willa Cather, Oscar Hijuelos, Studs Terkel, and Alice Walker wrote here; Aaron Copeland composed part of *Appalachian Spring* here; and Leonard Bernstein completed his Mass. Write for information from the MacDowell Colony, 100 High Street, Peterborough, NH 03458-2485 (☎ 924-3886; e-mail info@macdowellcolony.org). Farther along High Street is the **Peterborough Playhouse**, north of town, producing a summer of theater from Shaw to Neil Simon (PO Box 118, Peterborough, NH 03458; ☎ 924-7585). Weekends are also enlivened by **Monadnock Music** concerts of chamber music, opera, and virtuoso piano (PO Box 255, Peterborough, NH 03458; ☎ 924-7610 or 800-868-9613; e-mail monadmuse@aol. com). And the heart of the town can justly be said to be the bookstore: **Toadstool Bookshop** (☎ 924-3543), at 12 Depot Square, next door to the Peterborough Diner. Peterborough also has four antique shops in town and is surrounded by at least 20 more in the nearby villages.

Jaffrey

Jaffrey is home to Monadnock State Park but is also the final resting place of author **Willa Cather**, who wrote parts of *My Antonia* as she stayed quietly in a nearby inn. Her plain marker is in the far southwest corner of the **Old Burying Ground** on Route 124. The town was also the home of **Amos Fortune** (1710-1801), a prosperous former slave and tanner who left money to the town to hold the Amos Fortune Lectures yearly in the old meetinghouse; check on this year's date and speaker (Jaffrey Chamber of Commerce, PO Box 2, Jaffrey, NH 03452; ☎ 532-4549).

Rindge

Route 202 goes on south beyond Jaffrey to meet Route 119, where a left turn brings you to the **Cathedral in the Pines**. This outdoor memorial to all who have given their lives in service to this nation is also a spot of powerful and moving beauty; visitors can soak up the spiritual gift of the atmosphere. It's not surprising that weddings are sometimes held among the pines. Open from May to the week before Christmas with guided tours (☎ 899-3300; 75 Cathedral Entrance, Rindge, NH 03461). In July and August, outdoor organ meditations take place Monday through Friday from 11 to 3, weather permitting. Other musical recitals, church choirs, and services may also take place. Also here are a hilltop museum, belltower, chapels, and outdoor altar of the nation, as well as the paths through the pine trees.

New Ipswich

From Rindge or Jaffrey, return to Route 123/124 east to reach New Ipswich. Here the **Society for the Preservation of New England Antiquities** opens an 1800 Federal mansion, **Barrett House**, to the public on Thursday through Sunday in the afternoons, from June 1 to October 15. To find the mansion as you enter town, look for the right turn onto Route 123A (Main Street) and go a quarter-mile; the home is on your right, set on

100 acres of woods and meadows, its stately facade welcoming you to a taste of life enjoyed by the gentry in the early years of the nation. In addition to guided tours, there are occasional lectures, teas, and educational programs. Contact Barrett House, 79 Main Street, PO Box 358, New Ipswich, NH 03071; ☎ 878-2517.

Wilton

The small town of Wilton is almost at the eastern edge of the Monadnock Region, and once you go past it on Route 101 into Milford the Manchester-area traffic begins. Three miles north of Wilton is **Frye's Measure Mill**, a living museum village of a mill that made wooden products like boxes, hoops, and toys in the 1800s. Today water drives much of the mill with its upright turbine. The property is now on the National Register of Historic Places and can be visited Tuesday through Saturday from 10 to 5 (Sundays noon to 5) from April 1 to December 20; there are tours at 2 pm, and a museum shop and forge. Reservations are suggested for the tour (☎ 654-6581 or 654-5345). To get to Frye's Measure Mill from the Wilton business district, start north on Route 31. In 1½ miles you cross the railroad tracks and bridge and bear left at the fork; the mill is another 1½ miles ahead, on the right.

Greenfield & Francestown

A pleasant drive out of Peterborough to the northeast is to start out of town north on Route 202, then bear right on Route 136 and visit Greenfield and Francestown, two charming villages with plenty of hiking space around them. **Greenfield State Park** (☎ 547-3497) on Route 136 includes 401 acres around Otter Lake, and invites winter travelers on snowshoes, cross-country skis, and snowmobiles to also use the land. Nearby is **Crotched Mountain**, with three well-marked summit trails in the two-town region.

Hillsborough

After you've explored Greenfield and Francestown, make the left turn onto Route 47 and circle back to Route 202 to go a few miles farther north to the Hillsborough villages. (Note that town name spellings vary; "Hillsborough" alternates with the more modern-looking "Hillsboro.") Here are some of the earliest existing New Hampshire homes, clustered together and still in use, in Hillsborough Center. The **Franklin Pierce Homestead** is a national landmark, childhood home of the 14th US President, in Hillsborough Center, west of Route 202. From Route 9, turn north onto Route 31 and it's the second house on the right. Pierce was President during the bloody buildup to the Civil War; his homestead was a gathering place for individuals like Daniel Webster. Today it is managed by the **Hillsborough Historical Society** (☎ 478-3165), open summer and fall weekends (10 to 4 on Saturday, 1 to 4 on Sundays), and weekdays in July and August.

Hillsborough is also home to an **annual balloon festival** in mid-July, which includes a road race, pancake breakfast, "lumberjack" competition, and bicycling to chase the balloons (check dates and schedule with the Hillsborough Chamber of Commerce, open mornings, ☎ 464-5858).

Walpole

It's easy to miss the northwest corner of the Monadnock Region, unless you happen to be driving north from Keene. It's worth a special trip over to Walpole anyway. From Keene, take Route 12 north, stopping in Westmoreland (accent on the first syllable) to visit the **Summit Gift Barn** if you like. When you arrive in Walpole, signs direct you off the highway and into the quiet, elegant village. Founded in 1749 and issued a land grant in 1752, Walpole continues to treasure its heritage. Its most stately homes date from the early- to mid-1800s. The **Walpole Historical Society** (PO Box 292, Walpole, NH 03608) owns an 1831 building called the **Academy**, which houses two levels of meticulously documented collections and an admirable genealogical library. Genealogical information can also be exchanged with the museum's consultant; ask for her name and address when you visit.

The town's first residents were John Kilburn and his family, and many gracious homes were built by the Bellows family. Some of the houses are dated as 1788, 1791, and 1792; owners have often invested heavily in restoration, and a **walking tour** of the village is a pleasure. The loop from Route 12 is crossed by

Westminster Street, which in turn leads to Main Street, where the Historical Society is three buildings to the right of Westminster, on the opposite side of the street. It's open from June through September on Wednesdays, Saturdays, and Sundays from 2 to 4. If it's closed, leaflets on the walking tour may still be available at **John Cooper's**, a sandwich shop on Westminster Street. When you finish admiring the homes, stop at the shop of **L.A. Burdick Chocolate** on Main Street and sample the truffles or the trademark chocolate mice (☎ 756-3701 or 800-229-2419).

Where To Stay

Keene Area

One glance at the **Fitzwilliam Inn** is enough: love at first sight. Dream of sitting with a friend on the double porches on the Greek Revival inn on the common, staying in any of the 25 charming guest rooms, and indulging in good food (three meals a day are served). There's a fireplace in the pub, another in the dining room, and in February and March there are free Sunday afternoon concerts in the parlor. You are following a tradition that dates to 1796! And you can walk to more antique shops than you'll ever be able to explore. Reserve well in advance, especially for holiday seasons and fall foliage – late September, early October (in Fitzwilliam, ☎ 585-9000; $-$$). Also in Fitzwilliam, try the **Ashburn House** at Old England Enterprises, off the common (hosts David and Tina Ashton; ☎ 585-7198; $$), and the **Amos B. Parker House** bed and breakfast in an elegant Federal home (innkeeper Freda Houptl; ☎ 585-6540; $$).

Another wonderful lodging, overflowing with activities, is the **Inn at East Hill Farm** in Troy, southeast of Keene off Route 12 on Monadnock Street (hosts Dave and Sally Adams; ☎ 242-6495 or 800-242-6495; $$). This family vacation resort offers horseback riding, pony rides for children, lake and beach fun, tennis, outdoor pools, paddleboats on the pond, and in winter, cross-country skiing and indoor skating rink – plus fun with the farm animals, a game room, and much more. With 150 acres to play on, the inn offers lodgings that range from cottages to a redone sugarhouse, an English cottage, and the main inn. Ask about special seasonal packages, like choosing a Christmas tree in December.

The Fitzwilliam Inn.

Even Keene's bed and breakfast inns have a country feel. Try the **Carriage Barn Bed & Breakfast**, 358 Main Street (innkeepers Ellen and Peter Gammans; ☎ 357-3812; $), and the **Goose Pond Guest House**, on East Surry Road (innkeepers Stella Sise and family; ☎ 352-2828; $$). In Lake Spofford, the **Tower Light Inn & Motel** has some rooms facing the lake (host Walter Mulinski; ☎ 363-8154; $$-$$$). In Sullivan, east of Keene on Route 9, there's the **Post and Beam Bed & Breakfast**, overlooking Otter Brook (☎ 847-3330; $$). Harrisville, northwest of Dublin, offers the **Harrisville Squires' Inn**, which is close to the Monadnock-Sunapee Greenway, too (innkeepers are Pat and Doug McCarthy; ☎ 827-3925; $$).

Peterborough Area

East Jaffrey is a scenic drive away from Peterborough, and on Route 124 east, 2.3 miles from Jaffrey itself, is the **Benjamin Prescott Inn**. This is a meticulously restored 1850s farmhouse furnished with charm, and includes a honeymoon suite upstairs. Innkeepers are Barry and Janice Miller (☎ 532-6637; $$).

Peterborough has a modern motor inn, the **Jack Daniels**, on Route 202 north, within easy walking distance to the heart of the town. Reserve ahead, as it books up quickly (☎ 924-7548; $$). If you'd sample more of the traditional New England inn feeling, try the cozy comforts of **Apple Gate Bed and Breakfast** at 199 Upland Road (Route 123 south), in an 1832 Colonial nestled among gardens and orchards, serving candlelight breakfast by the fireplace (innkeepers Ken and Diane Legenhausen; ☎ 924-6543; $$). **Peterborough Manor** is right in town, at 50 Summer Street, and offers an affordable option with less elegance but a nice simplicity (☎ 924-9832; e-mail himanor @weaver.mv.com; $).

Visitors to the Cathedral of the Pines have the option of staying on the premises, in **Cathedral House**, a bed and breakfast inn with five guests rooms and a large common room with grand piano and fireplace (☎ 899-6790; $-$$). There's also ample lodging in the inn and lakefront cabins of the **Woodbound Inn**, which has its own restaurant as well as trails for hiking or cross-country skiing on 162 acres (☎ 532-8341 or 800-688-7770; $-$$$).

Temple is a small town just south of Route 101, between Peterborough and Wilton. It's reached by taking Route 45 south from Route 101 about two miles. Only three miles from the Temple Mountain ski area (alpine and Nordic), the **Birchwood Inn** (innkeepers Judy and Bill Wolfe; ☎ 878-3285; $$) offers many of the advantages of a small country inn – attractively furnished rooms, attentive innkeepers, a "blackboard" menu of ever-changing meals – but adds a generous serving of New England history. The inn first opened in 1775, although the present brick building probably dates to 1800. Among the overnight guests was Henry David Thoreau; the dining room mural is by itinerant New England painter Rufus Porter, 1825-1833.

Wilton, at the eastern edge of the Monadnock Region, offers three pleasant bed-and-breakfast inns: **Auk's Nest Bed & Breakfast** (rural tranquillity in a 1770s cottage; proprietor Anne D. Lunt; ☎ 878-3443; $-$$), **Stepping Stones** (19th-century home and garden; hostess Ann Carlsmith; ☎ 654-9048; $$), and **Final Folly Bed & Breakfast** (1791 home in tiny Wilton Centre, hosts Joan and George Andersen; ☎ 654-2725; $-$$). Call for directions from Route 101.

The **Greenfield Inn** is emphatically not a bed and breakfast; it offers modern luxuries along with the comfortable country decor rooms, so that fine china on the breakfast table and Mozart in the air mingle with a side order of business capability (innkeepers Barbara and Vic Mangini; ☎ 547-2418; $-$$). In neighboring Francestown is the **Inn at Crotched Mountain**, off Route 47 at 534 Mountain Road (hosts John and Rose Perry; ☎ 588-6840; $$-$$$). To the other side of Greenfield is Hancock, home of New Hampshire's oldest inn, the **Hancock Inn** (circa 1789). This inn describes its clientele as ranging from "cattle drovers and rum runners to aristocracy and a US President." There's an award-winning restaurant as well as Rufus Porter murals (circa 1824) and a village full of historic homes, close to the mountains, hiking trails, and wildlife sanctuaries (innkeepers Linda and Joe Johnston; ☎ 525-3318 or 800-525-1789; $$-$$$).

Hillsborough & Walpole

Hillsborough offers the **Inn at Maplewood Farm** (award-winning breakfast; ☎ 464-4242 or 800-644-6695; $$). In Walpole, the **Josiah Bellows House**, built in 1813 and furnished in spacious elegance, places you deep into the historic mood of this stately village. They have a well-stocked library, too. (Innkeepers Lois Ford and Lou Ciercielli; ☎ 756-4250; $$)

■ Camping

 **Emerald Acres Campground** on Cheshire Pond in Jaffrey is a pleasant family campground with boat, canoe, and paddleboat rentals and room for RVs; ask about weekly rates too (71 Ridgecrest Road, Jaffrey, NH 03452; ☎ 532-8838).

Options along the Monadnock-Sunapee Greenway include **Leighton State Forest** in Dublin, **Parker Hill** in Stoddard, **Fox Brook** by Pitcher Mountain, **Gen. Geo. Washington Campsite** just south of Washington, and **Moose Lookout** on the far side of Lovewell Mountain. **Greenfield State Park**,

Greenfield, one mile west of town via Route 136, has 252 sites with swimming, and pond fishing. It's open mid-May to mid-October (☎ 547-3497; reservations Box 203, Greenfield, NH 03047; ☎ 271-3628). **Monadnock State Park** in Jaffrey, four miles west of town off Route 124, has 21 tent sites, seven youth group sites and is open year-round (PO Box 181, Jaffrey, NH 03452; ☎ 532-8862 or 271-3628).

Where To Eat

Keene Area

 Stop in at **BrewBakers** at 97 Main Street to catch the Keene coffee shop mood. **Cifaldi's Market & Bakery** at 77 Main Street (☎ 358-3068) is a don't-miss-this deli with wonderful Italian baked goods (both breads and pastries). **Prime Roast** at 16 Main Street (☎ 352-7874) is a coffee shop with yummy strawberry scones; and around the corner at 333 Winchester Street is the area's bagel expert, **Einstein Bros**. (☎ 352-0408).

For gracious dining, visit **Mango's Café** on Main (81 Main Street, ☎ 358-5440) for lunch or dinner, which sometimes has live music in the evenings; and **Nicola's Trattoria** at 39 Central Square (entrance around on Winter Street side; ☎ 355-5242) for superb Italian cuisine. There are also several ethnic cuisine options, like curries and rice dishes of Northern India at **Paradise of India** (10 Central Square, ☎ 357-1959) and Greek fare at **Timoleon's Restaurant** (25-27 Main Street), Southwestern cuisine at **Bandido's** (Emerald Street, ☎ 355-4366), plus shops with pizza, Thai food, and more. Microbrew connoisseurs will want to stop at the Colony Mill Marketplace to visit **Elm City Brewery**.

In surrounding towns, visit the inns for memorable dinners, like the **Fitzwilliam Inn** (☎ 585-9000, Fitzwilliam, on the common). In Dublin there's a creative range of Italian dishes at **Del Rossi's Trattoria** on Route 137 (☎ 563-7195).

Peterborough Area

Steak and seafood at its best: the **Boiler House** restaurant in Peterborough (Route 202 by Noone Falls, ☎ 924-9486) will feed you well. To indulge in unforgettable epicurean cuisine of mixed ancestry (the restaurant calls it an "epicurean collage" and it tends to be either Mexican or Japanese!), seek out **Latacarta** in the heart of the town at 6 School Street (☎ 924-6878). Get together with other book lovers at **Aesop's Tables**, the coffee bar and tea room tucked into a corner of the Toadstool Bookshop on Depot Street. And don't forget those morning and noon nibbles at **Nonie's Restaurant and Bakery** at 28 Grove Street (☎ 924-3451), or at the **Peterborough Diner** (10 Depot Street, ☎ 924-6202). South of the village visit the **Kernel Bakery** on Route 202 just past the intersection with Route 101 (☎ 924-7930).

When you go exploring, stop in Rindge at **Lilly's on the Pond** for good food at affordable prices (Route 202, ☎ 899-3322) and in Jaffrey at **Michaels'**, the restaurant at the Jaffrey Inn (East Main Street, ☎ 532-8555). For lighter fare in Jaffrey, **Kimball Farm Ice Cream & Restaurant** is fun (Route 124, ☎ 532-5765; call ahead for takeout). Again, don't miss the inns for fine dining: the **Birchwood Inn** in Temple (☎ 878-3285) and the **Hancock Inn** in Hancock (☎ 525-3318) offer memorable meals.

Nearly at the Massachusetts border in Mason, on Nutting Hill Road, is **Pickity Place**, an entertaining blend of herb gardens, garden shop, greenhouse, bookstore, gift shop, and superb five-course gourmet luncheons in a 1786 cottage; be sure to reserve ahead (☎ 878-1151). **Parker's Maple Barn & Sugarhouse** offers New England hearty meals at 1316 Brookline Road in Mason (☎ 878-2308 or 800-832-2308).

Information Sources

Antrim Chamber of Commerce, Antrim, NH 03440; ☎ 588-2888.

Hillsborough Chamber of Commerce, Hillsborough, NH 03244; ☎ 464-5858.

Jaffrey Chamber of Commerce, Jaffrey, NH 03452; ☎ 532-4549.

Keene Chamber of Commerce, Keene, NH 03431; ☎ 352-1303.

Milford-Amherst Chamber of Commerce; Milford, NH 03055; ☎ 673-4360.

Monadnock Travel Council, Keene, NH 03431; ☎ 355-8155.

Peterborough Chamber of Commerce, Peterborough, NH 03458; ☎ 924-7234.

The
Merrimack Valley

From the Massachusetts border traveling north on Interstate 93, most of New Hampshire's truly urban areas line the highway. You may not see much of them, because the interstate is often "greened in" by trees and fields, but from south to the north, they are **Salem** and **Nashua**, **Manchester**, and **Concord**. Concord is the state capital, a small city with a pleasant historic walking district and the coffee shops and restaurants you'd expect to support a busy state legislature. Manchester is an industrial city at heart, but also has some large shopping malls, and the state's busy airport. Urban renovation may yet make a visitor-friendly place out of Nashua, but tourists from out-of-state cities are likely to find it a little too much like home to be a real vacation.

This urban strip of New Hampshire has some surprises, though: immediately to the east of Interstate 93 are two terrific state parks, Bear Brook and Pawtuckaway, that you may want to visit for their mountain biking and archery opportunities as well as hiking trails. There are preserved patches of green lands all through the region, too, thanks to many local efforts and often the management of the New Hampshire Audubon Society and the Society for the Preservation of New Hampshire Forests. Each of these two conservation-oriented societies has an interesting headquarters in Concord, worth visiting.

At the northern tip of the region is **Canterbury Center**, a town that has kept much of its pastoral character despite housing commuters for the cities. Here is a Shaker community, no longer active in membership but preserving the rural skills of this peaceable people as a living museum to visit.

TRAFFIC ALERT: *Commuter traffic around these cities is as frustrating as anywhere else. Stay off the roads at rush hours if you can, or drive on the interstate highways, where traffic is less likelay to bottle up. In winter, during ice storms, avoid even the interstates; find a nice restaurant or cozy lodgings and wait for road conditions to clear, which usually happens quickly.*

Adventures

■ On Foot

Concord

 Of the major cities, only Concord is really inviting for **walking tours**. Pick up a detailed brochure for $2 from the **Concord Chamber of Commerce**, either at the year-round office at 244 North Main Street (☎ 244-2508) just off Exit 15 from Interstate 93, or at the summer kiosk downtown by the statehouse. The Chamber of Commerce also has other maps of the city (by out-of-state standards it's more a large town than a city, with a population of 35,000) if you plan to explore beyond the small capital district. The walking tour takes you along both North and South Main Street and into the area around the statehouse.

New Hampshire's two major volunteer conservation societies have interesting nature trails to explore. To visit the **New Hampshire Audubon Society** headquarters, either navigate through the tangled roads of town with a map over to Clinton Road, or get there by taking Interstate 89 north to Exit 2 and going left onto Center Road (which began as Clinton back in town). Then go right on well-marked Silk Farm Road, and 0.2 mile to the Silk Farm Audubon Center, part of the **Silk Farm Wildlife Sanctuary** (☎ 224-9909; Audubon Society of New Hampshire, 3 Silk Farm Road, Concord, NH 03301-8200). This is open year-round, including Sunday afternoons. There are woods and wetland trails around nearby Great Turkey Pond, a

Merrimack Valley

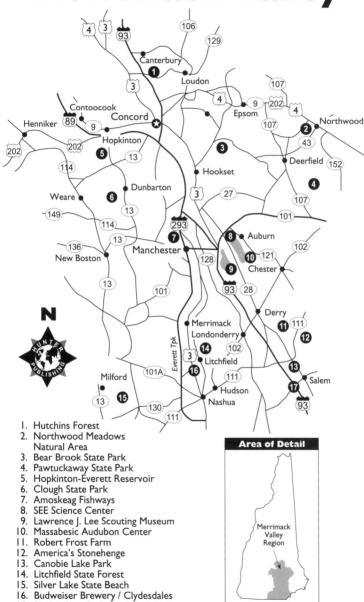

1. Hutchins Forest
2. Northwood Meadows
   Natural Area
3. Bear Brook State Park
4. Pawtuckaway State Park
5. Hopkinton-Everett Reservoir
6. Clough State Park
7. Amoskeag Fishways
8. SEE Science Center
9. Lawrence J. Lee Scouting Museum
10. Massabesic Audubon Center
11. Robert Frost Farm
12. America's Stonehenge
13. Canobie Lake Park
14. Litchfield State Forest
15. Silver Lake State Beach
16. Budweiser Brewery / Clydesdales
17. Rockingham Park

Area of Detail

Merrimack
Valley
Region

terrific research library, and a gift shop with arguably the best collection of field guides and trail guides around. Don't miss the "bird blind," where you can learn avian identification, or the video of birds with their taped calls. This is also the place to pick up trail guides to other Audubon properties, most of which are not advertised widely in order to protect them from overvisiting. Guides are 50¢ apiece.

It's a little harder to get to the headquarters of the **Society for the Protection of New Hampshire Forests** (SPNHF), but worth it for the chance to buy a map of the SPNHF's hundred protected properties in the state, many of which are off back roads, have few trails, and are not really noticeable in terms of signs or publicity. From downtown Concord, cross the river to the east on Route 9 and go a mile to the fast food strip, where you take Route 132 north 1½ miles to a brown sign on the left that says Conservation Center (it's a very modest sign). This road goes 0.2 mile to a center occupied by a half dozen private conservation-related groups, with the SPNHF the main one. There's an interpretive trail to take along the Merrimack River, and a gift shop where you can pick up your vital map to state-wide preserved properties.

Now it's time to get out of town!

Bear Brook State Park & Pawtuckaway State Park

It's incredible that a state park of 10,000 acres with 40 miles of trails is less than 10 miles from downtown Concord. Probably the easiest way to navigate from the state's capital is to take Route 9 east out of town and catch the right turn onto Route 3 south; when you reach Suncook (five miles), turn left on Route 28 and you'll be at the entrance to **Bear Brook State Park** in another three miles; it's on the right, well marked. A ranger or assistant at the toll booth will charge you a modest day fee and provide trail maps (or get them in advance: ☎ 485-9874 for maps and information). From the western entrance, where you drive in first, trails lead to the Hayes Marsh and to Catamount Hill. The eastern half of the park is a wildlife refuge and includes an outdoor archery range, and there's another entrance here, off Deerfield Road. Bear Hill Pond and the Old Reservoir offer are two additional hiking destinations. At the far eastern end of the park are two more ponds. A campground and three museums (family camping, snowmobiles, and the Civilian Conservation Corps or CCC) add to the attractions. Come early in the mornings on weekdays to avoid a crowd.

Pawtuckaway State Park (5,600 acres; ☎ 895-3031 for maps and information) is about 20 miles from Concord as the crow flies, but the routes are a bit indirect. Simplest is to take Route 9 east out of Concord all the way to Northwood (about 21 miles), go through the village, and take the right turn onto Route 152 south. In five miles drive through the village of Nottingham and, rather than bear left with 152, go straight ahead onto Route 156, which leads to the park entrance. Most people you meet in the parking lot will be headed to the beach and boating to your right; hikers park near the tollbooth and get maps, then head left toward South, Middle, and North Mountains.

Northwood

On Route 4 in Northwood, two miles west of Route 202, is the entrance to **Northwood Meadows Natural Area**. Filled with ponds and marshes, the 600-acre preserve is great for nature walks.

Canterbury

For a quiet woodland walk, discover the 88-acre parcel owned by the Society for the Protection of New Hampshire Forests called **Hutchins Forest**. The **Tree Farm Loop Trail** takes about an hour and meanders through wetlands, groves, and clearings; the **Burnham Brook Loop** includes old stone walls, evidence of regeneration in the forest that was logged here earlier, and signs of wildlife like wood ducks, beaver, deer, grouse, and fisher (a large weasel). Look for the marks of otter and mink along the brook. The land is now managed for careful timber harvests to allow the pine trees healthy growth; wildlife will be preserved. From Interstate 93 just north of Concord take Exit 16 and turn left on Route 132. The forest entrance is six miles ahead on the right.

Merrimack Valley

Note that a new Audubon Society Center at **Lake Massabesic** to the east of Nashua will soon provide hiking trails for this area; see *On Water*.

■ On Wheels

City Biking

 If you enjoy city biking, Nashua has a trail network for you. It focuses on **Mine Falls Park** but also includes miles around the surrounding city. Maps are just starting to be available at state rest stops; to order one, write to Urban Trails Alliance, Nashua Planning Department, Nashua City Hall, 229 Main St., Nashua, NH 03060.

Most of the roads in this area are too busy for happy biking, but **Route 3A** between Manchester and Nashua has some pretty spots along the Merrimack River.

Mountain Biking

Both **Pawtuckaway** and **Bear Brook state parks** allow biking, including mountain bikes, and provide miles of trail. There's serious mountain biking (on trails shared with pedestrians and trail bikes) at **Hopkinton-Everett Reservoir**. From Concord, take Clinton Street out of town past the turn for the Audubon Society Silk Farm Sanctuary, and stay on Route 13 to Pages Corner, where you turn left (south) with Route 13. Look for the Dunbarton Store and the right turn onto Winslow Road; parking is available here, by Stark Pond, and this is the bike access. The trail map that applies is the *New Hampshire ATV and Trail Bike Guide*, which may be obtained from the Department of Resources & Economic Development, Division of Parks and Recreation, Bureau of Trails, PO Box 1856, Concord, NH 03302-1856.

■ On Water

 Try for a chilly weekday when you visit **Pawtuckaway State Park** (directions in *On Foot*), to thin the number of paddlers you'll encounter. **Swimming**, **fishing**, and **canoeing** make great use of **Pawtuckaway**

Lake. There's a bass tournament here each spring. Angle for smallmouth and largemouth bass, as well as pickerel, horned pout, and yellow perch.

At **Bear Brook State Park** (directions in *On Foot*) there are **canoes** for rent at both Beaver and Catamount Ponds, with **rowboats** also available at Beaver Pond. Archery Pond is especially for **fly fishing** (brook trout); across the road from it is a kids' fishing pond (under age 12).

Manchester's **Lake Massabesic** ought to be a recreation area, and probably will be soon; the Audubon Society is opening a center at Battery Point with 130 acres of fields and woods, an old granite quarry, and direct access to the lake. Contact the center at ☎ 634-3313.

The *AMC River Guide to New Hampshire and Vermont* gives details on paddling the **Merrimack River**. The best section is from Franklin (north of this region) down to Concord, as it has a sandy bottom in this stretch. Flatwater, quickwater, and Class III rapids make this a lively excursion. Especially scout the old **Sewall Falls Dam** area, though, and a new set of standing waves there rated as Class III, with a Class II rapid after the dam, rocky in low water. A new launching ramp near the cloverleaf of Interstate 393 a mile above Bridge Street makes it easier to take out at Concord.

Looking for a **swim**? To the west of Nashua, in the town of Hollis on Route 122, **Silver Lake State Beach** offers a 1,000-foot sandy beach on a 34-acre lake, with swimming the top priority. There's another good-sized swimming beach to the southwest of Concord in Weare on Route 114: **Clough State Park** offers swimming in a 140-acre river pool with 900 feet of beach.

■ On Horseback

 Horse Haven isn't a place for a trail ride on someone else's horse. Instead, it's an unusual inn where you can bring your own horse or dog or both; the barn has ample room, and well-mannered canines may even stay in your room. Write to Velma Emery at Horse Haven, 462 Raccoon Hill Road,

Salisbury, NH 03268 (☎ 648-2101). There are 35 acres for trail rides and rambles with this comfortable bed-and-breakfast inn.

■ On Snow & Ice

 Bear Brook Park (directions given in *On Foot*) offers winter trails designed for **cross-country skiing** and **snowshoeing**; there is also a corridor for **snowmobiling** through the park. The skiers' parking lot is at the winter entrance to the park, on the Deerfield Road (1½ miles past the summer entrance) about three miles from Route 28.

■ In The Air

 Concord Aviation Services at the airport on Route 3 (south of Route 9) offers learn-to-fly discovery flights (☎ 229-1760).

Sightseeing

Salem

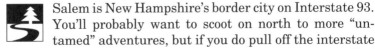 Salem is New Hampshire's border city on Interstate 93. You'll probably want to scoot on north to more "untamed" adventures, but if you do pull off the interstate here, there are three interesting sights. The first is called **America's Stonehenge**, and is a stone site in North Salem that may represent an astronomical construction like the British Stonehenge. At the site is a visitors' center, which displays stone artifacts as well as 18th- and 19th-century housewares found at the site. Admission is about $7. To find it, take Exit 3 from Interstate 93 for Route 111 east, which you follow for five miles to a right on Island Pond Road, which becomes Haverhill Road and goes to the entrance of Stonehenge. ☎ 893-8300; open daily from April through November, hours change seasonally.

Salem also has a **horse racing track**, **Rockingham Park**, at Exit 1 off the interstate; call for post times and reservations (☎ 898-2311). And finally, there's **Canobie Lake Park**, a traditional family amusement park at Exit 2, full of action excitement with a roller coaster, bumper cars, ferris wheels, and water rides. It's especially fun in the evening, offering colored lights and the scent of carnival food in the air. Open weekends from mid-April through May, then daily from Memorial Day through Labor Day (☎ 893-3506). Don't bring food or beverages; you have to buy them there.

Antique Trail

Along Route 101A from Nashua west to Wilton is a "treasure trail" of **antique shops**: 1,500 dealers in nine miles. Many of the shops are group endeavors and most are open daily. There's a lot of shopping offered here! Also see Northwood *Sightseeing* on page 305 for another antique dealer center.

Londonderry

Pause on the way north to get into the agricultural mood with a tour through the **Stonyfield Farm Yogurt Works**, where you'll see the moo-to-milk-to-yogurt process and get a taste treat too. Open Tuesday through Saturday, 9:30 am to 5 pm, with tours on the hour from February through November; closed in December except for the week between Christmas and New Year's. Call ahead to check on tours, especially during holiday weeks (☎ 437-4040, ext. 243).

Derry

Love poetry? Robert Frost readers will want to visit this small town off Interstate 93, where the poet and his family lived for a decade. Get off the interstate at Exit 4 and head through the town of Derry, reaching Route 28 at two miles from the interstate. Turn right and in another two miles you'll reach the **Robert Frost Farm**. It dates to 1900. There are guided house tours, a video presentation, exhibits, and a self-guided nature/poetry trail. Open June to October, daily 10 am to 6 pm (☎ 432-3091 or 485-2651).

Nashua

If for some reason you're staying in this business- and industry-oriented city for a while, **Mines Falls Park** in the center of town will offer some relief from streets under your feet. The 325-acre park includes walking trails, boating, and

Merrimack Valley

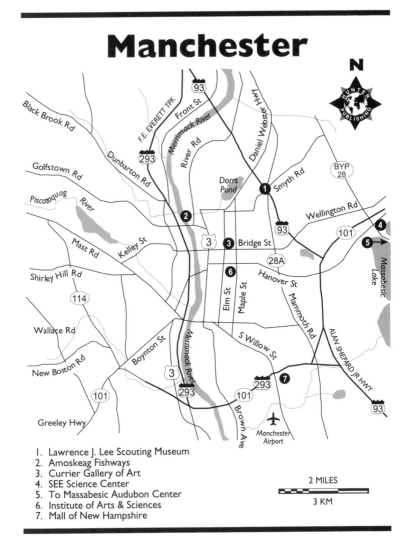

Manchester

N

1. Lawrence J. Lee Scouting Museum
2. Amoskeag Fishways
3. Currier Gallery of Art
4. SEE Science Center
5. To Massabesic Audubon Center
6. Institute of Arts & Sciences
7. Mall of New Hampshire

2 MILES

3 KM

cross-country ski trails. Call ☎ 594-3367 for information. At the
north end of town is **Greeley Park**, on Concord Street, where
many **Summerfest** events take place in a band shell; there are
more walking trails here.

Merrimack

Located between Nashua and Manchester, this busy city is the
home of a **Budweiser brewery**. For a look at the brewery and

a chance to see the magnificent Clydesdale horses here (even available for photos with you on the first Saturday of each month), come for a free tour daily from May through October (hours vary seasonally; ☎ 595-1202) and on Thursdays through Mondays from November through April. The brewery is at 221 Daniel Webster Highway – find Route 3 south of Manchester and take Exit 10 onto Industrial Drive going east. Watch for signs.

Manchester

Watch the springtime salmon run up the Merrimack River from an underwater window in the **Amoskeag Fishways**, and stop by in other seasons for city history, including that of the Native Americans who once lived here. There are tours and educational programs, too (call for exact dates and hours of operation; ☎ 626-3474). To get to the Fishway, take Exit 6 from Interstate 293 and bear right toward the Amoskeag (Abenaki for "great fishing place") Bridge. Turn right at the first light, Fletcher Street, and you've arrived. Owned by Public Service of New Hampshire, the Fishway is managed by the Audubon Society of New Hampshire in partnership with the state Fish and Game Department and the US Fish and Wildlife Service.

There are two museums and a science center in Manchester. The **Currier Gallery of Art** (☎ 669-6144) at 201 Myrtle Way. To get here, use Exit 8 from Interstate 93 and bear right onto Bridge Street; go 1½ miles and turn right onto Ash Street, then take the third left onto Myrtle Way; the museum is on the left. It's open Mondays and Wednesdays through Sundays with varied hours (call to check). The museum features European and American paintings, decorative arts, and sculpture by masters such as Picasso, Matisse, Monet, O'Keeffe, Calder, and Wyeth. Also part of the museum is a Frank Lloyd Wright house from 1950, Zimmerman House, with its original furnishings and the Zimmermans' collection of fine art.

The **Lawrence L. Lee Scouting Museum** (☎ 669-8919) is in a wooded setting seven miles from town on the shore of Long Pond; if you've been a Scout, you'll enjoy the collection and library. Open daily in July and August, and on Saturdays the rest of the year (from Interstate 93 use Exit 5 and take Route

Merrimack Valley

28A north to where it crosses back under the interstate to the museum.

Science Enrichment Encounters (SEE) is a great place to spend a rainy day, with its many hands-on science exhibits. It's at 324 Commercial Street. To get here, take Exit 5 from Interstate 93, turn right at the bottom of the ramp onto Commercial Street and look for SEE facing the river on the ground floor. Open to the public weekends from noon to 5 and Thursdays from 5 pm to 9 pm (☎ 669-0400).

The **Massabesic Audubon Center** is a brand-new focus on Lake Massabesic, east of Manchester. From Interstate 93 take the Exit for Route 101 east toward the seacoast, then immediately take Exit 1 and turn right at the end of the ramp onto Route 28 Bypass to the traffic circle. Go halfway around the circle and turn out of it there, to find Lake Massabesic on your left. Go exactly two miles more on Route 28 Bypass to Spofford Road, where you turn left. In a quarter-mile, when the road veers to the right, take the left turn onto Deerneck Road; the parking area is after the first house on the left. Expect trails, environmental programs, and lake access. For information, ☎ 634-3313.

Also underway in Manchester is an archaeology museum expected to be called the **Sargent Museum**. An 1841 schoolhouse at the corner of Lowell and Chestnut Street is already housing the collection.

Concord

The state's capital city offers historic sites, two historical museums, and a planetarium dedicated to the New Hampshire schoolteacher who dared to board a spaceship toward the stars.

For a comprehensive **walking tour brochure**, see the Concord Chamber of Commerce at its year-round office at 224 North Main Street, just off Exit 15 from Interstate 93. There's a summer information kiosk downtown by the statehouse, too. A shorter walking trail is the **Coach and Eagle Trail**, again with a brochure that the Chamber of Commerce distributes (☎ 224-2508). Be sure to go into **Eagle Square** on the North

Main Street; look for its fabulous wrought iron gateway. The **Museum of New Hampshire History** is the massive building at the back of the square, a place to travel through time and come face to face with Native Americans, early colonists, mill workers, and a US President. Open Tuesday through Saturday 9:30 to 5, Thursday evening 5 to 8:30, and Sunday noon to 5 (maximum family admission is $10 total; ☎ 226-3189). From Interstate 93, take Exit 14 and go west at the end of the exit ramp. Then turn right on North Main Street, take the next right into Storrs Street, pass under the bridge, and find the museum parking lot on the left.

The **New Hampshire Historical Society** has its own collection open to the public at 30 Park Street, off North State Street a block northwest of the Capitol. It's open Monday to Friday 9:30 am to 4:30 pm, and weekends noon to 4:30 (closed holidays); call ahead for special exhibits and programs (☎ 225-3381).

The **Capitol Building**, which is the State House, is easy to find downtown. The road in front of it is North Main, and the one behind it is North State Street. Don't miss out on visiting the **State House** itself. There's an exhibit of war-torn flags that can make your breath catch, some lovely portraits and, of course, the chance to see the striking architecture of this elegant building. Tours are available, or pick up the self-guided tour leaflet in the visitors center inside (☎ 271-2154).

The **Christa McAuliffe Planetarium** offers astro-adventures designed for young explorers, with a dramatic 92-seat theater and interactive exhibits. Public shows are on weekends and some mid-week afternoons; school groups get to use the planetarium the rest of the time. Call ahead for public hours (☎ 271-STAR). Closed Mondays and major holidays and the last two weeks of September. To find the planetarium, which is on the east side of town across the river, take Exit 15E from Interstate 93 or Exit 1 from Interstate 393, and follow the many signs.

Concord's cultural life often begins at the **Capitol Center for the Arts** at 44 South Main St. If you stay in town long, you'll want a schedule of Broadway shows, international dance

Merrimack Valley

troupes, family shows, and enrichment performances. The old theater was a stop on the vaudeville circuit in 1927, and was revived recently, even restoring the High-Hollywood Egyptian motif artwork. For a tour or programs, ☎ 225-1111 (www. ccanh.com).

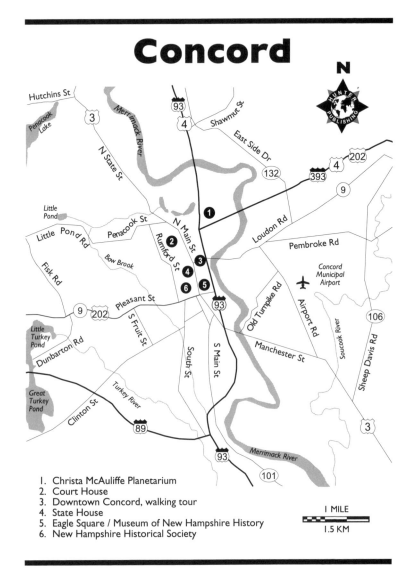

Concord

1. Christa McAuliffe Planetarium
2. Court House
3. Downtown Concord, walking tour
4. State House
5. Eagle Square / Museum of New Hampshire History
6. New Hampshire Historical Society

1 MILE

1.5 KM

If you're in Concord in the autumn, go west out of town to **Contoocook** and visit **Gould Hill Orchards**, where you can pick your own apples. It's 10 miles from Concord – take Interstate 89 to Exit 5 and Route 103 north, and watch for the right turn onto Gould Hill Road; the orchard is 1½ miles down this road (☎ 746-3811).

Loudon

Northeast of Concord on Route 106 is the town of Loudon, whose main attraction is the **New Hampshire International Speedway**. Visit their Web site (www.nhis.com) to get a schedule of races, or call ahead (☎ 783-4961). Races are mostly held on weekends, from mid-April to mid-October.

Weare

A very small nature center featuring collections, interpretive exhibits, library, and nature trails hides in the town of Weare, southwest of Concord. Special programs are offered all summer. You must make an appointment to visit. Contact the **Little Nature Museum**, 59 Boyce Road, Weare, NH 03281 (☎ 529-7180).

Northwood

From Concord, take Route 202 east for about 21 miles to reach Northwood, a little town known as **Antique Alley** for its corridor of antique shops. The town claims 800 antique dealers and craftspeople. Some of the number clearly comes from "group shops," but there are a lot of varied stores. Don't try to get around on foot, as traffic through town is fast and dangerous.

ANTIQUING IN NORTHWOOD

Here is a partial listing of special shops, all on **Route 4**:

- **R.S. Butler Trading Co**, antiques, furnishings, dried flowers, quilts, records, ☎ 942-5249.

- **Coveway Corner Antiques**, furniture "smalls" and unusual antiques displayed on three floors, quarter-mile west of Hudson's Restaurant, ☎ 942-7500.

Merrimack Valley

- **Nostalgia Antiques**, specializing in carpenter's hand tools, antiques fishing tackle, ☎ 942-7728.

- **Northwood Cordwainer House**, near the intersection of Route 152, jewelry, glass, porcelain, cameras, books, games, prints, ☎ 942-8111

- **Pioneer America**, three floors of country item.s, primitives, Victorian, 1930s, glass, china, ☎ 942-8588

- **American Traditional Stencils**, over 400 design.s, ☎ 942-8100.

- **Northwood Stoneware Pottery**, junction with Route 202, wheel-thrown stoneware, ☎ 942-8829.

One of the many shops of Northwood, along "Antique Alley."

Canterbury

"Hands to work, hearts to God" is the saying that expressed the Shaker way of life. Although the celibate religious group that lived here from the 1780s is now gone, with the death of the last Canterbury Shaker in 1992 (Sister Ethel Hudson, at age 96), the gentle and inspiring world of the Shakers lives on in **Can-**

terbury **Shaker Village**. Changing exhibits, guided tours through the simple buildings, and demonstrations of crafts like broom making, oval box making, woodworking, spinning, and weaving fill a day with activities. The museum is open daily from May 1 through October 1, 10 am to 5 pm; they are also open weekends (Friday to Sunday) in April, November, and December. The **Creamery Restaurant** interprets over 200 years of Shaker foodways and principles at luncheon, and there's a candlelight evening meal on Fridays and Saturdays (reservations required: ☎ 783-9511). Ask about holiday festivities, too; Herb & Garden Day, Wood Day, Mother Ann Day, Wool Day, Harvest Day, and a Canterbury Christmas are all special times to visit.

Where To Stay

Nashua

A number of lodging chains have spacious inns and lodges in Nashua: **Comfort Inn** at 10 Laurent Street (☎ 883-7700 or 800-228-5150; $$), **Holiday Inn** on Northeastern Blvd. (☎ 888-1551; $$), **Howard Johnson Motor Lodge** at 170 Main Dunstable Road (☎ 889-0173; $$), **Nashua Marriott Hotel** 2200 Southwood Dr. (☎ 880-9100; $$-$$$), **Red Roof Inn**, 77 Spitbrook Road (☎ 888-1893; $-$$), **Marriott Residence Inn** at 246 Daniel Webster Highway (☎ 424-8100; $$$), and **Sheraton Tara Hotel** on Tara Blvd. (☎ 888-9970 or 800-843-8272; $$-$$$). There's also the **Crowne Plaza Hotel** at 2 Somerset Parkway (☎ 886-1200; $$-$$$) and the **Merrimack Hotel** at 4 Executive Park in nearby Merrimack (☎ 424-8000; $$-$$$).

Manchester

Manchester also offers two customary city hotels, although the Holiday Inn building is called the **Center of New Hampshire** and offers an unusual degree of elegance (Route 293, Exit 5 onto Granite Street; ☎ 625-1000 or 800-HOLIDAY; $$-$$$$). **Howard Johnson** has a hotel and conference center at 298 Queen City Avenue (☎ 668-2600 or 800-654-2000; $$).

To find a really elegant lodging, slip out of town to Bedford, three miles southeast on Route 101. Here the **Bedford Village Inn** provides one of the state's most luxurious accommodations in a multi-million-dollar estate restoration. Fourteen rooms are decorated with period furnishings, custom fabrics, artwork, and oriental carpets, The inn has won such awards and titles as "best place for a romantic dinner." The Carte Blanche package includes dinner and breakfast in the eight intimate dining rooms, some with fireplaces. "Charolais in the surrounding pastures, a cup of tea with a generous slice of serenity. The inn offers you a natural balance of elegance and simplicity." That's the description from the inn, and it's accurate but falls short of just how lovely this place is. (If you're wondering about Charolais, they are elegant and placid cattle.) The inn is at 2 Village Lane; at the first set of lights on Route 101 in town, turn left to continue with Route 101, go straight through the next set of lights. About a quarter-mile farther on the right you'll see the yellow farm complex (☎ 472-2602 or 800-852-1166; $$$-$$$$).

Concord

Concord offers a **Holiday Inn** (172 North Main Street, ☎ 224-9534; $$), **Comfort Inn** (71 Hall Street, ☎ 226-4100; $$-$$$), **Centennial Inn** (96 Pleasant Street, ☎ 225-7102 or 800-267-0525; $$$), and **Hampton Inn** (515 South Street in Bow at Exit 1 off Interstate 89, ☎ 224-5322 or 800-HAMPTON; $$-$$$). For a complete change, **A Touch of Europe Bed & Breakfast** at 85 Centre Street (which is the continuation of Bridge Street at Exit 14 from Interstate 93; ☎ 226-3771; $$).

Chichester

Fifteen minutes from Concord on Route 202, Chichester offers a pleasant bed-and-breakfast inn: **Mural House** at 37 Suncook Valley Road, two miles north of the Epsom traffic circle (hosts Steve and Barbara Davis; ☎ 798-5813; $$). It's a convenient place to stay while exploring Antique Alley in Northwood.

Loudon

There couldn't be much more contrast with the New Hampshire Speedway in Loudon than the quiet country road where **Lovejoy Farm** offers bed-and-breakfast accommodations in a 1790

Georgian colonial with attached carriage house. Host Art Monty is an avid cyclist. From Route 106 north, turn left onto Hoit Road and bear right to stop sign, then right onto Village Road and left onto Lovejoy Road. The farm is 1.25 miles farther on the right (☎ 783-4007; $$).

■ Camping

Bear Brook State Park in Allentown is open from mid-May to mid-October and has 93 sites (☎ 485-9869). **Pawtuckaway State Park** in Nottingham is open the same season, has 193 sites, and offers waterview spots as well (☎ 895-3031).

There are also two campgrounds in Chichester: **Hillcrest Family Campground**, open from May 1 to October 15, on Route 4/9/202 (☎ 798-5124 or 800-338-9488), and the family campground at **Circle 9 Ranch** a quarter-mile south of Epsom's traffic circle (☎ 736-9656). There's a country dance hall on premises, with weekend entertainment.

Where To Eat

Nashua

How about dinner in New Hampshire's best Italian restaurant? That may be what you find at **Ya Mamma's** at 42 Canal Street at the north end of town. Dinner is served nightly, lunch on Thursdays and Fridays only. Be sure to make a reservation (☎ 883-2264); you don't want to miss the medallions of veal sautéed in olive oil with sliced mushrooms, flamed with Marsala wine, then topped with prosciutto and provolone cheese.

Mexican food for the family is at **La Hacienda del Rio** on the Daniel Webster Highway (southbound side) – reservations for larger groups are advised (☎ 888-3353).

Manchester

A downtown dining tradition is the **Café Pavone** at 194 Main Street (☎ 598-0500) for contemporary Mediterranean food, especially pasta.

Head out of town on Route 101 to Bedford and dine elegantly at the **Bedford Village Inn** (☎ 472-2001 or 800-852-1166; directions in *Where To Stay* on page 308). It's well worth the extra few miles to savor their chicken Andrea, deceptively simple and perfectly delicious. If you want a little less formality, the tap room menu is also excellent. A treat: lobster bake in the rough, available in summer on Mondays and Tuesdays.

Concord

Concord's restaurants offer a lively mix of casual dining, especially for lunch, with delicatessens and coffee shops along North Main Street. Stroll around Eagle Square, the historic park entered through the wrought iron gateway on North Main, to find the **Eagle Square Delicatessen** (☎ 228-4795) for a memorable sandwich.

In the evening, give in to the urge for fun at **Thursday's Roadhouse and Drinking Establishment** at 6 Pleasant Street, just off North Main (☎ 224-2626). There's everything from chips and salsa to Southwestern bruschetta to tender spareribs, and even crabcakes and Cajun catfish. There's music downstairs on the weekends.

Chichester

East of Concord on Route 202 is the town of Chichester. Take the turn onto Route 28 to find **Dominick's Pizza, Pasta and Things** (☎ 435-7370), an absurd-looking restaurant bedecked with pink flamingos but serving authentic Italian breads and a marinara sauce that satisfies deep longings. Fresh pasta, of course. It's casual, and you'd never guess how good the food is from just driving past.

Canterbury

Don't forget to make reservations to dine at the Canterbury Shaker Village if you're planning to explore it for the day (see *Sightseeing*, page 307). The **Creamery Restaurant** there offers candlelight dinners daily from May through October, and on weekends in April, November, and December (☎ 783-9511).

Information Sources

Concord Chamber of Commerce, Concord, NH 03301; ☎ 224-2508.

Derry Chamber of Commerce, Derry, NH 03038; ☎ 432-8205.

Hudson Chamber of Commerce, Hudson, NH 03051; ☎ 889-4731.

Londonderry Chamber of Commerce, Londonderry, NH 03053; ☎ 434-7438.

Manchester Chamber of Commerce, Manchester, NH 03101; ☎ 666-6600.

Merrimack Chamber of Commerce, Merrimack, NH 03054; ☎ 424-3669.

Nashua Chamber of Commerce, Nashua, NH 03060; ☎ 881-8333.

Salem Area Chamber of Commerce, Salem, NH 03079; ☎ 893-3177.

Southern New Hampshire Convention & Visitors Bureau, One Airport Road, Suite 198, Manchester, NH 03103; ☎ 645-9889 or 800-932-4CVB (outside NH).

Merrimack Valley

Seacoast Region

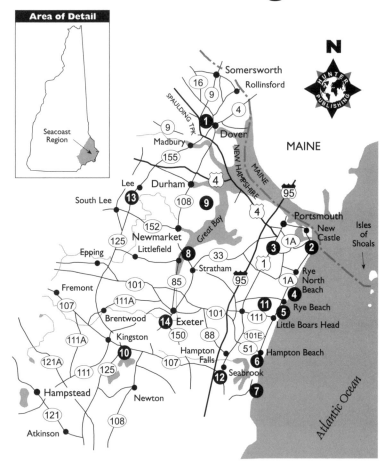

1. Salmon Falls Stoneware
2. Odiorne Point / Odiorne Point State Park
3. Water Country
4. Rye Harbor State Marina
5. Jenness Beach
6. Hampton State Beach
7. Seabrook Beach
8. Sandy Point Discovery Center
9. Adams Point
10. Webster Wildlife Natural Area
11. Fuller Gardens
12. Science & Nature Center / Seabrook Greyhound Park
13. Flag Hill Winery
14. American Independence Museum

The Seacoast

Eighteen miles of sandy beaches, with blue ocean, distant islands, and the haunting cries of seagulls over the slap of the waves. New Hampshire's seacoast is an oceanside delight, and much of the coast is state beaches. The city of **Portsmouth** is a blend of historic port and joyful self-indulgence in good restaurants, galleries, and gift shops, with music and another good bakery always waiting to be discovered.

Getting Around

Whether you're arriving up the coast on **Interstate 95** or **Route 1**, or from the interior of the state, head directly for Portsmouth and become immersed in the waterfront culture and stories. Then meander along the beaches on **Route 1A**, where the slow traffic is less of a hindrance and more of a gift to release you from hurry. There's a superb seacoast science center with park, and there are plenty of boats waiting to take you deep-sea fishing, whale watching, or to explore the Isles of Shoals that you can see across the blue water. Inland, a great Atlantic bay has become a preserve for wetlands and wildlife. Nearby, towns whose residents are descendants of participants in the American Revolution wait quietly for modern-day rebels and explorers to arrive and draw from their experience.

Adventures

■ On Foot

Portsmouth

Exploring **Portsmouth** is much more fun on foot than in a car. The small roads wind around in the oldest part of the city, and when you walk you're close to both the gardens and the sense of heritage that the colonial brick buildings send forth. Three hundred years old, the town used to be a sailors' place, rough and run down, but today it celebrates a seafaring heritage and a Revolutionary past as well as a festive present.

If you enter the city from Route 95 at Exit 7, the **Portsmouth Chamber of Commerce** is on your right almost immediately, just after you see the sign on the right for the *USS Albacore* (a submarine to tour). The chamber (☎ 436-1118; www.portcity. org) offers a free 48-page guide to the seacoast with clear maps, but to really appreciate the city's roots and architecture, get the $2 *Portsmouth Harbor Trail Walking Tour Guide and Map*. The city has three featured sections: the **downtown and waterfront section**, just past the chamber of commerce office; the **South End**, around the 10-acre Strawberry Banke living history museum; and the **Haymarket Square area**, where classic hotels rub shoulders with the library and older homes, even a mansion.

Parking is ample, both along the roads and in small lots scattered around the city. Try to start somewhere near **Market Square**, with its scrumptious bakery and small outdoor tables. You can still ride in a **horse and carriage** here, a fine way to tour in style! The carriage usually waits by North Church for riders in good weather. **North Church** is a reference point for touring, as you can see its high white spire from much of the city. Stroll the historic tour and plan to munch in **Prescott Park** on the waterfront, where there are outdoor vendors in the summer.

Odiorne State Park

When you've had your fill of town walking, drive out of town on Route 1 and take the "Beaches" turns for Route 1A, which in three miles comes to **Odiorne State Park**. There's a day fee charged at the tollbooth ($2.50 recently); park and head for the trails and the rocky waterfront. You can walk south to the cove, and north to Frost Point (total loop, two miles), with a visit to Audubon House afterward. This is an interesting rocky tidepool area; much of the rest of the New Hampshire coast is beach sand.

➔ **BEACHWALKS:** *Walking on beaches is great for stretching the leg muscles, as well as the soul. You won't find any dramatic hikes along this coastline, and the area of salt marshes now preserved near Hampton (62 acres) is sufficiently fragile that public use is discouraged. (You won't even see signs for it.)*

Great Bay National Estuarine Research Reserve

There's a wonderful inland bay of the Atlantic Ocean where the rivers meet the sea and much of the surrounding shore has been dedicated to a federal reserve as well as private conservation. This is **Great Bay**, a National Estuarine Research Reserve. The entire system of three river mouths and the ocean bay make up a living laboratory that visitors are invited to wander through. It's a refuge for 23 endangered species, a sanctuary to many more, and in it live oysters, clams, rock crabs, lobsters, herring, eels, smelt, and flounder, all of which have been harvested since the time of the Native Americans.

There are two points to enter the reserve: at the **Sandy Point Discovery Center** at the south end of the bay, reached from Depot Road off Route 33 near Stratham, and at the **Jackson Lab** on Adams Point, reached from Route 108 in Durham, by taking Bay Road to Adams Point. Jackson Lab can be toured by arrangement with the University of New Hampshire Marine Extension office (☎ 749-1565). There are walking trails at both locations. The one at Sandy Point is about a half-mile loop, including a graded gravel path and a boardwalk. The one at Adams Point has plenty of poison ivy (so wear protective clothes and watch where you step) and has some steeper sections, plus a viewing platform. You have a good chance of seeing birds like the great blue heron, and traces of deer, owls, fox, and coyotes (maybe even a snake or mouse!). For trail maps and information on species like wintering eagles, bluefish, rainbow smelt, and horseshoe crabs, contact Great Bay Reserve, 225 Main Street, Durham, NH 03824 (☎ 868-1095).

Wildlife & Natural Areas

Farther inland, away from the salt water completely, the Society for the Preservation of New Hampshire Forests manages two parcels that you might want to visit. One is in Kingston, the 89-acre **Webster Wildlife and Natural Area** with its cedar swamp, bog, and frontage on the Powwow River. From the junction of Route 125 with 107 and 107A in Kingston, go south on Route 125 for 2.2 miles. Turn left at the flashing light and immediately bear right. Go 0.1 mile and turn left on the gravel road. Go 0.5 mile and park on the left where the woods begin. After the sign, the woods road forks, with the right going to the bog and pond and the left looping through the property.

The second parcel is the **Smith Woodlot** in Newfields, 49 acres of white pine being used for forest management research. There are two miles of woods roads for pleasant walking or snow travel. Expect to see wildflowers in June; in winter watch for animal tracks. From Route 108 go south on Route 85 for 0.4 mile toward Newfields and turn right just past the railroad bridge. Go 300 feet and park just past the house; walk past the gate, bearing right, 600 feet to the property sign and wander along the trails.

■ On Wheels

Road Biking

If it weren't for the cars, Routes 1A and 1 would offer the perfect loop to bike, heading south down the seacoast on 1A, north through the villages (and past the shopping malls) on Route 1. There's even bike support on Route 1 as you head north again, at **Gus's Bicycle** (☎ 964-5445) on the right 0.2 mile before you reach Route 111. But the car traffic really is a drawback. Aim for April or early May, or else late August to September when the tang of autumn chill has sent the summer folk packing.

Bike Paths

There's also a bike path at **Odiorne Point State Park**, three miles from Portsmouth on Route 1A at the north end of the coast.

■ On Water

 Portsmouth Harbor is at the north of the seacoast; as you head south you reach **Rye Harbor** where the state marina is, then **North Hampton** and **Hampton**, and finally **Seabrook**. Prices for the various cruises and tours mentioned here are recent rates for adults; most companies offer senior discounts and lower prices for children, although rarely as low as half-price.

The barren-looking islands visible from the coast are the **Isles of Shoals**. Grand resorts once lured wealthy summer folk to these isles; author Celia Thaxter made them famous in 1893 with her book *An Island Garden*, as did painter Childe Hassam, who rendered the Thaxter gardens so romantically in pictures for the book. Today a walking tour of **Appledore Island**, where Celia Thaxter lived and welcomed so many illustrious guests, includes her garden – barren for 60 years, then painstakingly replanted in 1974 by a Cornell University professor and now nurtured by a local garden club. The haunted sense of the past on Appledore Island has also been captured in a recent novel by Anita Shreve, *The Weight of Water*. The isles are a summer place for visitors; only seafarers doggedly remain through the ice-encrusted and wind-torn winters there.

Cruises & Whale-Watching Trips

The **Isles of Shoals Steamship Co.** continues a 100-year tradition of taking guests to the Isles of Shoals, and offers historic cruises of the Isles and Portsmouth Harbor. They also have a ferry run with a morning walkabout on Star Island, a Star Island stopover trip, a Downeast (that means Maine) lobster clambake, and fireworks cruises all summer (mid-June through Labor Day). In the fall, through October, you can still get the Star Island walkabout or the Isles of Shoals cruise, and there's also an ocean expedition whale watch. On a whale watch you may see 50-ton whales leaping out of the water and gliding alongside the boat, watch dolphins cavort in the ship's wake, see seals sunning themselves on the rocks, and will probably spot sharks, bluefin tuna, and seabirds. There are also lighthouses and islands to see, and narrations of history and folklore from the captain. Call to confirm specific cruise dates and times

(☎ 431-5500 or 800-441-4620; www.islesofshoals.com). If you've arrived in town from Exit 7 of Interstate 95, the steamship company is on your left in three-fourths of a mile, just after you pass the Portsmouth Chamber of Commerce office on the right. There's a parking fee on the state dock, plus tickets for cruises from $8 to $25, depending on cruise and season; family passes and season passes are available.

Portsmouth Harbor.

Although Isles of Shoals Steamship Co. is the largest and best-known tour company on the water, there are a number of others, each with different charms. **Portsmouth Harbor Cruises** offers its boat, the *Heritage*, with more intimate cruises, also in the harbor, up inland rivers, during the evenings, and to the Isles of Shoals. Spring schedules (May 3 to mid-June) are variable; in summer and fall (to about the end of October) there are several cruises each day, and prices range from $7.50 to $15, with reservations encouraged (☎ 436-8084 or 800-776-0915).

Farther down the seacoast on Route 1A at **Rye Harbor State Marina** are more cruises and deep-sea fishing ships. **NH Seacoast Cruises** offers a tour of the nine islands of the Isles of Shoals on summer Wednesday evenings ($10 adults), and a whale watch ($20 adults); children's prices are lower. For whale watches, be sure to bring warm clothing and rubber-soled footwear, as well as a camera. Whale species sighted may include finback, humpback, sei, minke, and right whales. Call ahead for times and to make reservations (☎ 964-5545 or 382-6743; outside NH, 800-872-4753).

Deep-Sea Fishing

Deep-sea fishing, with the fresh salt wind and the challenge of landing a really big fish, is a terrific adventure. **Al Gauron** has a family business at the state pier at **Hampton Beach** with a fleet of fishing boats equipped for company: a single rental charge covers both bait and tackle, and off you go. From spring through October there are all-day deep-sea cruises to catch cod, haddock, and bluefin; half-day cruises closer to the coast vary with season, their targets are either cod or mackerel. At night in July and August go out for the bluefish. The Gaurons also offer daily party boats in July and August, with whale-watching trips in the morning, afternoon, and evening. If you really get hooked, try for one of the Monday fishing marathons scheduled throughout the three seasons. Call for times and reservations (☎ 926-2469 or 800-905-7820); parking is free. Prices for adults range from $12 to $36.

Also at the Hampton Beach State Marina is the *Tontine*, a private charter fishing and cruising boat that adds blue and mako shark to its list of catches. The *Tontine* also offers whale watching, night fireworks cruises, and night bluefishing. This is the boat you want for a group, rather than just one or two people. Helpful hints from the *Tontine* crew: wear rubber-soled shoes, bring a sweater or jacket, tote an old towel for wiping your hands, don't forget motion sickness pills and sunscreen if you need them, and bring a cooler to take home your fish fillets.

Sea Kayaking

Sea kayaking is a relatively new sport, with touring along the coast a special treat. **Adventure Learning** offers an intro to sea kayaking during the summer on Saturdays at **Little Harbor**, two miles from Portsmouth; call for schedules and rates (☎ 800-649-9728). Another kayak rental spot is at the Hampton State Marina, from **Sea Dogs Kayaks** (☎ 929-1288).

Snorkeling

Want to look under the water? **Atlantic Aquasport** of Rye offers snorkeling classes (☎ 436-4443). Note that the scuba providers mentioned in the *On Water* sections of other regions in this book often bring groups to the ocean.

Want to do something really wild? You can scuba dive under the ocean ice. To connect with the other crazy folks who indulge in this (especially to celebrate New Year's Eve), see the listings in *On Water* for the other regions of this book.

Swimming/Beaches

Of course, this wonderful strip of beaches is ideal for swimmers, beachcombers, sunbathers, and running through the waves. Hampton even offers seashell visitor information on the beach at Route 1A and F Street.

You can easily find all the beaches and picnic areas by driving down Route 1A. From the Portsmouth (north) end, popular ones are:

- **Wallis Sands**, a state park with large sandy beach; open weekends from mid-May to late June, then every day until Labor Day; fee charged; Rye's most popular beach; snack bar.

- **Jenness Beach**, another state beach, large and sandy, views to north and south, with money collected at the parking meters instead of at the beach; snack bar across the road.

- **North Hampton Beach**, smaller and quieter than the other Hampton beaches.

- **Little Boars Head**, with a two-mile path along the rocky promontory, waves crashing below; wild roses in summer.

- **North Beach**, mile-long sandy tidal beach, restrooms, metered parking.

- **Great Boars Head**, a scenic peninsula.

- **Hampton Beach**, where the southern part is a state park with store and RV parking; the next part north is a five-mile sandy beach with exceptional surf.

- **Seabrook Beach**, a favorite swimming beach of many locals.

Water Parks

The kids will point out to you that there's another choice besides saltwater for getting wet: **Water Country** calls itself New England's largest water park, and it's on Route 1, three miles south of the traffic circle at the south end of Portsmouth. Tube rides, wave pool, whirlpool, laser tag – it's wild entertainment, open daily from mid-June to Labor Day (☎ 436-3556).

How about a horse-drawn tour through historic Portsmouth?

■ By Horse & Carriage

The **Portsmouth Livery Company** (☎ 427-0044) offers tours of Portsmouth by horse and carriage, daily from mid-May through mid-October. The driver waits by North Church at Market Square. Advance reservations aren't needed; you can pick from the Strawberry Banke tour, Colonial tour, or "economy drive," a zippy view of downtown for

$2.50 per person, $10 minimum). You may also arrange for the driver pick you up at local lodgings, and drop you off at a restaurant after your tour; call ahead for this service.

■ In The Air

 Drive a little ways inland to **Newfields**, a picturesque town at the far side of Great Bay, and you can have a hot air balloon ride. **Puffin Air Limited** operates at the Ship to Shore Restaurant, Route 108, Newfields, NH 03856 (☎ 800-339-1161). Flights take off early in the morning or late in the afternoon when wind conditions are right; there are also tethered flights. No flights in rainy weather or strong winds. Costs are $160 per person or $600 for a party of four, with a deposit and advance reservation required.

Parasailing is both a water and air sport, and **NE Parasail & Jet Ski** gets you going (☎ 929-4174).

Sightseeing

 The **Seacoast Trolley Company** will give you rides from historic Portsmouth and Strawberry Banke to Wallis Sands State Beach, Odiorne Point State Beach, Rye Beach, and New Castle Common, with intermediate stops, too. The fare is $2 for all ages, daily from mid-June to Labor Day. Look for the marked stops.

Portsmouth

Portsmouth is a festival and celebration city. Look for the **music series** in **Market Square**; concerts and musicals at **Prescott Park**; and a **Shakespeare Festival** in August, plus single-day events like the September **apple cider day** at Jackson House, the state's oldest house. For dates and times check with the **Portsmouth Chamber of Commerce** (☎ 436-3988 or 436-1118; www.portcity.org).

Portsmouth

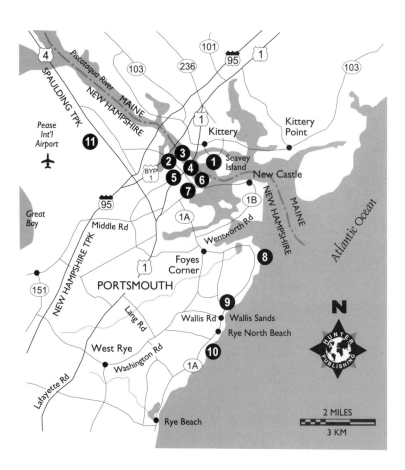

1. Portsmouth Naval Shipyard
2. Chamber of Commerce
3. Isles of Shoals Steamship Co.
4. Prescott Park
5. Portsmouth Brewery
6. Strawberry Banke
7. Portsmouth Children's Museum
8. Odiorne Point State Park and Seacoast Science Center
9. Wallis Sands State Beach
10. Rye Harbor State Park
11. Redhook Ale Brewery

Gift shop at the Strawberry Banke Museum.

When you tour the historic sections of town, you're bound to arrive at **Strawberry Banke**. (This was the first name Portsmouth had, thanks to the berries that greeted settlers along the river bank.) Strawberry Banke is a 10-acre living history museum open daily from May through October (☎ 433-1100; recent admission prices were $12 for adults, $8 for children seven-17, children ages six and under free, $28 for a family). It also reopens the first two weekends of December for a traditional **Candlelight Stroll** through the decorated grounds and houses. From almost anywhere in Portsmouth there are signs pointing to its location, opposite Prescott Park, which is on the bank of the Piscataqua River. The museum has 30 houses from the 17th to the 20th century, each allowed to tell a story about its inhabitants, a time period, or crafts and other parts of daily life. Special events include an annual decorative arts symposium, heirloom heritage plant sale, military encampment, boat-building demonstrations, and a brewers' festival in October.

At the start of the 20th century, Portsmouth was known as the ale-making capital of the country, and it now has several breweries. The **Portsmouth Brewery** is a brew pub at 56 Market Street (☎ 431-1115); **Smuttynose Brewing Company** (named after one island in the Isles of Shoals) is at 225 Heritage Way (☎ 436-4026); and **Redhook Ale Brewery** offers regular tours at 35 Corporate Drive (at the entrance to Pease International Tradeport off Route 16; ☎ 430-8600).

The **Children's Museum of Portsmouth** at 280 Marcy Street (☎ 436-3853) is a year-round science and arts museum with interactive exhibits, family-oriented performances and workshops. Hours are Tuesday to Saturday, 10 am to 5 pm; Sunday, 1 to 5 pm. In summer they are also open on Mondays from 10 am to 5 pm. Visit their Web site at www.rscs.net/children/home.html).

Bookstores abound, with antiquarian ones downtown: the **Book Guild of Portsmouth** (58 State Street, ☎ 436-1758), and the **Portsmouth Book Shop** (1 Islington Street, ☎ 433-4406). Don't miss the unusual collection of maps and travel books at **Gulliver's** (7 Commercial Alley, ☎ 431-5556; e-mail gullivers@ttlc.net; www.gulliversbooks.com). And for a thoroughly up-to-the-minute gathering of books, there's **Bookland** (☎ 433-1616) at the mall south of town.

Along the Seacoast

The **Seacoast Science Center** (☎ 436-8043) is at Odiorne Point State Park. It's open year-round, but hours change seasonally. Admission was recently just a dollar (in addition to the day-use fee for the park); exhibits reveal American Indian encampments, explore the wildlife of the park, and focus on the sea. The bookshop is terrific.

North Hampton offers a peaceful stroll through masses of estate gardens and 1,500 rose bushes at **Fuller Gardens** (☎ 964-5414). As you drive south on Route 1A, look for the sign on the right side of the road; if you reach the junction with Route 111, you've just passed the turn. Open daily 10 to 6 from early May through mid-October (nominal admission).

Hampton Beach is literally a playground, from the fireworks every Wednesday and holiday night all summer, to a casino and arcades, to free band concerts and, of course, the beaches themselves, full of swimmers, surfers, even parasailers. There's a five-day **children's festival** in August with sand castle contests, costume parade, free kites, and more. The annual **seafood festival** is held the first weekend of September. Get a vacation guide free; write to Hampton Beach Vacation Guide, PO Box 790B, Hampton, NH 03843-0790. Or call the Hampton

Area Chamber of Commerce, ☎ 296-8717 or 800-438-2826; e-mail hamptoncc@hamptonbeach.com.

Seabrook is home to New Hampshire's nuclear power plant, on Route 1. You can visit the **Science and Nature Center** (☎ 800-338-7482) at New Hampshire Yankee, Monday through Saturday, from March through Thanksgiving, from 10 am to 4 pm; open Monday through Friday the rest of the year. The center has educational exhibits about electricity, nuclear power, and the environment. Free admission. Seabrook also has a greyhound park on Route 107, with races on the weekends; call the **Seabrook Greyhound Park** for weekend packages that add lodgings and meals to the races (☎ 474-3065, ext. 234).

Inland

Some of New Hampshire's oldest towns are now small cities a few miles inland from Portsmouth. The history of **Exeter** is evocatively depicted, along with the rest of the state's, at the **American Independence Museum** at Ladd-Gilman House on Governors Lane, off Center Street and Ladd Lane. Open May through October, Wednesday to Sunday from noon to 5 pm (☎ 722-2622).

Durham is the home of the **University of New Hampshire**, with its agricultural fields and playing fields. Nearby is **Lee**, a very small town that is home to **Flag Hill winery**. It's at a farmhouse where four generations of the Reinhold family live. Tours are given daily from 10 am to 5 pm, or by appointment. Call for directions (☎ 659-2949).

Dover, a bit farther north and most directly reached from Portsmouth by taking the Spaulding Turnpike at the west side of town, is the home of **Salmon Falls Stoneware**, whose gray pottery with blue stenciled designs will immediately look familiar to you. Watch the potters in action. From Central Avenue (Route 108), turn east onto Oak Street at the Rite-Aid drug store. The pottery is at the Old Boston & Maine Engine House (☎ 800-621-2030).

Where To Stay

Portsmouth

You could stay in any of the big chain motels in Portsmouth, but why lose the chance to savor the city's real character? The **Sise Inn** (40 Court Street, walking distance to restaurants and sights; ☎ 433-1200 or 800-267-0525; $$-$$$) is one that stands out as different. Rooms are decorated in Victorian style, meeting rooms are similarly luxurious, and there's a charming breakfast room. Plus there's a library and a selection of classical cassettes to borrow during your stay.

The **Bow Street Inn** (121 Bow Street; ☎ 431-7760; $$-$$$) has a waterfront location with 10 cozy rooms and nice little luxuries. There are also a number of bed-and-breakfast inns in the historic districts: **Oracle House Inn** in a 1700s Colonial (38 Marcy Street, ☎ 433-8827; $$-$$$); the **Inn at Strawberry Banke** in an early Colonial home (314 Court Street; ☎ 436-7242 or 800-428-3933; $$); the **Martin Hill Inn**, comprised of two period buildings (404 Islington Street; ☎ 436-2287; $$-$$$); and a snug place with just one guest room, the **Cottage** (442 Islington Street; ☎ 431-3353; $$). If you cross the bridge of Route 1B to the charming and equally historic village of New Castle, you'll find **Great Islander Bed & Breakfast** at the center of town across from the church (62 Main Street; ☎ 436-8536; $$-$$$).

Along the Seacoast

Ashworth By the Sea is Hampton Beach's most luxurious resort, with a heated pool, three restaurants, and dancing and entertainment (295 Ocean Blvd., Route 1A; ☎ 926-6762 or 800-345-6736; www.ashworthhotel.com; $-$$$$). Also in Hampton, but on a smaller scale, the Oceanside Inn has 10 rooms furnished in high Victorian style, with many luxurious amenities (365 Ocean Blvd./Route 1A; ☎ 926-3542; $$-$$$$). For a taste of bed-and-breakfast comfort, try the **Victoria Inn** (430 High Street, between Routes 1A and 1; ☎ 929-1437; $$-$$$). Book well in advance for these seaside spots.

⊕ **SEACOAST ACCOMMODATIONS:** *Hampton has more accommodations than could possibly be listed. Send for the vacation guide from the Hampton Chamber of Commerce, for a generous attempt at getting them into print! Hampton Chamber of Commerce, 836 Lafayette Road, Box 790, Hampton, NH 03842.*

Points Inland

Hampstead is a on the way from Salem to the seacoast, if you take Route 111, and it has a pleasant bed-and-breakfast inn. Turn north in the middle of town onto Route 121, which is also Main Street, and go 3.7 miles to **Stillmeadow**, on the right (hosts Lori and Randy Offord; 545 Main Street; ☎ 329-8381; $$). It's especially nice in winter because there are cross-country trails nearby; the inn is also close to the Robert Frost Farm in Derry.

Savor deep luxury at the **Inn of Exeter**, an oasis of elegance that includes a superb restaurant. The inn is a traditional lodging for parents visiting their nearly grown children at nearby Phillips Exeter Academy, so book well in advance (90 Front Street; ☎ 772-5901 or 800-782-8444; $$-$$$$).

The 1809 Federal inn at Four Front Street, called simply **The Inn by the Bandstand** (☎ 772-6352; www.portsmouthnh. com/ lodging; $$-$$$), has taken pampering of guests to admirable heights. Many rooms have fireplaces, all have extras like down pillows, and parlor offerings include fresh-baked pastries and afternoon tea or sherry. The building is listed on the National Register of Historic Places.

■ Camping

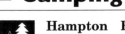 **Hampton Beach State Park** (on Route 1A; ☎ 271-3628) has a 28-site RV park with full hook-ups, open from mid-May to late September. Other campgrounds include **Wakeda Campground** on Exeter Road, Hampton Falls (back from the coast a couple of miles; ☎ 772-5274); **Shel-Al Campground** on Route 1 in North Hampton (not Route 1A, but Route 1, inland), open May 15 to

September 15 (☎ 964-5730); and **Tidewater Campground** on Route 1 in Hampton (☎ 926-5474).

Where To Eat

Portsmouth

This city has a reputation for food that rivals Boston's. And there's often music on the weekends to add to the pleasure of dining out. Surveying Portland restaurants took a long time and added pounds to your trusty author – but every mouthful was worth the effort!

For elegant dining, head for the **Oar House** (☎ 436-4025) at 55 Ceres Street, where the seafood is excellent and the piano bar lively. **The Metro** (☎ 436-0521) at 20 Old High Street also offers fine dining and a welcoming atmosphere, as well as live jazz. Another well-appointed and delicious place to dine is the **Porto Bello** (☎ 431-2928) upstairs at 67 Bow Street.

For a more casual night, try the Mexican food at **Poco Diablo** (☎ 431-5967), 37 Bow Street. **The Stockpot** (☎ 431-1851) at 53 Bow Street has been "serving good food cheap since 1982." Large families have fun at **Yoken's Thar She Blows** (☎ 436-8224), a mammoth restaurant on Route 1 south of town. The **Press Room** (☎ 431-5186) at 77 Daniel Street features live entertainment and music to go with its hearty burgers.

Dine at the sushi bar at **Sakura**, 40 Pleasant Street (☎ 431-2721), or be delightfully overwhelmed by all the choices at **Szechuan Taste & Thai Café** (☎ 431-2226), 54 Daniel Street. **Chiangmai Thai Restaurant** (☎ 433-1289) at 128 Penhallow Street is another favorite, especially for its curries.

Save room for dessert and migrate to the **Café Brioche** at 14 Market Square, where the cakes are outrageously rich and the plain pastries are still heaven. **Annabelle's** at 49 Ceres Street offers plenty of choices for good ice cream.

Along the Seacoast

Ashworth By the Sea, the luxury resort of Hampton, has one of the best restaurants as you go south on Route 1A, but beware of crowding during the peak beach season (☎ 926-6762). An excellent place for seafood, especially lobster, and steak is **Saunders at Rye Harbor**, on Route 1A at Rye Harbor (☎ 964-6466). When you turn inland at Seabrook on Route 286, stop at the - **Seabrook Lobster Pound** (☎ 474-3331) for a summer treat of "lobster in the rough," steamed and ready to eat picnic-style.

Route 1, the inland route, has the fast-food places your kids may be begging for, as well as **Road Kill Café** and **Tortilla Flats**.

Information Sources

Dover Chamber of Commerce, Dover, NH 03820; ☎ 742-2218.

Exeter Chamber of Commerce, Exeter, 03833; ☎ 772-2411.

Greater Portsmouth Chamber of Commerce, PO Box 239, Portsmouth, NH 03801; ☎ 436-1118.

Hampton Beach Village District, PO Box 7905, Hampton Beach, NH 03843; ☎ 926-8717 or 800-GET-A-TAN (800-438-2826).

Hampton Area Chamber of Commerce, PO Box 790, Hampton, NH 03842; ☎ 296-8717 or 800-438-2826; e-mail hamptoncc@hamptonbeach.com.

Index

Index